THE *Illustrated* COUNTRY ALMANAC

First published in Great Britain in 1982 by
Virgin Books Ltd., 61-63 Portobello Road,
London W11 3DD.

Printed in Great Britain by
Richard Clay Ltd., Suffolk.
Photoset by Typegeneration
Designed by Ray Hyden
Production services by Book Production
Consultants, Cambridge
Distributed by Hamlyn Paperbacks

ISBN 0 907080 53 7

THE *Illustrated* COUNTRY ALMANAC

A Day by Day history of Country Music

Richard Wootton

Virgin

Virgin Books

Foreword

I liked country music before I knew what it was called — the b-sides of fifties rock 'n' roll records by Jerry Lee Lewis, and the occasional country hit which had crossed over into the pop charts, including 'El Paso' by Marty Robbins.

The more I heard, the more interested I became. Country music is a huge and engrossing subject; born in the USA of multifarious influences brought by settlers from all over the world, it has developed and grown over several decades, picking up new ideas and styles along the way. Western swing, rockabilly, Cajun, honky-tonk, hillbilly and old-timey — all are part of country's rich and still changing sound.

I learnt about the early musicians while I was discovering the new, and it became quite natural to play modern country records side-by-side with the old; the gritty outlaw music of Waylon Jennings next to the rousing pre-war western swing of Bob Wills and his Texas Playboys, or Johnny Cash's gunfighter ballads after Hank Williams's sad, lonesome songs from the early fifties.

This book follows a somewhat similar pattern. In these pages country's past and present overlap and interweave. The biggest stars of today are next to the pioneers who paved the way for country to become so popular. It's been both informative and entertaining to compile, and I hope you'll find it the same to read.

Richard Wootton

J A N U A R Y

1st JANUARY

1953 Hank Williams died in the back seat of his powder blue Cadillac in the early hours of the morning. His driver, Charles Carr, a Montgomery teenager hired the previous day to take him to a concert in Canton, Ohio, didn't realise anything was wrong for several hours, despite the Tennessee highway patrolman who stopped him for speeding, looked in the back of the car and said, "That guy looks dead." Carr explained that his passenger was sedated, paid the $25 fine and drove off. At 5.30am he stopped at a gas station in Oak Hill, West Virginia, touched Hank's hand and found it quite cold. Williams was just 29, though the doctor who conducted the autopsy guessed 37. Death was due to heart failure, almost certainly caused by his excessive consumption of alcohol and pills. Williams seemed to know that he was on a self destructive course; he'd told his wife two days before his death, "I think I see God comin' down the road," and his songs were becoming increasingly pessimistic; the record on top of the country charts the day he died was his own, 'I'll Never Get Out Of This World Alive'.

1960 Johnny Cash's first free concert for the inmates of San Quentin Prison in California. He shared a bill with Larry and Lorrie—The Collins Kids, and some strippers. One of the prisoners was Merle Haggard, who had been jailed for burglary but would later become a very successful country singer. In his autobiography, *Sing Me Back Home,* Hag remembered, "The visit by Johnny Cash was probably the only good time I had during my entire stay. I remember he just looked terrible. He was hung over from the night before and his voice was almost gone—but hell, he came out on stage and just blew everybody away. Anybody who can actually make a group of men forget they're in San Quentin is some kind of magician." In January 1969 Cash made his third visit to the grim prison and the show was recorded for a TV programme and a live LP, *Johnny Cash at San Quentin.* He revealed a close affinity with the inmates and introduced a special song called 'San Quentin' with lyrics about the futility and destructiveness of the place. The prisoners stood on benches and tables and yelled him on. "I was really worried that they were going to riot," said June Carter later, echoing the fears of everyone except Cash. The LP was an enormous success, topped the charts for 20 weeks, was the Country Music Association's Album of The Year, and included the million selling single 'A Boy Named Sue'.

2nd JANUARY

1936 Roger Miller born in Fort Worth, Texas. He had great success in the sixties with a string of country-pop hits that were laced with sardonic humour, including 'England Swings' and 'You Can't Roller Skate In A Buffalo Herd'. Roger developed an early enthusiasm for music, Hank Williams being his biggest influence, and

began playing guitar and banjo as a youngster. When he enlisted in the Army he found himself in demand as an entertainer. He went to Nashville and started pitching songs, scoring his first success when Ray Price recorded his 'Invitation To The Blues' in 1968. Two years later Miller had his own recording contract with RCA and had minor hits, but it wasn't until he joined Smash in 1964 that he really broke through in a big way; 'Dang Me' being his first chart-topper with the label. Though he wrote all his most successful records, Roger has a good ear for other people's material and was one of the first to recognise the talents of Kris Kristofferson, recording the first version of 'Me and Bobby McGee', a small country hit for him in mid-1969. He's been less active as a performer in the seventies and eighties, though still records, and is now owner of a chain of motels, named after his biggest hit 'King Of The Road'.

1949 Tom Gribbin, Florida-based singer born. He achieved notoriety in 1981 as the first country singer to record a new wave song; a version of 'The Guns Of Brixton' written by British band The Clash.

1953 Country fans were stunned by the news of the death of Hank Williams. In his home town of Montgomery, Alabama, the *Daily Advertiser* devoted the whole of the front page to him. Those close to the singer were saddened but not very surprised. For Jerry Rivers, a member of Hank's long-suffering band The Drifting Cowboys, "The news was shocking but not unbelievable. The past months have been nothing but a series of surprises and disappointments for us, and this came almost inevitably as the closing chapter."

1974 Tex Ritter died of a heart attack at the Metro jail in Nashville, where he was trying to arrange bail for one of his band members.

Tex Ritter

3rd JANUARY

1917 Leon McAuliff born in Houston, Texas. One of the first people to use the steel guitar in country music, Leon worked alongside Bob Wills in the Light Crust Dough Boys (an early western swing aggregation), then joined Bob in his own Texas Playboys, who were based in Tulsa, Oklahoma for many years. He wrote 'Steel Guitar Rag'—a highlight of many Wills concerts and always introduced with Bob's catchphrase, "Take it away Leon"; and co-authored the western swing classic 'San Antonio Rose'. After the war he formed his own band and operated the Cimarron Ballroom in Tulsa.

1982 British rocker Elvis Costello fulfilled one of his greatest ambitions and played the Grand Ole Opry in Nashville, one of only three dates on an American tour to promote *Almost Blue,* an album of country standards recorded in Nashville with Billy Sherrill. The Sunday night audience was the youngest and loudest ever seen at the Opry House.

4th JANUARY

1923 WBAP IN Fort Worth, Texas broadcast 90 minutes of square dance music featuring a lively fiddler named M. J. Bonner. The station was deluged with requests for more and responded by launching the WBAP Barn Dance soon afterwards—the first regular barn dance show in the

US, pre-dating the Grand Ole Opry by nearly three years. WBAP is still broadcasting country music today.

1953 Hank Williams' funeral in Montgomery, Alabama drew over 20,000 mourners and caused a giant traffic snarl-up which prevented some of the official pall-bearers arriving on time. 2,700 people jammed into the Montgomery Municipal Auditorium, the rest listened outside in Perry Street as the service was relayed through hastily installed loudspeakers. Several country stars took part: Ernest Tubb sang 'Close To The Lord', Roy Acuff 'I Saw The Light', Red Foley 'Peace In The Valley', and a black gospel group, The Southwind Singers sang 'My Record Will Be There'. Hank's body lay in an open casket, dressed in a suit designed by his first wife Audrey and made by Nudie, the country and western clothes specialist. There was more traffic chaos as thousands tried to reach the Oakwood Cemetery Annex in time for the burial.

1960 Marty Robbins top of the pop charts with 'El Paso'. "I always wanted to write a song about El Paso," Marty told author Dorothy Horstman, "Because traditionally that is where the West begins. Western stories that I had read and stories my grandfather told me, inspired me to write it . . . Had I been born a little sooner, the cowboy life is the kind of life I'd have liked to have lived."

5th JANUARY

1923 Sam Phillips, the man who "discovered" Elvis Presley, Jerry Lee Lewis, Carl Perkins, Johnny Cash and others, then recorded their first discs for his Sun label, born on a farm near Florence, Alabama. After the death of his father, Sam took a job at a radio station in Muscle Shoals, moved to Decatur, then Nashville, before arriving in Memphis, Tennessee in the winter of 1944/45 and landing an engineering job at WREC. He became fascinated by the blues singers he heard on Beale Street and built a studio in a converted shop at 607 Union Avenue, with the express purpose of recording them. At first he leased the records to Chess in Chicago and Modern in Los Angeles, then in 1951 he quit the radio job and set up his own label, Sun Records. For the first three years he recorded mainly black artists, but also ran the Memphis Recording Service, where people could make 10 inch acetate records for $4. The young Elvis Presley came to the studio in the summer of 1953 to make a record for his mother. Within a year he was making records for Phillips' label, and their success brought dozens of other young musicians to the studios. Sam had an excellent ear for talent, as his son Knox Phillips explained, "If a guy came into the studio with a unique, distinctive sound and was himself, Sam heard it immediately, where most people would wince at it at first. Jerry Lee Lewis told me—and he had been to Nashville, and they all said to him, 'Man, get you a guitar'—Jerry Lee told me, Sam took one listen to his tape, and he didn't listen halfway through, and he said, 'You are a rich man', and he didn't mean in money, but in talent." Sam sold Sun Records in 1969 and today owns a radio station and has shares in another operation that started from humble origins in Memphis—the Holiday Inn chain.

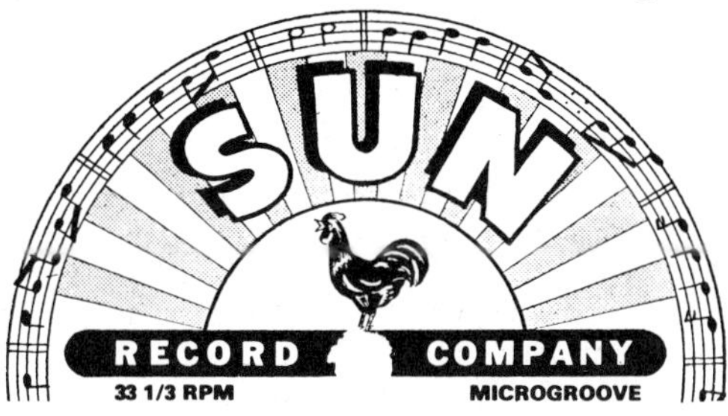

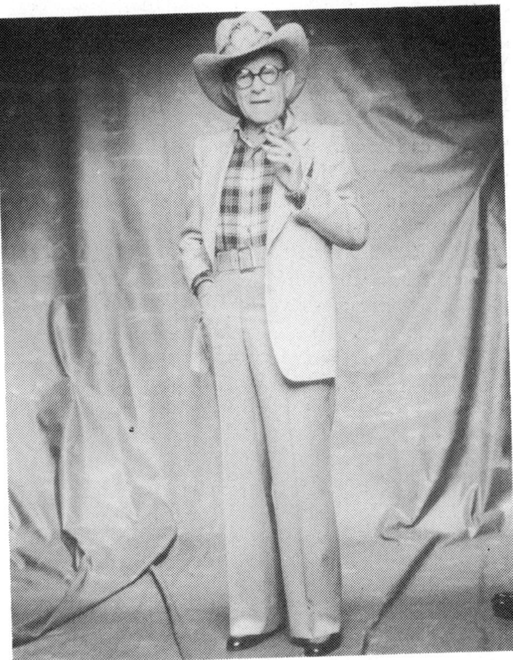

1980 Comedian George Burns made his country chart debut, at the age of 83, singing 'I Wish I Was Eighteen Again'.

6th JANUARY

1924 Earl Scruggs, "King of the Banjomen", born in Cleveland County, North Carolina.

Brought up in the foothills of the Appalachian Mountains, in a strong musical environment, Earl was playing the banjo at five, and by ten had invented the distinctive three-finger style that he developed while working with Bill Monroe's Bluegrass Boys, and which has influenced countless musicians ever since. Earl's great friend in Monroe's band was Lester Flatt, and in 1948 they formed their own group, The Foggy Mountain Boys. They played together for over 20 years, were part of the folk revival, and sold more records for CBS in the sixties than any other act except Johnny Cash. Their most popular recordings were, 'Foggy Mountain Breakdown' — which was used to great effect during the car chases in the film *Bonnie and Clyde;* and 'The Ballad Of Jed Clampett' — the theme from "The Beverly Hillbillies" TV series. In 1969 they split up, and soon afterwards the Earl Scruggs Review was formed, featuring Earl and his sons, and their music was a blend of progressive country rock and bluegrass.

1976 The David Grisman Quintet played their first gig, at Bolinas, California. Grisman, a gifted mandolin player, is generally recognised as the key figure in the music which combines bluegrass and swing jazz, a sound he has dubbed Dawg Music. David was brought up in New York and his musical heroes were Bill Monroe and Django Reinhardt. Before forming his influential Quintet, he worked in bands with likeminded newgrass musicians, Richard Greene, Peter Rowan and Clarence White; and did sessions for West Coast rock acts including Linda Ronstadt and James Taylor.

7th JANUARY

1930 Jack Greene born in Maryville, Tennessee. The "Jolly Giant" in Ernest Tubb's band, his solo spotlight, 'The Last Letter' on the album *Ernest Tubb Presents The Texas Troubadours,*

brought considerable airplay and launched a solo career. Jack scored eight Top Five hits in a row in the latter half of the sixties, and in the first year of CMA Awards was voted Best Male Vocalist of 1967. In the seventies he formed a duet act with Jeannie Seely.

1933 Radio station WWVA in Wheeling, West Virginia launched the long-running barn dance show which became known as the 'Wheeling Jamboree'. String bands were featured at first, then came the introduction of star vocalists like Just Plain John and the very popular Doc Williams and the Border Riders.

1943 Leona Williams (Leona Belle Helton) born in Vienna, Missouri. She became part of the Helton Family Band along with dad, mum and 11 brothers and sisters, and had her own radio show by the time she was 15. A year later she married Ron Williams and they worked together in Loretta Lynn's band. Leona launched a solo career in the late sixties and has recorded successfully for Hickory and MCA. In October 1978 she married Merle Haggard.

1978 Johnny Paycheck top of the country charts with David Allan Coe's anthem for down-trodden working people everywhere, 'Take This Job And Shove It'. The song inspired a movie in 1981.

8th JANUARY

1935 Elvis Presley born in a two-room shack in East Tupelo, Mississippi. He was one of twins, but his brother Jesse Garon was stillborn. Vernon

and Gladys Presley were extremely poor, but scrimped and saved to give all they could to their only son. Gladys pampered her little boy, and was obsessed with his safety; "My Mama never let me out of her sight," Elvis said later, "I couldn't go down to the creek like all the other kids. Sometimes when I was little I used to run off, Mama would whip me and I thought she didn't love me."

1946 Elvis wanted a bike for his 11th birthday, but he didn't get it, "I really wanted that bicycle, but daddy couldn't afford one. So he bought me a guitar for around twelve bucks. I know even this was a great sacrifice — he went without smokes for several weeks." Elvis learnt to play from his Uncle Vester, who knew a few chords, and from listening to the radio. He was never a particularly good player.

1979 Sara Carter, vocalist with the original Carter Family died in Lodi, California, after a long illness. She had been divorced from A. P. Carter in 1936 and married Coy W. Bayes in 1939, but had continued to perform with A. P. and their children until the early forties. She is buried near her first husband in Mount Vernon Cemetery, Virginia.

9th JANUARY

1941 Joan Baez born in Staten Island, New York. A leading figure in the sixties folk/protest movement, she first came to national prominence in the US with her appearance at the 1959 Newport Folk Festival — which included a shy duet on 'Wildwood Flower' with Earl Scruggs. Her large catalogue of folk recordings includes some country songs, written by some of the new wave of Nashville writers, Kris Kristofferson, Steve Young, Mickey Newbury and Willie Nelson. Her big hit 'The Night They Drove Old Dixie Down' was recorded in Music City.

Crystal Gayle

1951 Crystal Gayle (Brenda Gail Webb) born in Paintsville, Kentucky, a little sister for Loretta Lynn, who nicknamed her after the Krystal hamburger chain. From the age of four she was brought up in Indiana, where her mother worked at a hospital while her father fought a losing battle against black lung disease, contracted while he was a coal miner in Kentucky. "I grew up knowing I was going to be a singer," says Crystal and she was on the road singing back-up vocals for Loretta while still in her teens. Big sister helped her get started as a solo singer, and she had one hit single (written by Loretta) before her career foundered, only to be revived in 1973 when she signed with United Artists and was linked with producer Allen Reynolds. The country hits started almost at once, leading to 'Don't It Make My Brown Eyes Blue' in 1977, the first of several crossover pop hits.

1959 "Rawhide" debuted on American television. The western series introduced the young Clint Eastwood, later an international movie star, to a wide audience.

1982 Johnny Cash became the only person in Hendersonville, Tennessee to have a road named after him — Johnny Cash Parkway.

10th JANUARY

1935 Rock 'n' roller Ronnie Hawkins born in Huntsville, Madison County, Arkansas. He came from a country music background and his first band (formed when he was barely 16) played "hopped up hillbilly". He developed into a fully fledged rockabilly performer and with his band The Hawks (who went on to play with Bob Dylan and become The Band) recorded some classic singles for Roulette including 'Forty Days', 'Mary Lou,' and 'Who Do You Love', the latter featuring some superlative guitar work from Robbie Robertson. Unlike most of his contemporaries, Ronnie Hawkins didn't change his style to middle-of-the-road pop or country music, and when last heard of was still performing genuine rock 'n' roll.

1948 Thirteen-year-old Loretta Lynn married in Kentucky, despite strong objections from her family. "This is something you'll regret all your life," said her mother, though her father came to the Paintsville county courthouse to give her away. According to Loretta, "At our wedding, Doo wrote down his name as Oliver Vanetta Lynn, and I said 'Who's that?' See, I thought his real name was Doolittle." The traumatic early days of her marriage to Doo were recreated by Sissy Spacek and Tommy Lee Jones in the film version of Loretta's life story *Coal Miner's Daughter.*

11th JANUARY

1911 Tommy Duncan, vocalist with Bob Wills and the Texas Playboys born. A remarkably versatile singer, Tommy handled country, big band and blues numbers with equal skill, and never seemed to be put off by Bob Wills' interjections of approval and delight between his vocals. Duncan credited Jimmie Rodgers as his main influence and remains best known for the big-selling 'San Antonio Rose'.

1933 Goldie Hill, one of the most popular female country stars of the fifties, born in Karnes County, Texas. A regular on the Louisiana Hayride, then the Grand Ole Opry, she scored several hits for Decca including 'I Let The Stars Get In My Eyes' and 'Say Big Boy'. She met singer Carl Smith on a country package tour and they were married in 1957 when she was 24. Soon afterwards she retired from the music business, though has made occasional guest appearances and records since.

12th JANUARY

1905 Tex Ritter (Woodward Maurice Ritter) born near Murvaul, Texas. Although originally intending to become a lawyer, Tex chose a career in acting. He was one of the first people to introduce country and western themes to New York City, appearing in several radio serials in the thirties, including the original "Lone Ranger", "Cowboy Tom's Roundup" and "Tex Ritter's Campfire". He made over 50 cowboy films, then combined a recording career with acting when he signed to Capitol and scored numerous hits, like 'There's A New Moon Over My Shoulder', 'I Dreamed Of A Hillbilly Heaven' and the theme song from the 1952 movie *High Noon.*

Ray Price

1926 Ray Price born in rural Perryville, Texas — a few miles from Panola County where both Jim Reeves and Tex Ritter were born. He went to college with the intention of becoming a rancher or farmer, but was encouraged to develop his obvious talent as a singer. In 1949 he became a regular performer on the Big D Jamboree from KRLD Dallas, and soon had a recording contract with Bullet, the Nashville-based independent label. Two years later he moved to CBS, and after the death of Hank Williams hired most of The Drifting Cowboys for his own Cherokee Cowboys Band. He became a regular on the Grand Ole Opry and began a remarkable run of chart successes, scoring solo hits in every year from 1954 to 1979, including 'Crazy Arms' which stayed in the charts for 45 weeks. Willie Nelson joined his band as a bass player in the late fifties and provided Ray with his theme song, 'Night Life'. In the late sixties Price changed his sound radically from old-style hillbilly to smooth pop and began appearing with an orchestra and wearing a dinner jacket; but was back in jeans and a casual shirt for the Top Five duet album success, *San Antonio Rose,* with Willie Nelson in 1980.

1939 William Lee Golden, longest serving member of the Oak Ridge Boys, born in Brewton, Alabama. He played the guitar and sang with his sister on WEBJ, Brewton when he was just seven years old, and while at high school saw the Oak Ridge Quartet and decided that he wanted to be part of their organisation. A gospel group until the mid-seventies, the Oaks' heritage goes back to The Country Cut-Ups, who were formed during World War II in Knoxville, and performed at the atomic energy plant in Oak Ridge, Tennessee. They reformed in the mid-fifties as the Oak Ridge Quartet, and Bill joined the line-up in 1964.

13th JANUARY

1929 Wyatt Earp died in poverty in Los Angeles, aged 81. He's been depicted as both a brave and honest lawman who did much to tame the wild west, and as an unprincipled murderer, thief and conman. The truth is probably closer to the latter. Wyatt moved to LA in 1906 and by 1920 was penniless. He spent his last years hanging around Hollywood film studios, trying to get his life story published. Wyatt was befriended by cowboy actors William S. Hart and Tom Mix, but seems to have been exploited by producers and directors who used him for providing information about his past, but never paid him.

1967 Ed Bruce made his debut on the country charts with 'Walker's Woods'. He would have several small hits over the next decade, but didn't break through into the country music big-time until Waylon and Willie recorded his song 'Mammas, Don't Let Your Babies Grow Up To Be Cowboys'.

14th JANUARY

1929 Billy Walker born in the tiny Texas town of Ralls. He began singing and playing the guitar at an early age. When he was 15 he won a talent contest and the prize was a cake, two dollars and a guest appearance on KICA in Clovis, New Mexico. He was so well received that he was given his own 15 minute show each Saturday morning, which involved a weekly 80 mile hitch-hiking trip. A few years later he formed a band and toured the southwest and became a regular on the Big D Jamboree in Dallas where he assumed the persona of "The Travelling Texan—The Masked Singer Of Country Songs". A popular member of both the Louisiana Hayride and the Ozark Jamboree, he joined the Grand Ole Opry in 1960. Signed to CBS Records he scored his first number one hit in 1964 with 'Charlie's Shoes' and continued to make big-selling country records into the seventies.

1937 Billie Jo Spears born in Beaumont, Texas. She made her first record when she was 13, 'Too

Old For Toys, Too Young For Boys'. She had several small hits for Capitol records, starting with 'He's Got More Love In His Little Finger', but it wasn't until she joined United Artists that she broke into the big time. 'Blanket On The Ground' was a huge crossover hit in 1975. Billie is most successful in England, where she replaced Tammy Wynette as the best-selling female country singer at the start of the eighties.

15th JANUARY

1915 Folk music collector Alan Lomax born in Austin, Texas. Following the lead of his father John Lomax, Alan devoted himself to the task of recording folk artists for the American Library of Congress. Thanks to the Lomax's, many great musicians were brought to the public attention and many fine songs were preserved. Alan's discovery included the brilliant black musician Huddie Ledbetter, better known as Leadbelly, whose songs included 'Goodnight Irene'.

1925 The first use of the word "Hillbilly" to describe commercial country music. An anonymous string band comprising Al and Jo Hopkins, Tony Alderman and John Rector were recording in the New York studios of Okeh with Ralph Peer. They told him that he could, "call the band anything you want, we're just a bunch of hillbillies from North Carolina and Virginia anyway" So Peer named them the Hillbillies.

16th JANUARY

1946 Ronnie Milsap, one of the most popular contemporary country entertainers, born in Robbinsville, North Carolina. Blind from birth, he was raised by his grandparents until the age of six, when he was enrolled at the Raleigh State School for the Blind. He showed a strong aptitude for music; quickly learning to play the piano, violin and cello. But he had no great enthusiasm for classical music and, despite the discouragement of his teachers, formed a rock 'n' roll band with some fellow students. After leaving school he worked the Atlanta club circuit as an R&B singer, even scoring a one-off hit with 'I Never Had It So Good'. From Georgia, he moved to Memphis and did session work. He had a reasonably secure career but felt that his music was getting nowhere and decided to "go country". With his wife Joyce, Ronnie moved to Nashville in 1972 and secured a job playing at Roger Miller's King Of The Road motel. He then made demo tapes which impressed RCA boss Jerry Bradley, and led to a recording

contract. The country hits started with the very first release, and each of his subsequent singles has charted. 1977 was his most successful year, he swept the CMA Awards, winning Entertainer, Male Vocalist, and Album of the Year titles.

194? Jim Stafford, country-pop entertainer, born. He had his biggest success in 1974, with the David Bellamy song, 'Spiders and Snakes', which was an international multi-million-selling hit.

17th JANUARY

1972 The Southern part of Bellvue Street (also known as Highway 51 South) in Memphis, Tennessee re-named Elvis Presley Boulevard. Within days the city was having considerable problems with fans who were stealing the signs. The souvenir hunting continued no matter how or where the signs were fixed. One woman was arrested after demolishing a lamp post with an Elvis sign nine feet up. She'd fixed a chain between her car and the post and then driven away, bringing it crashing down. She was jailed for a night, then released. . . and given the sign to keep. The city no longer has the problem as they've stopped replacing the signs, and Elvis Presley Boulevard is now the only thoroughfare in America which doesn't display its name.

1976 Merle Haggard's 'The Roots Of My Raising', a future number one country hit, entered the charts. The song was written by Tommy Collins, a longtime friend of Haggard, and another

singer associated with the country music scene in Bakersfield, California.

18th JANUARY

1941 Bobby Goldsboro born in Marianna, Florida. After leaving university in 1962, Bobby joined Roy Orbison's band as a guitar player. He was signed to United Artists as a solo performer and had his first hit in 1964 with 'See The Funny Little Clown'. Most famous for his best-selling pop hits, 'Honey' in 1968, and 'Summer The First Time' in 1973, Goldsboro has been a regular visitor to the county charts and notched up over 15 entries.

1980 Kenny Rogers top of the charts with the multi-million selling single 'Coward Of The County'. The song title was later utilised for a TV movie in which Rogers himself starred, as a flamboyant, self-styled preacher in the story of a small-town youth who refused to fight during World War II. It was one of the most successful American TV programmes of 1981.

19th JANUARY

1919 Rollin' Oscar Sullivan, an original member of the country comedy duo Lonzo and Oscar, born. Lonzo and Oscar were favourites of the Grand Ole Opry audience for over 20 years from 1947 with their routines and songs like 'You Blacked My Blue Eyes Too Often' and 'Cornbread, Lasses and Sassafras Tea'.

1939 Phil Everly, the younger of the two Everly Brothers, born in Chicago, Illinois. The duo came to international prominence in 1957 with their hit single 'Bye Bye Love' on Cadence, but had already been performing together for 12 years, starting when Phil was six and Don eight years old at radio station KMA in Shenandoah, Iowa, and continuing with frequent appearances with their parents, Ike and Margaret Everly, who were local country favourites. The brothers went their separate ways in the early seventies, and Phil has recorded four solo albums and makes occasional personal appearances, usually at the famous Palomino Club, which is near his home in North Hollywood.

The Everly Brothers

1946 Dolly Parton (Dolly Rebecca Parton) born in a log cabin in Locust Ridge in the Tennessee Mountains, in the early hours of the morning. Her big sister Willadeene recalled. "It snowed the night she was born, then the sky turned bright blue the next day. She was the most beautiful baby I'd ever seen, the first in our

family with blond hair and fair, ivory skin". Doctor Robert F. Thomas attended the birth (he'd later be immortalised in a song by Dolly) and because the family were broke, he was paid with a sack of corn meal.

1960 Ralph Peer, successful music publisher, record company executive and the man who 'discovered' and first recorded Jimmie Rodgers and The Carter Family, died in Hollywood.

20th JANUARY

1924 Slim Whitman (Otis Dewey Whitman) born in Tampa, Florida. He had minor successes with records like 'Casting My Lasso To The Sky' in the late forties, but his biggest American hits came after he'd signed to Imperial Records in 1952, including 'Indian Love Call', 'Secret Love', 'Rose Marie', and 'Keep It A Secret'. His popularity was far greater, and lasted much longer, in England. In the seventies a Slim Whitman album went straight into the British LP charts at number one.

1973 Jerry Lee Lewis made his (belated) debut at the Grand Ole Opry. He interrupted his performance to invite singer Del Wood onstage. She was one of the very few people in Nashville who'd treated him with kindness when he'd first come to the city in the fifties.

1977 Jimmy Carter inaugurated President of the United States. The Charlie Daniels Band, The Marshall Tucker Band and James Talley (Rosalynn Carter's favourite singer) joined Guy Lombardo to perform at the Inauguration Ball.

21st JANUARY

1885 Folk hero Leadbelly (Huddy Ledbetter) born near Mooringsport, Louisiana. He travelled through Texas and Louisiana with his beloved 12 string guitar, playing on street corners and in brothels, linking up for a time with bluesman Blind Lemon Jefferson. Leadbelly had a fiery temper, was frequently in trouble and spent time in jail for murder. He was "discovered" in a Louisiana penitentiary in 1932, when he was 49, by folk collector John Lomax, who immediately recognised his talent. On his release he performed in New York, then toured the US with other legendary figures including Sonny Terry, Cisco Houston, Woody Guthrie and "Big Bill" Broonzy. Leadbelly's best known songs include 'Goodnight Irene', 'Pick A Bale O'Cotton', 'Rock Island Line' and 'Black Betty'.

1942 Mac Davis born in Lubbock, Texas. His family moved to Atlanta, Georgia in 1957, "to combat hoodlum tendencies and provide a college education", where he attended Emory University and "majored in beer with a minor in rock and roll". He had a variety of jobs including ditch-digger, gas station attendant, probation officer and record plugger, but wrote songs and played in a band during the evenings. Success came when Lou Rawls recorded his 'You're Good For Me' in 1967, and was consolidated when Elvis recorded 'In The Ghetto'—a performance that helped revive Presley's flagging career in the late sixties. Mac's breakthrough as a musician came with 'Baby Don't Get Hooked On Me', a pop success in 1972 which was followed by several country hits. An engaging live act, he performs frequently in Las Vegas and was named Entertainer of the Year by the Academy of Country Music in 1975, and has now become a popular film star, since his debut in *North Dallas 40* as an American footballer. Success as a singer, writer and actor has helped make Mac Davis one of the wealthiest country entertainers.

1957 Patsy Cline appeared on Arthur Godfrey's "Talent Scouts" TV show in New York, sang 'Walkin' After Midnight', and won. The idea of the show was for viewers to recommend performers, though Patsy's "scout" was her own mother, Mrs Hensley, who recalled, "There was an eternity of applause. Patsy cried and cried, this moment was everything she'd dreamed of — the recognition and receiving such fantastic exposure over national television".

22nd JANUARY

1959 Buddy Holly made his last recordings, alone in his New York apartment with his guitar and tape recorder. After his death additional instrumentation was added by Norman Petty with musicians from Jimmy Gilmer and the Fireballs.

1969 Glen Campbell awarded a gold disc for the single 'Wichita Lineman', a hit the previous Autumn. Glen was in the middle of a golden period — the albums *By The Time I Get To Phoenix, Gentle On My Mind* and *Wichita Lineman* had gone gold in 1968, and there'd be four more in 1969; *Glen Campbell Live, Galveston, Hey Little One* and the duet LP with Bobbie Gentry *Gentry/Campbell*.

23rd JANUARY

1957 An eventful day for Patsy Cline; she made her first appearance on the morning TV show "Arthur Godfrey Time"; then went to see Paul Cohen at Decca, who told her that she had a hit on her hands with 'Walkin' After Midnight', the song she'd first performed on television just two days before. Meanwhile in Maryland, her husband Gerald Cline filed for divorce.

1959 The first night of the Winter Dance Party, a tour featuring Buddy Holly, The Big Bopper and Ritchie Valens, which would end in tragedy. Buddy agreed to do the tour of the American midwest as a favour to his management. He left his pregnant wife Maria Elena at home in New York, and recruited the young Waylon Jennings, Tommy Allsup and drummer Charlie Bunch as his band. They were billed as The Crickets, though Jerry Allison and Joe Maudlin had the legal rights to the name.

24th JANUARY

1936 Doug Kershaw, whose autobiographical 'Louisiana Man' is one of the most frequently performed country songs, was born on a houseboat near Tiel Ridge, Louisiana. Brought up in true Cajun fashion, he spoke only French until he was eight, the age when he made his debut as a performer — singing with his mother, "Mama Rita" at the seedy Bucket Of Blood club in Port Arthur. At the age of 12 he formed The Continental Playboys with his brothers Rusty and Nelson "Pee Wee" Kershaw, and they played local dates. In the fifties Rusty and Doug performed as a duo and extended their popularity well outside of Louisiana after signing with Hickory Records and scoring hits with 'Hey, Sheriff', 'Louisiana Man' and 'Diggy Liggy Lo'. Doug went solo in 1964 and his lively stage performances, singing and playing the fiddle, earned him the nickname "The Ragin' Cajun". He has recorded for several different labels, appeared on dozens of TV shows, including Johnny Cash's TV Special with Bob Dylan; and in movies.

1937 Four-year-old Johnny Cash and his family were evacuated from their Dyass Colony homestead in Arkansas because of rising flood water. The memories would inspire Johnny's song 'Five Feet High And Rising'.

Ray Stevens

1941 Ray Stevens (Ray Bagsdale), versatile singer, writer and multi-instrumentalist, born in Clarksdale, Georgia. He studied music at the Georgia State University for four years, during which time he released several records on four different labels. In 1961 one of them reached the charts — 'Jeremiah Peabody's Polyunsaturated, Quick Dissolving, Fast Actng, Pleasant Tasting, Green and Purple Pills'. Ray moved to Nashville and recorded more novelty hits including 'Ahab The Arab', 'Gitarzan', 'Bridget The Midget (Queen Of The Blues)' and 'Harry The Hairy Ape'. In the seventies he began making more conventional country records, including the gospel-flavoured 'Turn Your Radio On', though can still be relied upon to turn up with a novelty smash hit every five years or so.

1981 Dolly Parton's theme song from the film *9 to 5* (in which she made her movie debut) top of the charts.

25th JANUARY

1975 Ronnie Milsap top of the country charts with '(I'd Be) A Legend In My Own Time'. Typically for a Milsap song, it had an "up" lyrical theme. "When I started in country music, it just seemed there was so much stress on pain and misery, cheating songs and drinking songs, and sadness in country music. And I thought there's gotta be people who are really happy, and wanna hear something about the good things in life. I guess I was one of the first in country music to sing only about the positive. I've been accused of being 'always happy', or even of being too happy, maybe, in my songs. But I'm a happy person. I got a lot to be happy about".

1982 A baby daughter, Chelsea Jane, for singer Rosanne Cash and her producer/husband Rodney Crowell, Rosanne is one of the few performers who manages to balance a successful career in country music with bringing up young children. Her albums *Right Or Wrong* and *Seven Year Ache* were successful even though she did little of the promotion work that's usually considered essential if a record is to be a hit. The proud grandfather of Chelsea Jane, the second daughter for Rosanne and Rodney, is Johnny Cash.

26th JANUARY

1900 Clayton "Pappy" McMichen born in Allatoona, Georgia. He was a revered and influential figure from the early days of country music; a singer, songwriter, comedian and band leader, but remains best known as a master of the fiddle — playing with Gid Tanner's Skillet Lickers on their classic recordings of 'Sally Goodin', 'Wreck Of The Old 97', and 'Down Yonder' in the twenties. He branched out on his own in the thirties leading a variety of groups, including The Georgia Wildcats, who played Dixieland jazz. He retired in 1954 and died in January 1970.

1932 Claude Gray, "The Tall Texan" born in Henderson, Texas. He was a musical enthusiast as a child and a popular performer at local events in his teens. In the late fifties his career took off through radio appearances and a recording contract which led to his first hit, 'Family Bible' in 1960. Claude had several other successful country singles in the sixties including 'My Ears Should Burn' and 'I Never Had The One I Wanted'.

Dave and Sugar

194? Dave Rowland born in Sanger, California. The son of a minister, Dave started singing in church at the age of four. His first important break came when he joined J. D. Sumner and The Stamps, the renowned gospel group, who were working with Elvis. After a year, Dave decided to change to country music and worked with a variety of aggregations, including the Four Guys and a country-rock band called Wild Oates, then hit upon the successful formula of working with two attractive female singers, as Dave and Sugar. "The first day I held auditions," recalls Rowland, "I knew the combination was magic. It was a great look and a great sound, and there was nothing like it in country music." Dave and Sugar existed from 1975 until early in 1982 (after several changes in Sugar) and their numerous hits included 'Tear Time' and 'Golden Tears'. Dave Rowland is now a solo performer.

27th JANUARY

1937 Buddy Emmons, one of the most accomplished session musicians in Nashville, born in Mishawaka, Indiana. He's probably best known to country fans as a steel-guitar player—on hundreds of LP's and in TV appearances, wearing his trademark bowler hat; but he's also a gifted pianist and bass guitarist. He had lengthy periods on the road with Ernest Tubb, Roger Miller and Ray Price; was based in Los Angeles for a few years, working with the likes of Linda Ronstadt; but has spent most of his time since 1973 doing sessions in Nashville.

Buddy Emmons

1956 Elvis Presley's 'Heartbreak Hotel' released. It was his first record for RCA and would launch his career well beyond the country market—where he'd had his first hits, on Sun, and been nominated Best Newcomer of 1955. 'Heartbreak Hotel' was written by Mae Boren Axton (the mother of Hoyt Axton) and Tommy Durden, and Elvis' version eventually topped the country and pop charts and also reached the Top Five in the rhythm and blues charts—a rare feat.

28th JANUARY

1936 Bill Phillips, singer, songwriter and guitarist, born in Canton, North Carolina. Having decided to become a country performer, Bill didn't immediately make the obligatory trip to Nashville, Tennessee, but headed south to the sunny climes of Miami, Florida in 1955, where he became a regular on the Old South Jamboree which was broadcast over radio station WMIL and later WMIL TV. Then, having established a reputation for himself, Bill went to Music City, secured a contract with Columbia Records and had chart success in the sixties with 'Put It Off Until Tomorrow', 'Words I'm Gonna Have To Eat', 'Little Boy Sad' and several other self-penned compositions. More recently Bill has been a popular member of the Kitty Wells/ Johnny Wright roadshow.

1976 Red Steagall entered the country charts with the rousing 'Lone Star Beer And Bob Wills Music', a song which added to the growing interest in western swing and all things Texan;

a revival that had been fuelled by Waylon Jennings' hit 'Bob Wills Is Still The King' (in 1975) and records by young Austin-based bands Asleep At The Wheel and Alvin Crow and The Pleasant Valley Boys.

29th JANUARY

1928 Jimmy Sizemore, at the peak of his fame one of the youngest stars in country music history, born in Paintsville, Kentucky. He was part of a sentimental act (of a kind very popular in the thirties) with his father — they were billed as Asher Sizemore and Little Jimmy, and were regulars at the Grand Ole Opry from 1933 (when Jimmy was five years old) until 1942. Asher boasted that his son could "sing from memory more than two hundred songs and there were numerous others that he joins in with Dad on the chorus." Their specialities were sentimental "heart songs" (some of which were immortalised on wax for Victor's Bluebird label) and included 'How Beautiful Heaven Must Be', 'The Dying Girl's Farewell', 'Shake Hands With Mother Again' and 'The Dying Cowboy'.

1977 Kenny Rogers, a "has been" best known for his hits with the First Edition entered the country charts with a song called 'Lucille'. Within weeks it was the most popular in America, then started selling in vast quantities abroad. Kenny Rogers was back in the big time. He consolidated his success with the follow-up 'Daytime Friends' and within three years was the most successful country star in the world. The song 'Lucille' was born in the bar of the Greyhound Bus station in Toledo, Ohio (date unknown I'm afraid) when songwriter Hal Bynum noticed a couple having an argument. Then the man got up and said, "All I can say is, you picked a fine time to leave me". Suitably inspired, Bynum started writing on a table napkin, and then teamed up with Roger Bowling in Nashville to complete the song.

30th JANUARY

1938 Norma Jean, the singer who worked with Porter Wagoner on his very popular country music TV show in the sixties, born in Wellston, Oklahoma. Brought up on a farm and surrounded by a family of C&W enthusiasts, she was singing from a very early age, was a pre-teen star at Oklahoma City barn dances, and began a three-times-a-week radio show over KLPR on her 13th birthday. In 1958 she began making regular appearances on the Ozark Jubilee TV show and was invited to join the Opry two years later. Here she met Porter Wagoner who invited her to be his TV partner. A spell on Columbia Records produced no hits but a move to RCA brought chart success with songs 'Let's Go All The Way', 'Go Cat Go', 'I Wouldn't Buy A Used Car From Him' and 'Put Your Arms Around Her'. Norma Jean married in 1967, left the TV show and cut back on her recording and performances. Her replacement on Porter's show was the very young Dolly Parton.

1940 Jerry Badley, chief executive of RCA in Nashville, born.

19?? Jeanne Pruett born in Pell City, Alabama. She came to Nashville in 1965 with her husband Jack, a guitar player with Marty Robbins. During the sixties Jeanne made some records for RCA and Decca and wrote several songs for Marty, including 'Count Me Out', 'Waiting In Limbo' and 'Lily Of The Valley', then scored a major crossover pop hit with 'Satin Sheets' in 1973. She was surprised, but pleased, to be named one of the best "new" singers in the 1973 CMA Awards — ten years after she'd made her first record! Jeanne joined the Opry in 1974 and is frequently described as the best cook in Nashville.

31st JANUARY

1976 'Convoy' by C. W. McCall, one of the biggest selling country records of the seventies, came to the end of a six week run at the top of the charts. McCall's recitation had appeared at the height of the CB Radio craze in America; a craze which began after President Nixon imposed a 55mph speed limit to save fuel during an oil crisis, and motorists began communicating over the Citizen's Band to warn of police speed traps. 'Convoy' became very successful abroad, including countries where CB Radio was an unknown quantity, and DJ's had to translate the jargon to their listeners. The record later inspired a successful movie, which starred Kris Kristofferson and Ali MacGraw.

F E B R U A R Y

1st FEBRUARY

1937 Ray Sawyer, eye-patched vocalist for Dr. Hook, born in Chicksaw, Alabama.

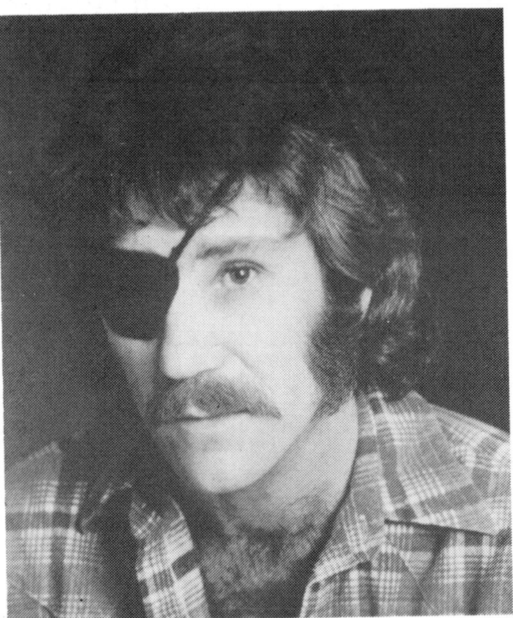

1937 Don Everly, elder half of the Everly Brothers, born in Brownie, Kentucky. The Everly's made one record for Columbia in 1956, then signed a management deal with Wesley Rose in Nashville and joined Cadence—a very fruitful association with several hits written by Felice and Boudleaux Bryant (including 'Bye Bye Love' and 'All I Have To Do Is Dream') and produced by Chet Atkins. The partnership ended in 1960 when the Brothers signed to Warner Brothers, scored some huge international hits, but then suffered a decline in popularity which coincided with the arrival of The Beatles and the "British Invasion" of the American charts. Don now lives in Nashville where he performs regularly with his curiously named Dead Cowboys Band, and has made several solo albums, including the well-received *Brother Jukebox*.

1981 Scotty Wiseman, one of the pioneering acts in country music history, died of a heart attack in Gainsville, Florida. Wiseman was part of the duo Lulu Belle and Scotty who performed as "The Sweethearts Of Country Music" for 25 years on the WLS Barn Dance.

2nd FEBRUARY

1902 Lester McFarland, the mandolin playing half of Mac and Bob, one of the early mandolin/guitar duos, born in Gray, Kentucky. Lester met his partner Robert Gardner when both were students at the Kentucky School for the Blind. Mac and Bob were regulars on the WLS National Barn Dance and were influential predecessors of The Delmore Brothers, The Blue Sky Boys and others. Lester retired from the music business in the early fifties.

Mac and Bob

194? Howard Bellamy, eldest of The Bellamy Brothers duo, born in North Florida. Their big country hits have included 'If I Said You Had A Beautiful Body, Would You Hold It Against Me' and 'Dancin' Cowboys'.

3rd FEBRUARY

1950 Linda Hargrove born in Tallahassee, Florida. One of the best of the singer/songwriters who came to Nashville in the early seventies. Linda worked with Mike Nesmith and Pete Drake and made some solo albums, including 'Blue Jean Country Queen' for Elektra, and 'Love You're The Teacher' for Capitol, which brought critical acclaim, but low sales. Linda is now a born again Christian and no longer sings her secular material.

1959 Buddy Holly, the Big Bopper (J.P. Richardson) and Ritchie Valens killed in a plane crash en route from a concert at Clear Lake, Iowa to Moorhead, Minnesota. Atrocious weather had slowed the progress of the Winter Dance Party tour bus and everyone was tired and their clothes dirty, so Holly decided to charter a private plane for his band to fly to the next date; but Holly's co-stars wanted to fly too. Buddy's young bassist Waylon Jennings gave up his seat to the Big Bopper, who had a cold, and Tommy Allsup flipped a coin with Valens, who called "heads" and won. When the rest of the tour party heard about the tragedy, they decided that the Winter Dance Party should continue. A local band, The Shadows, were added to the bill. It was the first important break for the band's 17-year-old leader, Bobby Velline; later he changed his name to Bobby Vee and rose to pop fame with a vocal style very similar to Holly's.

4th FEBRUARY

1978 A new album *Waylon and Willie* (RCA), recorded by Waylon Jennings and Willie Nelson at the peak of their popularity, stormed the album charts. In *Billboard*'s listings, it took just three weeks to top the country charts, then stayed there for 11 weeks; though in other magazines it entered at number one. Whatever the chart placings it sold in large quantities and soon achieved platinum status. The album packaging was ingenious—the brown cover had a raised, carved effect which looked like hand-tooled leather, and there were wildly ecstatic sleeve notes by Chet Flippo (associate editor of *Rolling Stone)* who observed, "I've not always approved of everything they've recorded, but when these two guys really crank it up, nobody—but nobody—can touch them. One listen to these songs made me a believer again. Waylon and Willie invoke the sheer beauty and power of real, honest country music as no one else does." There were 11 songs—five were duets, including Ed Bruce's 'Mammas Don't Let Your Babies Grow Up To Be Cowboys' which became a number one single and earned them a Grammy Award in 1979. In March Waylon and Willie went on tour together and outgrossed every other music act on the road at the time. A large proportion of the audiences were young, very young. "I think the kids are looking for something real to turn to," said Waylon, "Willie and I have been called crazy and wild and everything, but I guess the kids know we do stand up for what we believe in."

Waylon Jennings

5th FEBRUARY

1933 Claude King, best known for the hit 'Wolverton Mountain', born in Shreveport, Louisiana. He bought a guitar when he was 12, for just 50 cents, learnt to play and became a popular teenage entertainer at local social events. Suitably encouraged by the enthusiastic response he received, Claude began a musical career and eventually landed a CBS contract in 1961 and had a string of hits, including 'Big River, Big Man', 'The Comancheros' and, in 1962, 'Wolverton Mountain'.

Mervyn Conn

1935 Mervyn Conn born in Hackney, London, England. A leading British impresario, Mervyn can take credit for building a substantial market for country music in Britain, having brought almost every American star of note to the UK for his festivals, held annually at the Wembley Arena in London. He staged his first festival in 1969, "I had been booking people like The Moody Blues, The Rolling Stones and The Hollies, but country music intrigued me, so I put virtually every penny I had into staging the first one-day festival at Wembley," he recalls, "my friends and associates all thought I was mad but I have vindicated my decision." Conn's Easter festival now runs for several days in London, and also involves tours of several European countries.

1941 Henson Cargill born in Oklahoma City. His parents wanted him to become a lawyer, but Henson wanted to be a rancher, though when he came back from college he had doubts about both so worked briefly as a deputy sheriff, then decided to develop his keen interest in music and become a professional writer and performer. He scored with his very first record, 'Skip A Rope', which went to number one in early 1968. Subsequent releases did less well, though the country hits continued into the seventies, by which time Henson had achieved his ambition of becoming a ranch owner.

6th FEBRUARY

1955 A big country and western concert held at the Auditorium in Memphis drew a large crowd for a strong bill featuring some of the biggest acts of the time—Faron Young, Martha Carson, Ferlin Husky and The Wilburn Brothers. Bottom of the bill was a young singer from Memphis who'd end the year voted "Most Promising Newcomer of 1955" by country radio DJs—Elvis Presley.

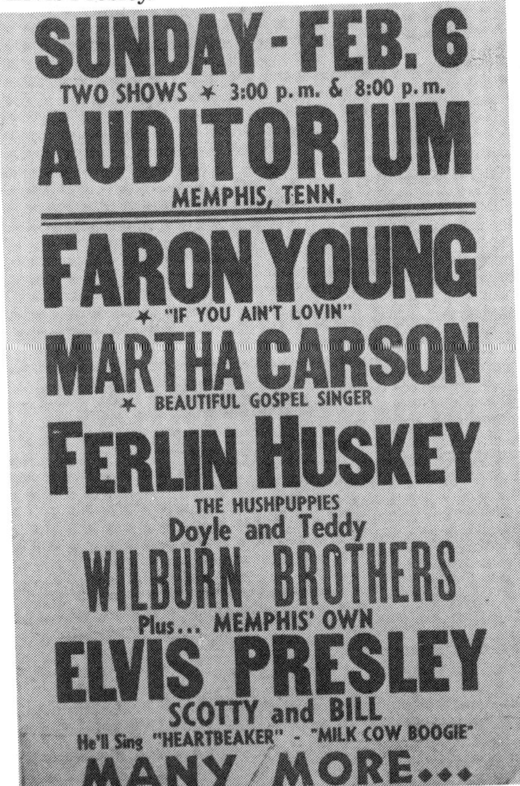

1971 Conway Twitty and Loretta Lynn made their debut in the country charts as a duo with 'After The Fire Is Gone' (Decca). They proved to be a very successful combination, scoring numerous hits including 'Lousiana Woman, Mississippi Man' and the memorable 'As Soon As I Hang Up The Phone', which involved Conway as a man trying to break up a love affair, and Loretta as the partner blissfully unaware of what he's trying to say. The pair were voted "Vocal Duo Of The Year" on four separate occasions by the CMA. Many country fans found their records too convincing; as Loretta explained in her biography *Coal Miner's Daughter*—"I'm always getting letters from Conway's fans who say I'm responsible for breaking up his marriage. Those fans hear Conway and me singing on our records, or they know we're partners in a talent agency. But that's the *only* way we're partners."

7th FEBRUARY

1898 Dock Boggs born in West Norton, Virginia. He prefected a quite unique banjo style and made some fascinating recordings of ballads and blues for Brunswick in the twenties. Unfortunately, his wife considered banjo playing sinful and persuaded him to stop performing so he became a coalminer. Boggs was rediscovered during the sixties when there was a revival of interest in Appalachian music amongst folk enthusiasts, and performed at concerts and recorded for Folkways.

1921 Wilma Lee Cooper born in Valley Head, West Viginia. Her family were a very popular religious singing group, The Leary Family, and Wilma Lee was performing with them from a very tender age. In 1939 she married Stoney Cooper, who had joined The Leary Family as a fiddle player, and after several years working within the group, they left and began performing as a duo. They were featured regularly on the WWVA Wheeling Jamboree from 1947 to 1957, then became members of the Grand Ole Opry. Wilma Lee and Stoney had several country hits including 'There's A Big Wheel' 'Come Walk With Me' and 'Big Midnight Special'. Stoney Cooper died in 1977, but Wilma has continued to perform and remains an Opry regular.

1959 The body of 22-year-old Buddy Holly buried in the Lubbock City Cemetery after a funeral service at the Tabernacle Baptist Church. There were 1,000 mourners and pall bearers were musician friends: Bob Montgomery, Sonny Curtis, Joe Mauldin, Niki Sullivan, Jerry Allison and Phil Everly. One of Buddy's favourite records, 'I'll Be All Right' by The Angelic Gospel Singers was played during the service. His gravestone has the correct spelling of his last name — Holley.

8th FEBRUARY

1902 Harold "Pappy" Daily, successful producer and record company executive, born in Yoakum, Texas. A country fan for many years before he became involved in the business side of recording, he formed Starday in Houston in the early fifties, and the young George Jones was an early signing. He was involved with handling Mercury's country product from 1955, then moved to United Artists in the sixties where he had great success managing the careers of George Jones (again), Melba Montgomery and Gene Pitney.

1952 Webb Pierce began a remarkable run of country music hits with 'Wondering' on Decca. He had records in *Billboard*'s country listings for 21 consecutive years from 1952 until 1972. Newcomers to country music probably know Webb better for his famous "guitar shaped" swimming pool, which was specially built at his home in Curtiswood Lane, Nashville and became a very popular tourist attraction. Webb (standing on the diving board) and pool are featured on the best-selling postcard in Nashville.

9th FEBRUARY

1914 Ernest Dale Tubb born on a cotton farm in Crisp, Texas. He wanted to be a musician at the age of 13, when he first heard Jimmie Rodgers. His enthusiasm for "The Singing Brakeman" was almost fanatical. Tubb moved to San Antonio and was singing Rodgers' songs on an early morning KONO radio show, when he discovered that Jimmie's widow lived in the same city. She took a keen interest in his career, lent him Rodgers' guitar and arranged an audition and recording session with RCA. Despite all the help from Mrs Rodgers, the records were not a success and RCA showed little enthusiasm for continuing with the young singer. But Tubb persisted with his career as an entertainer and in 1940 signed with Decca, who gave him a lot of support, and within two years he'd scored a million-selling hit, 'Walking The Floor Over You'. Ernest became an Opry regular the following year, appeared in several films and toured with his Texas Troubadours. In 1974 he opened his (now famous) record store in Nashville, and began the Midnight Jamboree radio show, which was broadcast from the store each Saturday night after the Opry. Tubb has always loved playing before a live audience and frequently spends upwards of 300 days a years on the road. His old bus, Green Hornet No. 1, is supposed to have travelled over two million miles, before being replaced by Green Hornet No. 2.

1947 Joe Ely, one of the most promising new singers to emerge from Texas in the late seventies, born in Amarillo, Texas, then brought up in Lubbock. He was in the acoustic country band The Flatlanders (with other Texas country cult figures Butch Hancock and Jimmie Dale Gilmore), travelled the world, then formed his own band and recorded the *Joe Ely* album for MCA, in 1977, which drew widespread critical acclaim but minimal sales. Ely and band are very popular as a live act in Texas and Europe but haven't had a hit record yet, probably because their high-energy material falls in the no-man's-land between country and rock radio formats.

1981 Bill Haley, the first star of rock 'n' roll, died in his sleep, at home in Harlingen, Texas. He was 56.

10th FEBRUARY

1943 Ral Donner, one of the better Elvis sound-a-likes from the early sixties, born in Chicago. His biggest hit was 'You Don't Know What You Got'.

1979 Eddie Rabbitt top of the country charts with 'Every Which Way But Loose', the theme song from an extremely successful Clint Eastwood film, which grossed over $100 million. The soundtrack spawned four number one singles and a platinum album, and encouraged a spate of movies with country music soundtracks and themes. *Every Which Way But Loose* also launched producer Snuff Garrett into the lucrative world of film scoring — "For the last twenty years I'd been hitting up the studios to let me do something," said Snuff, "I always wanted to do film and music and I took people to lunches, dinners, meetings, but in those days film and music didn't jell and I didn't score." Garrett's break came when Clint Eastwood called him during the shooting of *Loose* saying he was unhappy with the music and could Snuff help? Snuff didn't need asking twice and organised everything within the two week deadline.

Eddie Rabbitt

11th FEBRUARY

1918 Wesley Rose born in Chicago, Illinois. He played a key role in the expansion of the Acuff-Rose publishing company in Nashville which his father (Fred Rose) had set up with Roy Acuff in 1943. Wesley was instrumental in getting pop artists to record Hank Williams' songs he signed up great writers like Felice and Boudleaux Bryant, John D. Loudermilk, Marty Robbins and Roy Orbison and did much to help the fledgling career of the Everly Brothers, Don and Phil.

1935 Gene Vincent (Vincent Eugene Craddock) one of the great rock 'n' roll vocalists, born in Norfolk, Virginia. Before he became a performer, Gene was in the US Navy, and while in Korea was very badly injured in the left leg. Doctors wanted the leg amputated, but he insisted on keeping it, and suffered pain and a pronounced limp for the rest of his life. Vincent entered a talent contest in 1956 which had been organised by Capitol Records, who were looking for someone to rival Elvis Presley. He won with the song 'Be Bop A Lula', which remains his best known hit. Gene Vincent died in October 1971.

1936 Burt Reynolds, one of the top box-office movie stars in the world, born in Waycross, Georgia. The son of a Florida police chief, Burt progressed from TV stuntman, through nude centrefold of an American women's magazine, to film stardom in a series of country music-related movies — *Gator, White Lightening, WW And The Dixie Dance Kings* (which also featured the Ryman Auditorium, Jerry Reed and a hatless Don Williams), the enormously successful *Smokey and the Bandit* and *The Best Little Whorehouse in Texas*. Reynolds seems to have played almost identical parts in several films — an easy going, good humoured, though useful with his fists character; but proved that he could be taken seriously as a actor with the movie *Deliverance* Burt's relationships with famous women have brought him considerable publicity, including a spell when he was seen regularly with Tammy Wynette. Her autobiography *Stand By Your Man* contains a dramatic account of his collapse in her bathroom with a severe case of hypoglycemia (a blood sugar infection).

12th FEBRUARY

1911 Stephen Sholes born in Washington D.C. He worked for RCA Victor for nearly four decades, and can take much of the credit for establishing the first major record company office in Nashville. Steve played a very important role in developing the careers of several major names, including Chet Atkins, Eddy Arnold, Hank Snow, Hank Locklin, Jim Reeves, Roy Rogers and Elvis Presley.

Moe Bandy

1944 Moe Bandy, popular honky-tonk singer, born in Meridian, Mississippi. He came from a musical family, father played the guitar and mother was a pianist, while his grandfather had worked on the railroads with Jimmie Rodgers and had a huge collection of Rodgers' records, which Moe listened to during childhood. Bandy liked the idea of being a guitarist and singer but was also attracted to being a rodeo rider. A series of broken bones while bronco-busting persuaded him that music was the more preferable option and he formed a band called The Mavericks, then went solo in 1973 and his self-financed single 'I Just Started Hating Cheatin' Songs Today' brought him his first taste of success. He made a few singles for the small GRC label, including the autobiographical 'Bandy The Rodeo

Clown', then moved to CBS where he scored with 'Hank Williams You Wrote My Life'. For many people, Bandy's music is seen as a welcome return to country music basics; it's hardcore, 100 per cent proof stuff of the kind that used to blow out of West Texas honky-tonks in the forties and fifties before the Nashville Sound took country music uptown and gave it a more sophisticated image and softer sound. "I really think my songs are about life," says Moe Bandy, "There's cheatin' and drinkin' and divorcin' going on everywhere. I believe that's what good country music is all about. And there's a definite need for good hardcore country. Sure, the music has changed,and it's brought in more fans, but I'm trying to go back for the feel of original country, and that's why I've stayed with it."

13th FEBRUARY

1919 Tennessee Ernie Ford (Ernest Jennings Ford) born in Bristol, Tennessee. His ambition to become a DJ was fulfilled, after many days spent hanging around his local radio station WOAI, when he was given a job as announcer. He was a great success and soon progressed to bigger and better stations in Atlanta and Knoxville. After war service he moved to California where bandleader Cliffie Stone noticed his talents as a singer (something Ernie was only doing "for fun") and arranged an audition with Capitol Records. They liked what they heard, signed Tennessee Ernie Ford to a contract, and in 1949 he had his first big hit with 'Mule Train'. His 1950 hit 'Shotgun Boogie' was an early and very successful example of the fast-paced hillbilly-boogie style which predated rock 'n' roll, and it remains a cult favourite with rockabilly enthusiasts today. 'Sixteen Tons' was his biggest hit, while *Hymns,* an album of religious songs (one of several that he made) became the first country LP to sell over a million copies.

1920 Boudleaux Bryant, male half of one of the most successful songwriting teams in popular music history, born in Shellman, Georgia. He came from a classical music background, studied violin as a child, but subsequently played in all manner of pop aggregations rather than the symphony orchestras one might have expected. Boudleaux was in a family band that featured jazz and folk, played the fiddle with a country group and had periods where he was a "Spanish guitarist" in a Latin band and a "Filipino" with an Hawaiian group. In 1945, while touring with a jazz outfit, Boudleaux stayed at an hotel in Milwaukee and met Felice, who was working the elevator. They married three months later and began writing country songs together for fun. One such song found its way to Acuff-Rose and Boudleaux and Felice were invited to Nashville. Since then there's hardly been a week when one of their tunes hasn't been in the charts. They think they've now written over six thousand, and four hundred different artists have recorded them, including Dylan, Presley, Simon and Garfunkel and almost every country star of note.

1927 Jim McReynolds, guitarist and vocalist in the bluegrass duo Jim and Jesse, born in Coeburn, Virginia. Their traditional bluegrass performances have made them favourites at festivals for many years. They've had several chart entries (unusual for a bluegrass team) including 'Diesel On My Trail', 'Better Times A-Coming' and 'Freight Train'.

14th FEBRUARY

193? Razzy Bailey, christened Rasie after his father's first name of Erastus, born. Now a very successful star of contemporary country music, Razzy has certainly "paid his dues". He grew up in poverty as his folks struggled on small farms in Alabama, New Mexico and Texas, and he had his first band when he was 15, but lacking any know-how of the music business it was years before he'd be anything more than a local club favourite. He spent nearly two decades on the Georgia, Alabama and Florida honky-tonk curcuit and had several frustrating and unsuccessful attempts at making hit records, including twice forming his own labels—Aquarian (after his star sign) and Erastus (after his dad). Razzy became so disillusioned that he gave up music for a time, and his personal life began to fall apart. "I started to get up and have a drink in the morning, just to try and figure out how I was going to face the day, thinking all the years of effort wasn't going to develop into anything," he recalls. "My son began to get into trouble and then my wife said she couldn't stand the pressure and was going home to her mother." But a change of fortune was just around the corner; in 1976 Dickey Lee recorded a song

Razzy had written ten years before, '9,999,999 Tears' and it rose to the top of the charts. Dickey's record company RCA took an interest as Razzy as a performer and he finally broke into the country music big time in 1978 with 'What Time Do You Have To Be Back In Heaven' —the first of a long string of Top Ten hits.

1953 'Kaw Liga', Hank Williams' first posthumous release entered the country charts. According to Wesley Rose, "Hank stayed at a fishing lodge in South Alabama called Lake Kowaliga. The name struck him as a good Indian name and also a good title for a song".

1973 The film *Gospel Road* had its world premiere in Charlotte, North Carolina. A feature length documentary on the life of Jesus Christ, it was written, produced, narrated and financed by Johnny Cash. "I really wanted to zero in on Christ," said Cash, "I had never seen a film on Christ that I could relate to, one that was really believable." Songs for the movie were contributed by Kris Kirstofferson, Joe South, John Denver, Larry Gatlin and Cash himself.

1982 Johnny Lee married Charlene Tilton (actress from the popular TV series "Dallas") at Tony Orlando's home. Mickey Gilley, co-owner of Gilley's Club in Houston where Johnny fronted the house band for years, was the best man.

15th FEBRUARY

1918 Hank Locklin (Lawrence Hankins Locklin) born in McLellan, Florida. His is the familiar story of the boy who grew up on a cotton farm, loved singing country songs, and was impressing his family and friends with his skill on the guitar before he'd reached his teens. He retained ambitions of becoming a successful musician through the difficult days of the Depression when he worked on farms and as a road worker, and performed whenever he could. His perseverance paid off after World War II when he was featured on the Louisiana Hayride, and began making records, first for Decca then Four Star. Hank's first Top Ten success came with 'Let Me Be The One' in 1953, then came a four year gap before a move to RCA Victor brought a long run of chart entries. The best known songs associated with Hank Locklin are 'Geisha Girl' (his first number one), 'Send Me The Pillow You Dream On' and 'Please Help Me I'm Falling'. In the sixties Hank returned to McLellan, bought a large ranch ("The Singin' L") which incorporated the cotton field that he'd worked in as a child, and became so popular with the locals that he was elected mayor!

Hank Locklin

1958 Don Gibson's double sided country hit 'Oh Lonesome Me'/'I Can't Stop Lovin' You' entered the charts. It stayed there for 34 weeks.

16th FEBRUARY

1914 Jimmy Wakely born in a log cabin in rural Arkansas. He grew up in Oklahoma, became a ranch hand and impressed his friends with his singing. He was persuaded to enter a local talent show and the response he received encouraged him to form the Wakely Trio. They had their own radio show which impressed a visiting Gene Autry and resulted in Jimmy joining the famous cowboy star in California—where the trio were featured on the Melody Ranch show and Jimmy began appearing in films. In the forties Wakely left Gene Autry and formed a band comprised of some future country music notables: Spade Cooley, Merle Travis, Cliffie Stone and Wesley Tuttle, and they appeared in over 30 movies. Jimmy started making records in the forties as a solo performer, but had his biggest hits when he teamed up with Margaret Whiting. Their successful collaborations included 'Slippin' Around', 'Wedding Bells' and 'Broken Down Merry-Go-Round'.

Jo Walker-Meador

1924 Jo Walker-Meador, executive director of the Country Music Association, born in Orlinda, Tennessee. Jo helped build up the CMA from humble beginnings in 1958 to the prestigious, influential and respected organisation it is today.

17th FEBRUARY

1931 Uncle Jimmy Thompson, the fiddle player who was the first musician featured on WSM Barn Dance (later called the Grand Ole Opry) died aged 83.

1936 Bill and Charlie Monroe's first recording session, at the Southern Radio Building in Charlotte, North Carolina. RCA A&R man Eli Oberstein was determined to record the pair and sent them a telegram reading WE MUST HAVE THE MONROE BROTHERS ON RECORDS STOP WON'T TAKE NO FOR AN ANSWER STOP ANSWER REQUESTED, which they ignored, but which he followed with telephone calls until they agreed. Bill and Charlie recorded ten songs including several which have become their best known and loved—'What Would You Give In Exchange', 'My Long Journey Home', 'Nine Pound Hammer Is Too Heavy', 'On Some Foggy Mountain Top' and 'New River Train'.

1965 The Tennessee State Legislature declare 'The Tennessee Waltz' a state song. There are four others—'My Tennessee', 'My Homeland Tennessee', 'When It's Iris Time In Tennessee' and 'Rocky Top'.

1969 Johnny Cash and Bob Dylan recorded together at Columbia studios in Nashville. One of the songs, 'Girl From The North Country', turned up on Dylan's *Nashville Skyline,* though most of the material was never officially released (but appeared on the bootleg LP *The Dylan/Cash Session).*

18th FEBRUARY

1914 Frank "Pee Wee" King, singer, writer and bandleader, born in Milwaukee, Wisconsin, of Polish origin—his dad led a polka band. Pee Wee played the accordion and fiddle, and was leading a band and performing on the radio while still in his teens. After working with Gene Autry (before he went to Hollywood) and then the Log Cabin Cowboys, King formed his Golden West Cowboys in 1936 and they appeared regularly on the Grand Ole Opry and had a daily radio show on a Knoxville station. At various times his band included such up-and-coming country stars as Ernest Tubb, Eddy Arnold and Cowboy Copas. From 1947 Pee Wee King began a TV show on WAVE in Louisville, Kentucky, which ran for ten years, the last two being networked by NBC. He had some chart hits but his greatest successes came as a song-writer. His best known songs are 'Slow Poke', 'Walk Me By The River', 'Napoleon's Retreat', and 'Tennessee Waltz', which he co-wrote in 1948 with Redd Stewart. Pee Wee King was elected to the Country Music Hall Of Fame in 1974.

1978 Hattie Louise "Tootsie" Bess, owner of Tootsie's Orchid Lounge, died in Nashville after a long battle with cancer. For years unknown pickers and singers (fresh off the Greyhound Bus) came to Tootsie's little beer joint in Lower Broadway, Nashville in the hope of being discovered by some of the country stars who patronised the bar between performances at the nearby Ryman Auditorum, home of the Grand Ole Opry until 1974. Tootsie was famous for ejecting troublesome customers with the aid of her long hat pin, supposedly given to her by Charley Pride. Among the many floral tributes at her funeral was a heart made of flowers from Ernest Tubb with a giant hat pin stuck through the centre.

19th FEBRUARY

1924 Movie tough guy Lee Marvin born into a wealthy family in New York City. Lee's films have included *Cat Ballou, The Man Who Shot Liberty Vallance* and *Paint Your Wagon* in which he proved he couldn't sing, but nevertheless scored an international hit with 'I Was Born Under A Wandering Star'.

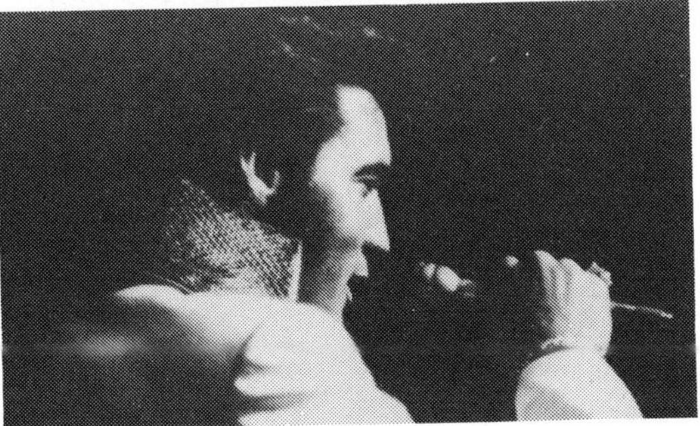

1977 Elvis Presley top of the country charts with 'Moody Blue'. RCA had tremendous difficulty getting Elvis into the recording studio in the last years of his life, but then solved the problem by bringing the recording equipment and musicians to Graceland, Presley's home in Memphis. 'Moody Blue' was recorded there in early February of 1976.

20th FEBRUARY

1925 Film maker Robert Altman born. His credits include *Nashville,* the 1975 movie which used country music as the metaphor to examine the state of Americana in the seventies. The film annoyed many music people in Nashville, but was praised to the heights by most film critics, including Jay Cocks of *Time* magazine who noted, "The movie satirizes country and western people—audiences and performers alike—but without condescension and with a palpable affection for their fine, flaky spirit".

1941 Buffy Sainte-Marie, a folk singer who has edged over into country on several occasions, born in either Canada or Sebago Lake, Maine of Cree Indian parents. She was fostered and never knew her mother and father (hence the confusion about her birthplace) and was raised in Massachusetts. Buffy came to prominence as a performer in folk clubs in New York's Greenwich Village. Her best known songs include 'The Universal Soldier' and 'Now That The Buffalo's Gone'. In 1968 she came to Nashville to record the album *I'm Gonna Be A Country Girl Again,* and had a small hit with the title track, but scored a much bigger success with the theme song from *Soldier Blue,* a particularly violent movie about a massacre of American Indians.

21st FEBRUARY

1976 Waylon Jennings and Willie Nelson top the country charts with 'Good Hearted Woman', a track from *Wanted:—The Outlaws* an extremely successful compilation album devised by Jerry Bradley at RCA to capitalise on the enthusiasm for "outlaw" country stars. It was cleverly packaged; the brown sleeve looked like a "Wanted" poster and featured grainy photographs of the artists: Waylon, Willie, Tompall Glaser and Jennings' wife Jessi Colter. *Wanted:—The Outlaws* sold well over a million copies—largely to non-country fans; and became the first certified platinum album in country music history. Ironically, it isn't a particularly good record; none of the artists are represented at their best and the only outstanding track is 'Good Hearted Woman'. The song topped the country charts for three weeks, and was later voted CMA Single Of The Year.

Willie Nelson

22nd FEBRUARY

1910 Spade Cooley (Donell Cooley), western swing bandleader, born in Grand, Oklahoma. He came from a musical family and made his debut as a public performer at the age of eight. Spade's western swing band were very popular in the California area during the forties, and made several records. His career came to a dramatic halt when he was arrested and subsequently convicted of murdering his wife.

1920 Del Wood (Adelaide Hazelwood) born in Nashville. A piano player in the old fashioned ragtime/barrelhouse style, she had a big hit in 1951 with 'Down Yonder'. The tune, and singer were great favourites of Jerry Lee Lewis. Del became a member of the Grand Ole Opry in 1952 and has been appearing there regularly ever since.

1959 Loretta Lynn, living in Washington with Mooney and her young family, learned that her father had died, after waking from a dream when she'd seen him lying in a wine-coloured coffin. "I was still dreaming when Clyde Green knocked on the door and said there was a phone call for me. People didn't usually call me that early. Sure enough, it was Mommy, telling me Daddy had gone. They said he died of a stroke but I figured the coal mines done it."

23rd FEBRUARY

1946 Rusty Young, an original member of the country-rock band Poco, born in Long Beach, California. Brought up in Colorado, his parents were big country fans and they started little Rusty on the pedal steel guitar when he was just six. He was in a popular Colorado band called Boenzee Cryque from 1964 to 1968, then moved to Los Angeles where he played pedal steel on one of the last recording sessions of Buffalo Springfield. He was asked to join the Flying Burrito Brothers but plumped instead for Poco (originally called Pogo after a cartoon character but changed when the cartoonist threatened legal action). The original line-up of Poco, who made their debut at LA's famed Troubadour club, were Jim Messina, Rusty, George Grantham, Richie Furay and Randy Meisner—only Rusty remains in the band today. They were one of the best country-rock outfits and deserved big hits with songs like 'Rose Of Cimarron' and 'Good Feelin' To Know', but they didn't win large-scale public acceptance until they changed their style to contemporary soft rock in 1979.

1957 Porter Wagoner joined the Grand Ole Opry.

24th FEBRUARY

1979 Anne Murray's album *New Kind Of Feeling* (Capitol) entered the country album charts. 1979 was a good year for Anne, but it was also a frustrating year of "almosts". The *New Kind Of Feeling* album would stay on the listings for almost a year—51 weeks; and almost make number one—it was at two for nine weeks. Anne scored three chart-topping country singles in 1979: 'I Just Fall In Love Again', 'Shadows In The Moonlight' and 'Broken Hearted Me', which were pop successes too, but by the year's end she was just pipped at the post by disco star Donna Summer as America's most successful female artist in *Billboard*'s chart breakdown of the top records. Despite her enormous success in the field, Anne doesn't associate much with other country artists or the fans, and considers her music only partially country. "I don't play for country audiences;" she told an English journalist, "I think I've played maybe three specifically country events in my life and I found them awful! They have thirty performers and it's like a cattle call. I didn't enjoy them at all. You see, I don't like going out and presenting just one part of me, and country music is only one part of what I do, I can do without people yelling abuse because I'm not doing a pure country act—so I stayed away from that kind of show. I do include country songs on all my albums, but that's because I like to. Some have more than others, but usually I don't have more than two or three that are country flavoured. I really don't know what country is any more. Take 'I Just Fall In Love Again' for instance. That was the biggest country single of 1979 and it wasn't what I'd call a country song!"

25th FEBRUARY

1927 Ralph Stanley, one of the great Stanley Brothers who were legendary figures in bluegrass music, born in Stratton, Virginia—in the Clinch Mountain area which also produced The Carter Family and The Stoneman Family. Their early musical experiences were with traditional country music, and their mother taught Ralph and his elder brother Carter harmony singing at a very early age. While Carter learned to play the guitar, Stanley became adept with the banjo and they formed a teenage group The Stanley Brothers and The Clinch Mountain Boys, who played old-timey music and had their own radio show on WCYB Bristol, Tennessee. In the mid-forties they changed to the bluegrass style popularised by Bill Monroe, but continued with their radio show and built a very strong local following at concerts. In the fifties they began touring the US, and then accepted invitations to travel abroad, introducing bluegrass to a large international audience. They made several records for a variety of labels including Starday, King, Mercury and Columbia. The partnership ended when Carter died (in 1966) but Ralph continued to tour and make records. Emmylou Harris has done much to popularise their music in recent years, singing some of their material and recording Ralph's classic 'The Darkest Hour Is Just Before Dawn' on her bluegrass album *Roses In The Snow*.

Ralph Stanley

1932 Faron Young born in Shreveport, Louisiana. He started singing and playing guitar at an early age, and by the time he entered high school could apparently perform almost all the big country hits of the day. He worked regularly on The Louisiana Hayride radio show (which was broadcast from his home town) and it was there that he met Webb Pierce, who took him on tour and gave him some much needed exposure outside of Louisiana. He signed to Capitol in 1952 and began an almost unbroken run of hit singles from 1953 through to the seventies. Somebody worked out that between his first hit 'Going Steady' and the hugely successful 'Four In The Morning' in 1971, Faron had been on the country charts for 742 weeks! 'Four In The Morning' was a hit around the world, reaching number three on the English pop charts in 1972. The hits continued through the seventies, though Faron was less of a permanent fixture, but was still very active in country music both as performer and businessman.

26th FEBRUARY

1845 Buffalo Bill (real name William Frederick Cody) born in LeClaire, Scott County, Iowa. He became famous for his adventures as chief scout with the 5th US Cavalry; then entered show business, starting Buffalo Bill's Wild West Show, which toured America and even visited Great Britain for Queen Victoria's Jubilee. Cody's star attractions in London included Annie Oakley, Buck Taylor "the first cowboy hero" and Chief Sitting Bull. Cody can take credit for being one of the first to romanticise the "Wild West" and its cowboys and Indians.

1932 John R. Cash, one of the all-time country greats, born in Kingsland, Arkansas. John's father was a sharecropper who lost his livelihood during the Depression, but was fortunate to be chosen for a government resettlement programme at the Dyass Land Colony, near the banks of the Mississippi River. John helped his father in the fields throughout his boyhood and teens, then left home and joined the Air Force, where he formed his first band and met his first wife, Vivian Liberto. The couple married and moved to Memphis where they started a family, eventually comprising four girls, including Rosanne, who's now a successful country singer. Johnny sold vacuum cleaners, but had keen aspirations to become a musician. He auditioned at Sun Records, but Sam Phillips turned him down. Then Cash met Luther Perkins and Marshall Grant (The Tennessee Two) They teamed up and had developed the distinctive sound of their first Sun Records by the time of the second audition, where Phillips was immediately impressed by Johnny's song, 'Hey, Porter'. Cash's success and status grew in leaps and bounds, particularly after he'd signed with CBS in 1958. There were frequent tours and numerous hit records, but the hard work and constant travelling took their toll and Johnny became addicted to pills. By the mid-sixties many people feared that he would go the same way as Hank Williams, but he pulled himself back from the brink with help from a doctor and June Carter, his second wife (Vivian having divorced him in 1966). By the end of the sixties, Johnny Cash was back in good health, and the hits have continued ever since.

27th FEBRUARY

1936 Charles "Chuck" Glaser, of Tompall and the Glaser Brothers, born on the family ranch in

Spaulding, Nebraska. The brothers travelled to Nashville in 1957 and brazened their way into a Marty Robbins concert where they impressed the star with their harmonies and songwriting. "We were three brassy brats," remembers Chuck, but the approach worked and Marty signed them to his own label and publishing company. After a long career, the trio split in the early seventies, and Chuck formed the Nova booking agency. He wasn't a novice in the backstage world of country music, having been involved in management and production duties while still a performer. He co-produced John Hartford's classic recording of 'Gentle On My Mind' and he managed the bizarre Kinky Friedman. In 1975, Chuck suffered a massive stroke which paralysed his entire left side, including his vocal chords and doctors thought he might never talk or walk again. With great determination, Chuck recovered the use of his voice, though two full years passed before he could carry a tune.

1971 'Kentucky Feb. 27, '71' is one of the tracks on Tom T. Hall's *In Search Of A Song,* the true story of Tom's visit to see an old man.

28th FEBRUARY

1911 Jim Denny born in Buffalo Valley, Tennessee. One of the hardest working men in country music history, he helped the careers of many artists as Grand Ole Opry talent scout, publisher and booking agent. James was born into a poverty stricken family and moved to Nashville when he was 11 to live with an aunt. He sold newspapers, delivered telegrams and worked as a messenger for the National Life and Accident Insurance Company which owned station WSM and the Grand Ole Opry. Denny worked his way up inside the company, finally becoming the Opry booker in 1951. He started the very successful Cedarwood publishing company in 1954, then set up his own booking agency—Jim Denny Artist Bureau.

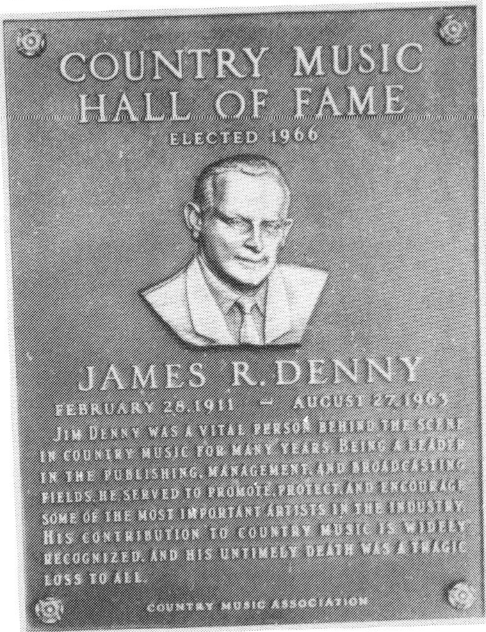

1940 Joe South, multi-talented musician and songwriter, born in Atlanta Georgia. He made his name as a session guitarist with Bob Dylan, Simon and Garfunkel and others, then began making his own records and scored country hits like 'You're The Reason', and had an international best-seller with 'The Games People Play'. His biggest successes as a writer have been 'Rose Garden' (for Lynn Anderson). 'Down On The Boondocks' (for Billy Joe Royal), 'Hush' and 'Walk A Mile In My Shoes'.

M A R C H

1st MARCH

1917 Cliffie Stone (Clifford Gilpin Snyder) born in Burbank, California. His father was a country entertainer and used the name Herman The Hermit. Cliffie didn't immediately follow his father's footsteps but was a bassist with a dance band and then a DJ, before switching to country music and becoming a bandleader, comedian, singer, and host of radio shows like "Hollywood Barn Dance" and "Lucky Stars". During World War II Cliffie was introducing more than 20 different country radio shows each week. After the war he signed to Capitol Records, where he was both an artist and talent scout, and he earned the company's lasting gratitude when he "discovered" Tennessee Ernie Ford. Cliffie Stone had his own 'Hometown Jamboree' TV show on a Los Angeles station for several years in the fifties, then dropped out of performing to concentrate on building up his publishing company and talent booking agency. The skills of the multi-faceted Stone also extended to song writing, and he was co-author of several hits, including 'Divorce Me C.O.D.' and 'So Firm, So Round, So Fully Packed'.

1934 Jim Ed Brown born in Sparkman, Arkansas. Jim has had country chart success as a solo artist; as part of an award winning duo, with Helen Cornelius; and as a member of The Browns, a family trio that featured his sister Ella Maxine and Bonnie. The Browns had begun performing in the early fifties and their career was building slowly and surely when they had a huge international hit in 1959 with 'The Three Bells', a French song about a fictional 'Jimmy Brown'. They disbanded in the mid-sixties and Jim had solo success with 'Pop A Top' and 'Morning'. The Jim Ed Brown and Helen Cornelius combination was extremely successful in the seventies and they were voted Vocal Duo of the Year by the CMA in 1977.

1968 A week after winning a Grammy award for their recording of 'Jackson', Johnny Cash and June Carter were married in Franklin, Kentucky. Merle Kilgore, who co-wrote 'Ring of Fire', was the best man. The marriage coincided with the successful conclusion of Cash's fight to quit the tranquilizer pills that he was addicted to and had almost killed him. Cash came off with help and support from June and his doctor, Dr. Nat Watson, who observed "I've never seen anybody come off pills with the guts that he showed. He was really fighting. But he was fighting on his terms. A miserably low percentage of people who are hooked can make it. I have a feeling that he's made it. Relapses are possible, but I don't think he'll ever have trouble again. I wouldn't make that statement about anybody else I know who has ever been on drugs."

2nd MARCH

1923 Doc Watson (Arthel Watson), blind guitarist and banjo player, and one of the most respected traditional-style country musicians, born in Deep Gap, North Carolina. He developed an early love for traditional songs, which he learned from his family, and was an accomplished musician by his teens. Doc was educated at the Raleigh School for the Blind (where Ronnie Milsap was a student years later), and after the completion of his studies, he became a popular local musician. In 1960 he was "discovered" by musicologist Ralph Rinzler, who was on a field trip to North Carolina. Concert appearances in New York and Los Angeles followed, and then a series of albums for Vanguard. Since 1965 Doc Watson has been performing with his son Merle, and his fame has spread further through appearances at international festivals and concerts.

1952 Grand Ole Opry favourite Uncle Dave Macon admitted to a Murfreesboro hospital with a throat ailment. The hospital was deluged with cards and the switchboard become so overloaded that a local radio station began giving regular bulletins on Uncle Dave's condition.

Uncle Dave Macon

3rd MARCH

1960 The day Elvis Presley came to Great Britain. It was an extremely brief visit; "The King" was on his way home to America after his army service in West Germany and his transport 'plane landed at Prestwick Airport in Scotland. Elvis got off for just a few minutes.

1966 Seminal country-rock band Buffalo Springfield (Neil Young, Stephen Stills, Richie Furay, Bruce Palmer and Dewey Martin) formed after a chance meeting in a traffic jam on Sunset Boulevard in Hollywood! According to Richie Furay (quoted in Peter Frame's *Rock Family Trees* book), "Stephen and I were driving down Sunset Boulevard when we got caught up in a traffic jam. As we sat there, we noticed that the car in front was a hearse bearing Ontario plates — and Stephen, knowing that Neil used to drive around in an old hearse, shouted, 'That has just got to be Neil!' Well, we rushed out and sure enough there sat Neil and Bruce Palmer. Neil had come to Los Angeles looking for us and, being unable to find us, was just about to got off to San Francisco."

1970 A baby son for Johnny Cash and June Carter — John Carter Cash, born just after midday at the Madison hospital.

4th MARCH

1932 Betty Jack Davis born in Corbin, Kentucky. In the late forties she formed a singing duo with her close friend Mary Francis Penick (who changed her name to Skeeter Davis) and they appeared as The Davis Sisters. They were signed to RCA by Steve Sholes in 1950 and scored a huge hit in 1953 with the song 'I Forgot More Than You'll Ever Know'. Later that same year, on August 2, they were involved in a terrible car accident and Betty was killed. Skeeter went on to have a very long and successful career as a solo artist.

1980 The film verison of Loretta Lynn's autobiography *Coal Miner's Daughter* premiered in Nashville. Directed by Michael Apted, an Englishman, the film starred Sissy Spacek as Loretta, Tommy Lee Jones as Doolittle Lynn and Beverly D'Angelo as Patsy Cline. Much of the movie was shot on location in the poverty-stricken East Kentucky area where Loretta was born. "It's the other America, an area even most Americans think of as a foreign country," said Apted. "We had a huge 100-man crew, 40-foot trailers. I insisted on Sissy doing some singing live, so we had all that equipment too. We had to travel a mile over unmade roads to reach the location every day, and if something like the camera had broken down, there was no help available . . . We had terrible resistance to overcome. The country and western people in Nashville were furious about Robert Altman's film *Nashville,* so they were very suspicious of it. Then there were the local Appalachian people, the poor whites themselves, who felt that Hollywood and the media in general always showed them as hillbillies and ignorant clowns." But the problems were overcome, *Coal Miner's Daughter* was very successful, and Sissy Spacek won an Oscar for her performance.

5th MARCH

1940 Tommy Cash born at Dyess, Arkansas. The younger brother of Johnny Cash, also a country songwriter and performer, he's had several country hits including 'Rise and Shine' and 'Six White Horses'.

Patsy Cline

1963 Between 6 and 7pm a twin-engine Comanche piloted by Randy Hughes and carrying Patsy Cline, Hawkshaw Hawkins and Cowboy Copas back to Nashville after a benefit concert in Kansas City, crashed. Everyone on board was killed. A report that the 'plane was missing was broadcast by Grant Turner over WSM. Roger Miller was one of those listening, "I used to cruise around town in my old 'forty-nine Dodge and think and write music. Grant promised to keep listeners posted, so I stayed tuned. Then, at one point, Grant announced the flying time from Dyersburg to Nashville and pinpointed an area around Camden where a farmer had seen a 'plane that looked like it was in trouble and also where an explosion had been reported. It was said that when a communications check by radio had failed to locate the plane or bring any response, Federal Aviation officials, the state and local police, and the Civil Air Patrol were forming a search party. I suddenly realised that I had to join them." Carl Perkins was another musician who heard the reports and left Nashville to join the search party.

6th MARCH

1905 Bob Wills, "The King of Western Swing", born on a farm in Limestone County, East Texas. He led the Texas Playboys, one of the finest and most innovative bands in the history of popular music. Over 20 years before the arrival of rock 'n' roll Bob successfully fused country with black dance music. He grew up on a number of different farms, began playing fiddle at the age of eight as the result of a bet, and made his first public performance when he was ten, deputising for his musician father who was drunk! After a brief spell as an entertainer with a travelling medicine show, Bob was featured on Fort Worth radio in 1929 leading the Wills Fiddle Band on one station and playing with the Aladdin Laddies on another. In 1931 he began an association with W. Lee O'Daniel, and helped him advertise flour, changing the name of the Wills Fiddle Band to the Light Crust Dough Boys. Bob quit in 1933 and formed the Texas Playboys. A year later they moved to Tulsa, Oklahoma and became firmly established with a radio show over KV00 which continued for many years. Wills made over 550 recordings over a 44 year time span, from 1929 until 1973.

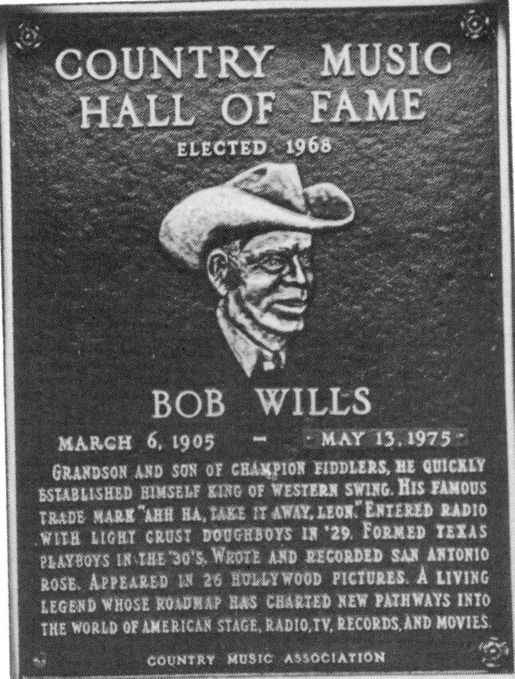

1937 Doug Dillard born in Salem, Missouri. With his brother Rodney, Mitch Jayne and Dean Webb, he formed the bluegrass group The Dillards. They left Missouri for Los Angeles in 1962, recorded some fine albums for Elektra and appeared regularly on the Andy Griffith TV show as the mentally-backward but musically forward Darlin Family. By the mid-sixties The Dillards had begun using electrified instruments at bluegrass festivals. This horrified traditionalists but won even more young fans to the music. It also helped to kick off the country rock movement. Doug left the band and, after touring for a time with The Byrds, joined forces with Gene Clark for the Dillard and Clark expedition. This short-term collaboration produced a unique combination of country and rock. In the seventies Doug worked as a solo artist and guested with other musicians, also finding time to do some acting and write a banjo anthology.

1963 The wreckage of the plane carrying Patsy Cline, Hawkshaw Hawkins and Cowboy Copas was discovered at daybreak. Grant Turner began his 6.00am announcement on WSM, "Ladies and gentlemen, this is the hardest thing I've ever had to to do . . ." Roger Miller was one of the first to arrive at the scene of the crash. "I walked up to it and wanted to turn back. It was ghastly. That's the only way to describe it. The plane had crashed nose down, it just plowed into the earth on this steep hillside. It was all twisted metal and pieces of bodies. It was especially horrible when you knew them all." The news had a devastating effect on Nashville musicians, including Loretta Lynn — "That just about broke me up, to think that someone as good as that was gone. And I guess I was selfish enough to mourn as much for myself as for her. I was upset because who could I turn to? Patsy was like a mother and a sister to me. When she died, I just about gave up. I thought this was the end for me, too."

Townes van Zandt

1963 Jack Anglin, of the Johnny and Jack duo, killed in a car accident en route to a prayer service in Nashville for Patsy Cline. Teddy Wilburn of the Wilburn Brothers (quoted in Ellis Nassour's biography *Patsy Cline*) is one who will never forget that Thursday prayer service — "You literally had to fight your way through the surging crowds in the street and the crowd inside. We were standing there, milling around, talking in low, hushed tones. Suddenly there was this commotion and word filtered in that Jack had died . . . I totally broke down, I absolutely lost control. A lot of people were upset and horrified at the news . . . The country music industry had gone for almost ten years without any tragedy. Everyone was living on and on, and no one tremendously important in the business had died since Hank Williams passed on. It was amazing, especially in view of the way we travelled — no buses to speak of, everyone mostly driving Cadillac limos and pulling trailers with costumes and equipment. The law of averages caught up with us, but it didn't make it any easier to accept."

7th MARCH

1924 The first string band recording (if two people can be said to constitute a string band). Gid Tanner and Riley Puckett recorded with fiddle and banjo for the Columbia Phonograph Company in New York.

1944 Townes Van Zandt born in Fort Worth, Texas. Best known as a writer, his compositions include 'Pancho and Lefty' and 'If I Needed You', Townes also has a strong cult reputation as a performer. He's credited as a major influence by several country writers, including Guy Clark, Rodney Crowell, and Mickey Newbury who said that he ". . . writes like Hank Williams probably would have written, but I tell ya', I think Townes is better. I consider him in the same category as Dylan and McCartney."

8th MARCH

1938 Lew DeWitt, one of the four Statler Brothers, born in Roanoke County, Virginia. The tenor vocalist with the group, Lew wrote their 1965 hit 'Flowers On The Wall' which went into the Top Five of the pop charts. The Statler Brothers, now the most acclaimed country music vocal group in history, came together "years ago" when they sang at the Lynhurst Methodist church near Staunton, Virginia. They got their first break in 1963 when they met Johnny Cash in Roanoke. The foursome had come up at the request of the show's promoter and met Johnny, who told them to come to his Sunday concert which was being held in Berryville, Virginia. The four dutifully showed up, and Cash asked them to open the show for him. They did, he liked them and, nine months later, the quartet was working full-time for Cash. At this point, the group officially adopted the name of The Statler Brothers, taken from a box of tissues in a hotel room. Harold Reid says that they could just as easily have been named the Kleenex brothers! Poor health forced Lew to quit the group in July 1982.

1946 Randy Meisner born in Scotts Bluff, Nebraska. The grandson of a Russian classical violinist, Randy left Nebraska in the mid-sixties, spent time in Colorado, then moved to the West Coast where he played a leading role in the development of the California country-rock sound of the seventies. He was a founder member of Poco, Rick Nelson's Stone County Band and The Eagles. He quit The Eagles in 1977 to go solo.

9th MARCH

193? Mickey Gilley born in Ferriday, Louisiana. He grew up with his cousins Jimmy Swaggart and Jerry Lee Lewis and they shared an interest in music and sang together at the local church. By their mid-teens they'd gone their separate ways — Jerry Lee went to Memphis, Tennessee and became a rock 'n' roll star, Jimmy became a minister and found fame as a radio and TV evangelist, and Mickey went to Houston and found work as a construction worker. Life as a grease monkey didn't appeal to Mickey much when he discovered how well his cousin was doing in the music business, so he decided to try and do the same thing. For 18 years he worked the Houston clubs and recorded for local labels — Jerry Lee style rockers that never sold well though became cult favourites in Europe. Mickey's life changed in 1970 when he was approached by an eccentric, self-made millionaire named Sherwood Cryer, who offered him a share in a club he was opening in the Houston suburb of Pasadena. "Gilley's" was an instant success with the local blue collar workers and quickly expanded in size as its fame spread. Mickey had no ambition to be a national star and was quite happy running the club, but in 1974 he suddenly found himself with a huge country hit — 'Roomful Of Roses'. Since then he's had success beyond his wildest dreams, a long run of country chart-toppers, and legendary status for the club in the wake of the *Urban Cowboy* movie which was shot at Gilley's.

1974 The last Saturday night performance of the Grand Ole Opry from the Ryman Auditorium in downtown Nashville. A week later the show moved to a purpose built theatre at the Opryland park, several miles from the centre of town. The Ryman had strong memories for many country stars, but most were pleased to move from the cramped dressing rooms and limited facilities of the old building.

10th MARCH

1923 Jethro Burns (Kenneth C. Burns) born in Knoxville, Tennessee. A child musician — he played the mandolin — Jethro met his partner Homer (Henry D. Haynes) when both were youngsters growing up in Knoxville. Their combination of music and humour made them an instant success. They were featured on the Renfro Valley Barn Dance show, toured for a time with their own tent show, were regulars on the National Barn Dance and guested on every other radio show of note, including the Grand Ole Opry. Homer and Jethro had a long career as recording artists for RCA and their speciality was parody versions of big hits, including three Elvis Presley spoofs of 'Hound Dog', 'Heartbreak Hotel' and 'Are You Lonesome Tonight'.

1938 Johnnie Allan, leading Cajun country and rock 'n' roll performer, born in Rayne, Louisiana. He came from a musical family, his great uncle was Joe Falcon, who recorded the first Cajun record in New Orleans in 1928, 'Allons A Lafayette'. Johnnie's big sellers have included 'South to Louisiana', a Cajun reworking of the Johnny Horton hit 'North To Alaska' and 'Promised Land', a 100mph version of the Chuck Berry classic, which was popular in Britain.

1938 Guitarist Norman Blake born in Chattanooga, Tennessee. A leading session musician, Blake has worked with Johnny Cash, Kris Kristofferson and Bob Dylan, and also made albums of his own, for specialist labels like Flying Fish and Rounder.

1963 Patsy Cline's funeral. An estimated 25,000 people lined the four mile route from Winchester to the Shenandoah Memorial Park. There were unprecedented scenes at the graveside when onlookers started to take souvenirs. According to a report in the *Winchester Star* — "The effect of the first stolen flower hit the crowd like an electric shock. The people — jammed in close to the small tent over the grave — began snatching, literally from the side of the grave, everything and anything they could lay their hands on, short of the gold finished coffin . . . . . But it's unlikely that Patsy would have minded. These were "her people", her fans, the people who made her famous."

11th MARCH

1890 W. Lee "Pappy" O'Daniel born in Malta, Ohio. He was working for Burris Mills & Elevator Co. in Fort Worth, Texas when Bob Wills approached him and offered to promote the company's flour with his music. The Wills Fiddle Band became the Light Crust Doughboys and played on radio station KFJS. They made some records for RCA, then switched to Vocalion. Bob quit in 1933, but the band continued with "Pappy" stepping in for a couple of years as MC. When he was standing for election as Governor of Texas he persuaded the Doughboys to give him their musical support, and it's generally agreed that they played a vital role in his successful campaign.

1939 Leading Tex-Mex accordionist Flaco Jiminez born. Known in the San Antonio area as El Ray (the King) de Texas, Flaco has been featured on albums by Doug Sahm, Peter Rowan and Ry Cooder.

1972 Freddie Hart top of the country charts with 'My Hang Up Is You'. He stayed put at the top for six weeks.

12th MARCH

1976 Joe Stampley's tribute to rock 'n' roller Chuck Berry — 'The Sheik Of Chicago' — entered the charts. Joe had more country hits than anyone in 1976; four on Epic, and four on his previous label, ABC/Dot. "Every time I put out a new record, ABC would release one of my old tracks," recalled Stampley. "This meant that I kept having two records competing with each other. Sometimes this meant that neither would make the Top Ten, or in one case an old song, 'All These Things', went to number one while my new release didn't. It was a little frustrating."

1977 Charley Pride top of the country charts with 'She's Just An Old Love Turned Memory'. Pride released three singles in 1977 — the others were 'I'll Be Leaving Alone' and 'More To Me' — all went to number one and all stayed on the *Billboard* charts for 14 weeks.

13th MARCH

1930 Liz Anderson (Elizabeth Jane Haaby) born in Rosean, Minnesota. As a singer she had several country hits in the sixties, and as a songwriter found particular success with songs written for Merle Haggard including 'My Friends Are Gonna Be Strangers' and 'The Fugitive'. Country singer Lynn Anderson is her daughter.

1932 Jan Howard born in West Plains, Missouri. She moved to Los Angeles with the ambition of becoming a singer, but she met and married songwriter Harlen Howard, gave up thoughts of singing professionally and devoted herself to bringing up their three sons. But Jan still got the chance to sing, on the demo tapes Harlan made to introduce new songs to producers. The demo of 'Mommy For A Day' led to a contract with Challenge Records, and her first releases were duets with Wynn Stewart, one of which, 'The One You Slip Around With' was a Top Ten single. Jan subsequently made solo records, and teamed up with Bill Anderson for tours, TV and hit records, including 'If It's All The Same To You' and 'Someday We'll Be Together'. Then came tragedy; two of her sons died, one killed in Vietnam, two weeks after Jan had recorded a song about him called 'My Son'. She retired from the music business for a time, but then returned, making regular appearances at the Opry.

1975 George Jones and Tammy Wynette divorced.

14th MARCH

1953 Marty Robbins made his chart debut with 'I'll Go On Alone', on Columbia. He had been recommended to the label by Little Jimmy Dickens, who had worked with Marty in a Phoenix night club.

1972 Merle Haggard granted a full and unconditional pardon by Ronald Reagan, the governor of California. Hag had been convicted in the Superior Court of the State of California on January 30 1958, for the crime of burglary and "escape without force". He served 2 years 5 months in San Quentin, and was then on parole for 2 years 3 months. Reagan granted the pardon in view of what he described as "favourable recommendations and indications that the applicant is now a fully rehabilitated member of society and entitled to a pardon."

15th MARCH

1927 Carl Smith born in Maynardsville, Tennessee. A very popular country singer in the fifties and sixties, Carl was married for a time to June Carter and is the father of Carlene Carter. He was a regular performer on WROL (which broadcast out of Knoxville, Tennessee) in the forties. He joined the Grand Ole Opry in 1950 and a year later won a recording contract with Columbia. He was with the label for 24 years, sold about 15 million records, and was rarely absent from the country charts in two decades. His long string of hits included 'Let Old Mother Nature Have Her Way', 'Don't Just Stand There', 'Hey, Joe' and 'Loose Talk'. Carl has now virtually retired from the music business and devotes most of his time to his large ranch in Franklin, Tennessee, where he lives with his wife Goldie Hill (they were married in 1957).

1947 Ry Cooder born in Los Angeles, California. While still in his teens Ry developed a keen enthusiasm for the regional music forms at the root of American rock 'n' roll. He learned directly from bluesmen like the Rev. Gary Davis, then played with Taj Mahal in The Rising Sons, and developed an awesome reputation as a session guitarist. His solo career began in 1970 with the first in a series of highly acclaimed albums for Warner Brothers, which featured long-forgotten or little-known gospel, old-timey country, Cajun and blues tunes given a very distinctive treatment. Ry's personal musical favourites include the West Virginia mountain fiddler Blind Arthur Reed, who wrote the songs 'How Can A Poor Man Stand Such Times and Live' and 'Always Lift Him Up'. One of his finest LP's is *Chicken Skin Music,* which introduced Tex-Mex music to a wide audience, and featured accordionist Flaco Jiminez and his Conjunto musicians from San Antonio. For the movie *The Long Riders,* Ry recreated the western music which was played in saloons during the gunfighter era of Jesse James and Cole Younger.

16th MARCH

1897 Robert Gardner born in Olive Springs, Tennessee. A member of Mac and Bob, one of the first mandolin-guitar duos, he met his partner Lester McFarland when both were teenage students at the Kentucky School for the Blind.

1922 WSB in Atlanta, Georgia went on the air. It was the first high-powered radio station in the South, and was probably the very first to feature country music. Fiddlin' Johnny Carson and gospel singer Rev. Andrew Jenkins are known to have performed on the station during the first few months. Old-timey country music became very popular with the listeners and other radio stations began featuring similar string band performers.

1942 Jerry Jeff Walker (Paul Crosby) born in Oneonta, New York. He came from a musical family — "My parents were square dance people and my mother sang in local trios and choirs. There were always family get-togethers where we'd all pick and sing." After a period with a band called Circus Maximus, he took off with his guitar and rambled around the US, drifting from town to town playing folk clubs or street corners. "I travelled for six years and a hundred thousand miles under the flag of itinerant footloose," he recalls. Over a long weekend in a New Orleans jail he met a man who gave him the inspiration for his best known song 'Mr Bojangles'. In the seventies he moved to the Texas capital Austin and became closely associated with the progressive "outlaw" country movement, though Jerry Jeff was no outlaw, rather a good-natured rapscallion with a special talent for projecting his happy-go-lucky attitude to life through music. Walker has made over a dozen albums, mostly for MCA.

Jerry Jeff Walker

1951 Ray Benson, leader of the Austin-based western swing band Asleep At The Wheel, born.

1974 The premiere performance of the Grand Ole Opry at the new purpose-built, 4,400 seat Opry House. President and Mrs Richard Nixon were among the guests and at one point Nixon joined Roy Acuff on stage and was taught the art of the YoYo. As country historian Charles Wolfe pointed out in *The Illustrated History of Country Music*: "For many fans of country music, the spectacle of seeing the President appear alongside Roy Acuff, and of hearing 'Hail To The Chief' played on a fiddle, banjo and steel guitar, seemed the final proof that the music's long struggle to gain respectability was won. Acuff himself, who had barely 20 years earlier heard a Tennessee governor complain that the Opry and the hillbilly image were embarrassing to the state, admitted that he felt that in spite of the later Watergate scandal, Nixon's visit to the Opry stage was the greatest thing that had ever happened to country music."

17th MARCH

1932 Dick Curless born in Fort Fairfield, Maine. Dick was a popular teenage singer/guitarist as "The Tumbleweed Kid", then gained further fame as "The Rice Paddy Ranger" after his induction into the army during the Korean war. Back in the US his career went into a decline, only to pick up dramatically in 1965 with the hit 'A Tombstone Every Mile' which brought him two surprising, but welcome "Best Newcomer" awards. He had several more hits for Tower and then Capitol Records.

1944 John Sebastian born in New York City. He was very active in the Greenwich Village folk scene in the early sixties, then formed The Lovin' Spoonful in 1965. They were an appealing four-piece group who played good-time music which combined folk, jug-band sounds, country, gospel, ragtime and blues. Sebastian was lead vocalist, played autoharp, and wrote much of the band's material including their hits like 'Nashville Cats' (which included the immortal line "There's thirteen hundred and fifty two guitar pickers in Nashville"), 'Summer In The City', 'Darlin' Be Home Soon' and 'Do You Believe in Magic'.

18th MARCH

1938 Charley Pride, country music's most successful black artist, born on a cotton farm in Sledge, Mississippi. "My colour says I'm supposed to shine shoes and sing the blues," says Charley, "But I don't fit that image, you see, because I'm Charley Pride the man, not a black man singing white man's music. I'm an American singing American music. I worked out those problems years ago — and everybody else will have to work their way out of it too." Baseball was Pride's biggest love, but he also enjoyed singing.

In 1965 he was playing semi-pro ball by day and country music by night, when he caught the ears of Red Sovine and Red Foley with his version of 'Lovesick Blues' and they suggested he audition in Nashville. A recording session was arranged and Chet Atkins brought the resulting demo tape to a meeting of top RCA A&R men. Charley was signed to the label and cut his first single, 'Snakes Crawl At Night' which was very well received. Only then did country fans, radio DJ's and most of the RCA staff discover that the talented newcomer was black. Since then he's made over 40 albums and 50 singles (14 of which were consecutive number one's). Despite a deliberately low-key and straightforward style, Charley Pride has become one of the best known stars of country music. He has also played an important role in helping several other country singers, including Ronnie Milsap, Dave and Sugar, Gary Stewart, Sylvia and Janie Fricke.

1943 Dennis Linde born. Most successful as a writer, composing 'Burning Love' for Elvis Presley and 'Long, Long Texas Road' for Roy Drusky, he's also shown promise as a producer, most notably with Kris Kristofferson's *Jesus Was A Capricorn* LP, and as a solo performer, including his two Elektra albums *Dennis Linde* and *Trapped In The Suburbs*. According to his good friend Kris Kristofferson, "Dennis Linde may be a genius, he certainly is weird . . . possibly the most creative and prolific songwriter in the business."

19th MARCH

1921 Martha Lou Carson (Martha Ambergay) born in Neon, Kentucky. She was one of the few female stars of country music in the forties and fifties. She came to prominence on radio shows like the Renfro Valley Kentucky Barn Dance and the WSB Barn Dance, and through touring with her husband James Carson. In the fifties she joined the Opry and began making frequent TV appearances. A prolific songwriter, she recorded at various times for RCA, Capitol and Cadance.

1942 Richard Dobson, singer/songwriter, born in Tyler, Texas. His most successful songs include 'Piece Of Wood And Steel', for David Allan Coe, and 'Baby Ride Easy' for Dave Edmunds and Carlene Carter.

1964 Tom T. Hall married "Miss Dixie", a lady from Birmingham, England whose real name is Iris. As he explained in his highly-readable and very amusing autobiography *The Storyteller's Nashville* (Doubleday) — "The day dawned cold and clear. Just like in the movies, I forgot the preacher's name, but he was not all that excited about marrying two show-business people. He said it as if he were about to join two people from outer space in matrimony. I remember asking him if he would take some pictures of us. He refused. We were married in the Brentwood United Methodist Church. The building was later torn down, and a bank sits there now."

20th MARCH

1937 Jerry Reed (Jerry Hubbard) born in Atlanta, Georgia. The perennial version of the American good ole boy, Reed has been successful as songwriter, session-guitarist, singer and (most recently) movie star. He worked in a cotton mill by day and performed in bars at night. In 1955 he met Atlanta musical entrepreneur Bill Lowery and landed a recording contract. "I was too young to be makin' records," he remembers, "I didn't know what to do." But his songs had already started to impress people, including Brenda Lee, and Gene Vincent who recorded 'Crazy Legs'. In the sixties Jerry moved to Nashville and worked as a session musician, a job which inspired the song 'Guitar Man', later a hit for Elvis Presley. Chet Atkins had signed Reed to a solo RCA contract in 1965 and between the session work he'd made a few records, including 'Tupelo Mississippi Flash', one of the best songs ever written about Elvis. His solo career hit top gear in 1970 with the number one country hit 'Amos Moses' which won him awards and a regular spot on the televised "Glen Campbell Goodtime Hour". More hits followed, including 'When You're Hot You're Hot'. He accepted a dare to audition for a part in the movie *W.W. and the Dixie Dance Kings* and was hired, impressing the star Burt Reynolds who described Jerry as "the most natural actor I've ever worked with". Several films followed this success including the original *Smokey and the Bandit, Gator* and *Hot Stuff*.

1957 "Fraulein" by Bobby Helms entered the country charts. It stayed there a whole year (52 weeks) and was the longest-running chart record in the fifties.

21st MARCH

1882 Bascom Lamar Lunsford, an important early folk collector, born in Mars Hill, North Carolina. In 1928 Bascom instigated the first Mountain Dance and Folk Festival at Asheville, North Carolina, and he organised the event for many years. The annual old-timey country and folk music event still takes place and is one of the longest-established and most colourful festivals in America.

1919 Eddie Kirk born in Greeley, Colorado. He grew up on a ranch, loved singing western songs, and was a dab hand at roping cattle before he'd reached his teens. Eddie joined the California-based western group, the Beverly Hillbillies in the thirties, and was vocalist and guitarist. Kirk won the National Yodelling Championship in 1935 and 1936, appeared in several films, performed regularly on the Gene Autry show, but didn't start making solo records until the late forties. His biggest hits were 'The Gods Were Angry With Me' and 'Candy Kisses'. He was concerned to improve the image of country music and, despite the name of his first group (or perhaps because of it), he was very active in the struggle to get the term "hillbilly" replaced by "country".

1981 Alabama entered the album charts with *Feels So Good*, which would rise rapidly to the top spot. One of the biggest country music success stories of the eighties, Alabama had spent the seventies on a musical roller-coaster ride, and most of the time they seemed to be down. There were at least three times when the group was totally resigned to giving up; from personnel changes, injuries, to utter disillusionment. Things suddenly clicked for them in early 1980 when the single 'My Home's In Alabama' (on the small MDJ label) started climbing the charts and all the major record companies, who'd turned them down before, took an interest. Within months they were the most successful country band in America.

22nd MARCH

1892 Charlie Poole, one of the early pioneers of country music, born in Almance County, North Carolina. He was vocalist and banjo player with the North Carolina Ramblers, and they made some historic string-band recordings for Columbia in 1925, including the very popular 'Don't Let Your Deal Go Down Blues'. Poole made over 100 recordings, but his career was short. He drank to excess and by the thirties seems to have lost most of his enthusiasm for performing. He died of a heart attack, aged just 31, after a particularly heavy drinking bout.

1918 Western swing bandleader Hoyle Nix born in Texas. Most of his contemporaries gave up playing western swing when rock 'n' roll came along in the fifties, but Hoyle Nix and his Cowboy Band, who formed in 1946, just kept on going. They're a household name in the 250-mile radius of their tiny home town of Big Spring, Texas, where they've been performing every night for over 30 years at Hoyle Nix's Stampede Club.

1952 Uncle Dave Macon, the "Dixie Dewdrop" of the Grand Ole Opry, died at Rutherford Hospital, Murfreesboro, Tennessee. He was 81, and had been ill for some weeks.

1956 Carl Perkins injured in a car crash at Delaware while travelling to appear on the Ed Sullivan Show. His recording of 'Blue Suede Shoes' was high on the pop, country and R&B charts (it would eventually top them all) and the prestigious TV appearance was seen as his 'big break' to becoming a teenage idol, like former Sun Records artist Elvis Presley. Carl never made the show and, perhaps because he was laid-up for six months after the crash, never became a big star. Quoted in Colin Escott and Martin Hawkins' *Sun Records,* Perkins recalled, "I was a poor farm boy and with 'Shoes' I felt that I had a chance but suddenly there I was in hospital". But he added philosophically, "Elvis had the looks on me. The girls were going for him for more reasons than music. Elvis was hitting them with sideburns, flashy clothes and no ring on that finger. I had three kids. There was no way of keeping him from being the man in that music but I've never felt bitter, always felt lucky to be in the business. Most kids from my background never get to drive a new car."

23rd MARCH

1868 Fiddlin' John Carson born in the Blue Ridge Mountains of Fannin County, Georgia. A fine singer as well as stylish fiddler, John was one of the most popular early stars of country music. He was a jockey in his teens, then worked in a cotton mill, but in his spare time entertained with a fiddle which, according to legend, had been brought to America from Ireland by a great-grandfather in a flour sack. He built a reputation in the Atlanta area in the 1910's and was chosen "Champion Fiddler of Georgia" several times. He made his radio debut over WSB in Atlanta in 1922, perhaps the first time that country music was broadcast, and a year later made a pioneering first recording for Ralph Peer and Okeh. The resulting disc sold very well and alerted record company executives to the enormous potential market for the folk music of the American South.

1926 Maybelle Addington married Ezra Carter (brother of A.P.) and thereby joined The Carter Family. She brought with her a talent for playing the autoharp, banjo and guitar.

24th MARCH

1957 Carson Robison, popular country singer and bandleader, died at his farm in Pleasant Valley, New York. He had continued to make records until very late in life. In April 1956 he recorded the tongue-in-cheek 'Rockin' and Rollin' with Granmaw', which became a cult favourite with rockabilly enthusiasts in the UK over 20 years later.

1958 Elvis Presley inducted into the US Army. His pay dropped from $100,000 to $78 a month.

1973 Barbara Fairchild top of the country charts with 'Teddy Bear Song', her first big hit.

25th MARCH

1934 Johnny Burnette born in Memphis, Tennessee; a contemporary of Elvis, he attended the same school and worked for the same electrical company. He formed a rockabilly trio with his elder brother Dorsey and friend Paul Burlison. They were rejected by Sam Phillips at Sun, but found some success in New York when they won a TV talent show and were signed to Decca/Coral. None of their records were hits, though they are prized today by rockabilly connoisseurs. Johnny signed to Liberty as a solo artist in 1960 and, with producer Snuff Garrett, made several hits including 'Dreamin', 'Little Boy Sad' and 'You're Sixteen'. He was drowned while fishing in 1964.

Hoyt Axton

1938 Hoyt Axton born in Commanche, Oklahoma — his mother is Mae Buran Axton, a songwriter who wrote 'Heartbreak Hotel' for Elvis. He's an engaging, happy-go-lucky entertainer who's been making folk/country albums for over two decades. When he couldn't get a satisfactory new record deal in 1978 he set up his own label, Jeremiah, and proved music industry sceptics wrong by scoring two bit hits, 'Della and the Dealer' and 'Rusty Old Halo'. Hoyt's biggest successes have been as a songwriter, most notably 'Greenback Dollar' for the Kingston Trio, 'Joy To The World' for Three Dog Night (his record label is named after Jeremiah, the bullfrog in this song), and 'The Pusher' for Steppenwolf.

1939 The American trade magazine *Billboard* published its first list of top-selling Hillbilly Records, though pointed out that "double-meaning records are purposely omitted from this column". Smutty hillbilly songs were very popular in the thirties and several well known country names recorded them, as Nick Tosches revealed in his book, *Country — The Biggest Music In America*.

26th MARCH

1942 Larry Butler, top-notch producer, songwriter and occasional performer, born in Pensacola, Florida. His songwriting credits include 'Another Somebody Done Somebody Wrong Song' and 'Lullaby Of Love', and he has produced many successful country records including several of Kenny Rogers' million-selling hits.

194? Ronnie McDowell born in Portland, Tennessee, one of ten children. He developed a talent for vocal impressions and while in the US Navy was a popular entertainer, performing authentic versions of songs by Elvis Presley, Johnny Cash, The Platters and Ernest Tubb. He moved to Nashville and began recording for Scorpion, but his records went nowhere until Elvis died and he recorded a tribute, 'The King Is Gone' using Presley's distinctive vocal style. It was an instant success and Ronnie has been a regular fixture on the country charts ever since, though he's made a determined effort to shake-off the 'Elvis imitator' tag and is now recognised for his own talents, both as writer and singer.

Dean Dillon

1955 Dean Dillon born in Lake City, Tennessee. He was profoundly influenced by the songs of Merle Haggard, some of which seemed to tell the story of his own troubled childhood, and he began writing when he was a teenager. After scuffling around Nashville in the time honoured tradition of trying to break into the music business, he was eventually signed to Pi-Gem as a writer and composed songs for Barbara Mandrell, Johnny Rodriguez, and 'Lying In Love With You', a number one hit for Jim Ed Brown and Helen Cornelius. Through the exposure gained from 'Lying' he gained the attention of RCA Nashville boss Jerry Bradley, who signed Dean to the label and produced his first records. He's had several hits, including 'I'm Into The Bottle' and 'Nobody In His Right Mind' and has collaborated as part of a duo with Gary Stewart.

1956 Charly McClain (Charlotte Denise McClain), contemporary country glamour girl, born in Jackson, Tennessee. She was in a band with her brother when she was just nine, Charlotte and The Volunteers, and they played local dates and had a regular slot on a small TV station. "At gigs we did primarily country songs of the time, from my favourites like Tammy, Loretta and Connie Smith. I remember the first song I ever did on TV was 'D-I-V-O-R-C-E'. Then later we started to bring a little country-rock into our stage performances." The band stayed together for five years until brother Mike was drafted into the army. After leaving school she was a model, then became a regular singer on the Mid-South Jamboree where, despite her protests, her name was changed from Charlotte to Charly. A meeting with Memphis-based producer Larry Rogers provided her "big break" and she was signed to Epic in 1976. Her successful career has been built up by a series of Rogers-produced LP's and in 1980 she was voted Most Promising Female Country Vocalist by the readers of *Music City News*. Since then she's been dubbed the "Princess of Country Music" by George Jones, scored several big hits, including 'Sleepin' With The Radio On', 'Surround Me With Love' and 'Who's Cheatin' Who', and made TV appearances.

27th MARCH

1909 Moon Mullican (Aubrey Moon Mullican), the "King of the Hillbilly Piano Players", born on his father's farm in Polk County, near Corrigan, Texas. His enthusiasm for playing keyboard instruments began after his father brought a pump organ into the house — when Moon was just eight. He was determined to become a professional musician and was making money as a piano player by the time he was 11. Later he moved to Houston, formed a band, then toured Louisiana and Texas honky-tonks. His long and successful recording career began in the thirties, and he was at his peak in the late forties/early fifties with hits like 'New Jole Blon', 'Goodnight Irene', 'I'll Sail My Ship Alone', 'Mona Lisa' and 'Cherokee Boogie'.

1940 Janis Martin born in Southerlin, Virginia. Female singers who could match the energy and excitement of the great male performers were a rare breed in the early days of rock 'n' roll — Janis Martin was one of the few. She had been singing since she was small, had her own radio show when she was 13, performing mainly country and bluegrass, and was discovered by RCA A&R man Steve Sholes when she was just 15, just a few weeks after the signing of Elvis Presley. He thought he'd struck gold again — another youngster from a humble background with a remarkable and refreshing talent. She was dubbed "The female Elvis", and several records were released between 1956 and 1958, featuring musicians like Chet Atkins, Floyd Cramer and Shorty Long; but all failed, presumably because American record buyers weren't ready for wild rock 'n' roll from a girl. She retired in 1958 after having a baby and though she resurfaced a couple of times to make new records, her career was effectively over.

19?? Leon Everette born in South Carolina, but raised in Queens, New York. He wasn't involved in music until he joined the US Navy, on an aircraft carrier with a crew of "Southern boys" who spent their off-duty hours playing bluegrass music. Their pastime, coupled with long, boring hours at sea, prompted Leon to buy a guitar while on leave in the Philippines and teach himself to play. After his tour of duty was completed, Leon returned to South Carolina and was an employee at a gas company, then quit after a row with his boss and organised a band. He worked extremely hard at building a career in music and was eventually rewarded when a Florida trucking executive decided to invest in him, forming Orlando Records, with Leon as the featured singer. Now signed to RCA records, Everette has become one of the most successful new country performers of the eighties.

Brenda Lee

1957 Brenda Lee made her debut in the country charts with 'One Step At A Time'. She was just 12 years old.

1982 Dave and Sugar played their final live date together. Dave Rowland then went solo and made an album called *Sugar Free*.

28th MARCH

1941 Charlie McCoy, highly respected Nashville harmonica player, born in Oak Hill, Virginia. He's made solo albums, was featured in the band Area Code 615 (his playing is featured prominently on their 'Stone Fox Chase', the theme tune from the BBC TV series "The Old Grey Whistle Test"), and as session man he's worked with Bob Dylan, Joan Baez, Ringo Starr, Joe Simon and hundreds of others. Al Kooper, in his book *Backstage Pass* described a typical Charlie McCoy incident which took place during the sessions for Bob Dylan's *Blonde on Blonde* album. One song called for a trumpet part, which should have been an easy overdub, except that Dylan didn't like overdubs. So McCoy, while playing bass guitar with his left hand, played trumpet with his right, without missing a beat. Kooper points out that Dylan stopped in the middle of the song, amazed.

195? Reba McEntire born on a cattle ranch near Chockie, Oklahoma. "I'm a third generation rodeo brat," she laughs. "My daddy rodeoed, and his daddy before him. I was a barrel racer myself until I gave it up for singing. Now I'm married to a rodeo rider." When an opportunity arose for Reba to sing the national anthem at the National Finals Rodeo in Oklahoma City, she grabbed it, and there was no turning back. It was at that event, in her senior year at college, that she met her mentor, Red Steagall, who took her into the studio to cut the demo session that led Reba to signing with Mercury/PolyGram Records in late 1975. She's been with the company ever since and has scored several hits including 'Runaway Heart', 'Sweet Dreams' and '(You Lift Me) Up To Heaven'.

29th MARCH

1960 Tootsie's Orchid Lounge opened in Nashville. The small bar at 422 Broadway became world famous when it was patronised by country stars between Grand Ole Opry shows at the nearby Ryman Auditorium, and has been featured in movies (including *Coal Miner's Daughter*) and TV.

1975 Dolly Parton's 'The Bargain Store' reached the top of the country charts despite being banned by some radio stations, where the lyrics were thought too suggestive.

30th MARCH

1913 Frankie Laine (Frank LoVecchio) born in Chicago, Illinois. The big-voiced pop singer used country music to flavour his hit records in the fifties, including 'High Noon', 'Jezebel' and the theme from the American TV series 'Rawhide'.

1945 Eric Clapton, extremely talented British rock guitarist, born in Ripley, Surrey. He's known to be a big fan of Don Williams; he joined him on-stage during a London concert in the mid-seventies, and has successfully covered Don's country hit 'Tulsa Time'.

1974 Young Tanya Tucker topped the country charts with the David Allan Coe song 'Would You Lay With Me (In A Field Of Stone)'.

31st MARCH

1928 Lefty Frizzell (William Orville Frizzell) born in Corsicana, Texas. As a child he appeared on radio station KELD, El Dorado, Texas and by his mid-teens was an adept and experienced professional performer. Music and boxing seem to have been equally important to him for a while; he acquired his nickname because of a powerful left hook. A demo-recording of his song 'If You've Got The Money, I've Got The Time' won him a contract with Columbia Records in 1950, and it became his first hit. "I was working in West Texas at a night club and I had a friend from Oklahoma to come visiting. He wanted to go somewhere and he said 'Lefty, you want to go?' and I said, 'Well if you got the money, I got the time!' and it dawned on me this would be a beautiful idea for a song." His numerous hits in the fifties and sixties included, 'I Love You A Thousand Ways', 'Always Late', 'Mom and Dad's Waltz' and 'Saginaw, Michigan'. Lefty died after suffering a stroke, in 1975.

Lefty Frizzell

1934 John D. Loudermilk born in Durham, North Carolina. A very successful songwriter and sometime recording artist, though he rarely performs in public. He wrote 'A Rose and Baby Ruth', which helped make George Hamilton IV a star, 'Sittin' In The Balcony', which gave Eddie Cochran his first taste of chart success, and several classic songs including 'Waterloo', 'Ebony Eyes', 'Talk Back Trembling Lips', 'Abilene' and 'Tobacco Road'.

A P R I L

1st APRIL

1908 Bob Nolan, leader of the Sons of the Pioneers, born. The original line-up in the early thirties was a trio comprising Bob, Roy Rogers and Tim Spencer. Roy left to concentrate on a movie career; the group expanded to a six-piece and had several best-selling records, many written by Nolan, including 'Cool Water' and 'Tumbling Tumbleweeds'.

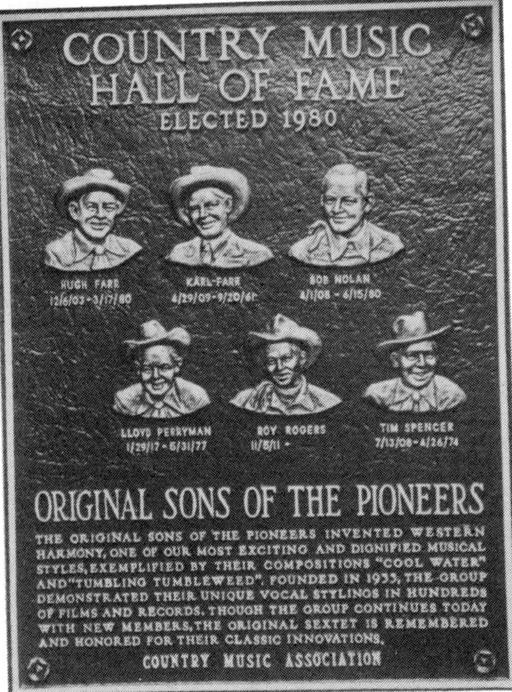

1967 The Country Music Hall of Fame and Museum opened at 4 Music Square West, Nashville. The Hall of Fame was originally the main exhibit area, with the plaques of each country personage elected displayed next to a case containing ~~selected~~ objects relating to their careers and a specially painted portrait. Gradually the museum has expanded; it now covers a 17,500 square foot area, with a wide range of exhibits that emphasise the historical aspects of country music. There are musical instruments, costumes, souvenirs, artifacts, photographs and rare records. Two theatres show vintage films of early artists such as Jimmie Rodgers, Hank Williams and Gene Autry. The most popular exhibit seems to be Elvis Presley's 1960 "Solid Gold Cadillac", which has the roof cut open to reveal golden upholstery, a gold brush and comb set, gold records . . . and a black and white TV.

2nd APRIL

1938 Warner Mack (Warner MacPherson) born in Nashville, Tennessee — one of the few singers to start their lives in the country music capital. His family moved soon afterwards to Mississippi, where Warner, as a schoolboy guitarist in Vicksburg, first took an active interest in music. When his studies were over he became a professional musician and was soon a regular performer on the Louisiana Hayride. Kapp Records signed up the promising newcomer, but he had only limited success. In the sixties he switched to Decca and began a long run of big country hits with 'Sittin' In The All Nite Cafe', followed by 'The Bridge Washed Out', his first number one.

1941 Leon Russell, the rock multi-instrumentalist who has been involved with country music on a number of occasions, born in Lawton, Oklahoma. As a teenager he worked with Jerry Lee Lewis, Ronnie Hawkins, Glen Campbell, James Burton (who taught him to play the guitar), Dorsey Burnette and many others. Leon became one of the first "super-sessionmen" of rock, working on most of the classic Phil Spector singles and The Byrds' 'Mr Tambourine Man'. He became a rock star in the seventies with the success of the Mad Dogs and Englishmen tour, with Joe Cocker. In 1973 he adopted the persona of "Hank Wilson" for a country album titled *Hank Wilson's Back,* and in 1979 made *One for the Road,* a duet LP with Willie Nelson.

1941 Sonny Throckmorton, one of the most prolific and successful of Nashville's songwriters, born in Carlsbad, New Mexico. He's made some records, including a version of his classic 'The Last Cheater's Waltz'.

1949 Emmylou Harris born in Birmingham, Alabama. "I didn't actually get turned on to country 'til late in my life, but obviously it was there inside me. My brother was a country fan and I'd hear country music all the time, listening to WWVA a lot travelling to see my relatives from where I was living. I used to look down on country at the time because I was heavily into folk protest stuff. But I couldn't help being drawn into some of it — like Hank Williams. Country was always creeping in. Like I was an Ian and Sylvia addict. They had a lot to do with my musical inspiration. Their music was so original, it had a lot of guts and a lot of powerful beauty. Their harmonies and choice of material suggested a country approach to some extent. I seemed to take a really roundabout path to where I am today. There were all kinds of little seeds starting from the beginning, but it was only when I met Gram (Parsons) and I started working with him that I got really interested in country. That was the turning point of my life." After Gram's tragic death in 1973, Emmylou launched a solo career. Her debut album, *Pieces Of The Sky* was an immediate critical success, and live shows — with an expensive and very talented crew of musicians she tagged the Hot Band — helped build her popularity with both rock and country fans.

3rd APRIL

1928 Don Gibson born in Shelby, North Carolina. A professional performer from the age of 14, Don soon built a regional following by frequent touring and radio shows. He settled in Knoxville and was very popular locally, but his first national success came as a songwriter; he wrote 'Sweet Dreams', a country classic that was first taken into the charts by Faron Young (and later by Don, Patsy Cline, Reba McEntire and Emmylou Harris), and 'I Can't Stop Lovin' You', originally a hit for Kitty Wells and later a huge international best-seller for Ray Charles. Gibson signed to RCA Records in the late fifties and began having hits of his own, starting with the double-sided number one 'Oh Lonesome Me'/'I Can't Stop Lovin' You'. Don Gibson became a chart regular through the sixties with songs like 'Sea Of Heartbreak', 'Just One Time' and 'Lonesome Number One'.

Don Gibson

1929 Johnny Horton born in Tyler, Texas. He harboured a desire to be a fisherman, but wound up as a singer, though with the nickname "The Singing Fisherman". After working in California for several years, on radio shows and on Cliffie Stone's televised "Hometown Jamboree", Johnny moved east and became a regular on the Louisiana Hayride. He became one of the star attractions of the show, signed to Columbia Records, and had several hits including 'I'm A Honky Tonk Man', 'When It's Springtime In Alaska' and 'The Battle Of New Orleans'. His successful career came to a sudden and tragic end when he was killed in a car accident on November 5, 1960, while driving from Louisiana to Nashville.

1948 The very first Louisiana Hayride broadcast from radio station KWKH in Shreveport, Louisiana. The show brought stardom to many performers, including Elvis Presley, Jim Reeves, Hank Williams, Webb Pierce, Red Sovine, George Jones and Kitty Wells.

1975 Debut performance of the Hot Band with Emmylou Harris, at the Boarding House in San Francisco. Emmy's manager Eddie Tickner persuaded Warner Brothers to underwrite the hiring of a "hot band of musicians". The line-up was James Burton, guitar; Glen D. Hardin, piano (they'd both taken time off from Elvis Presley's band); Emory Gordy, bass; Hank DeVito, pedal-steel guitar; John Ware, drums and Rodney Crowell, rhythm guitar and backing vocals.

4th APRIL

1951 Steve Gatlin, the middle Gatlin brother, born in Texas. Larry, Steve and Rudy sang together as youngsters until Larry moved to Nashville and became a country star. After getting a university degree, Steve began working with Rudy, singing back-up vocals for Tammy Wynette, and also recording with Larry. In 1976 the three brothers began working together on a full-time basis. In addition to recording, performing, arranging and producing, Steve also assists in the overall management of the Gatlin Brothers Band.

1953 Jim Reeves made his chart debut with 'Mexican Joe' on Abbott Records. It eventually rose to number one.

1980 Red Sovine, famous for his trucking songs and recitations, killed in an auto-accident in Nashville.

5th APRIL

1927 Darby and Tarlton's first recording session. A pioneering country music team, Tom Darby and Jimmie Tarlton were duet singers. Jimmie played the steel guitar and was one of the first people to use the instrument on a hillbilly recording. According to country music historian Bill Malone, he had originally played the instrument bottle-neck style, but learnt the correct technique from some Hawaiians who he met in California during World War I.

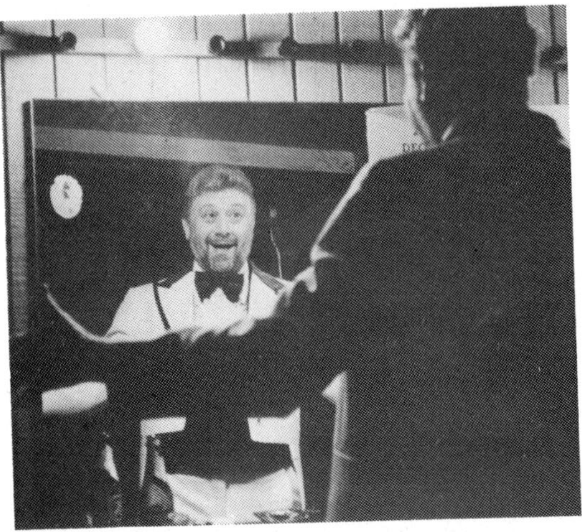

1931 "Cowboy" Jack Clement, producer, songwriter, publisher and occasional performer, born in Memphis, Tennessee. Jack began his musical career as a country singer in the early fifties, then joined Sam Phillips at Sun Records and produced Jerry Lee Lewis, Johnny Cash (also writing his big hit 'Ballad Of A Teenage Queen') and others. In the sixties Clement moved to Nashville, built his first studio, produced numerous country hits and helped up-and-coming stars including Charley Pride and Don Williams.

6th APRIL

1883 Vernon Dalhart (Marion Try Slaughter), who made the first million-selling country record, born in Jefferson, Texas. Details of his early life are obscure, though it's known that his father was knifed to death by a brother-in-law when Vernon was 11, and a 1929 CBS press release says that he "was punching cattle and crooning cowboy songs" at 12. Dalhart moved to New York in 1920 with ambitions of becoming an opera singer, but when he began recording for Thomas Edison's phonograph company in 1916 he sang mostly light opera and Al Jolson-style "Mammy" songs. In 1924 RCA Victor persuaded him to record the Southern folk song 'The Wreck Of The Old '97', coupled with 'The Prisoner's Song', which Vernon wrote from traditional sources with his cousin Guy Massey. Country music had been recorded before, but Dalhart's release made the genre commercial — it was a best-seller throughout the US and in

Europe and Australasia. Vernon (who took his name from two Texas towns, Vernon and Dalhart) recorded for almost every New York company under a variety of names and is thought to have made several thousand masters.

Vernon Dalhart (right) with Carson Robison

1892 (William) Henry Whitter born in Grayson County, Virginia. A multi-instrumentalist by the time he was 20, Henry entertained locally, then travelled to New York in 1923 to record for the General Phonograph Corporation. It's not known whether he was actually invited to make the trip north, but personal motivation certainly played a key role and encouraged other Southern musicians to approach record companies. His debut recordings were shelved, but after the success of Fiddlin' John Carson's first release, Whitter was recalled to New York in December 1923 and made his first disc — 'The Wreck Of The Old Southern '97'. This was shortly before Vernon Dalhart recorded a version of the same song; Henry's version probably inspired that release. He made several more records that sold well in the South, and formed one of the earliest string bands — Whitter's Virginia Breakdowners. His importance in country music history is as a pioneering recording artist, rather than for singing or musicianship. As Norm Cohen has observed, "His guitar work was often deficient. Much of the time the instrument was out of tune . . . Whitter's singing style was bland at least, now and then pitched in too high a key for him to keep in control."

1937 Merle Haggard born in Bakersfield, California. His parents had moved from the Oklahoma dust-bowl three years before he was born, in the hope of bettering themselves, but they were still very poor. Young Merle was frequently in trouble with the law, partly because "Somewhere along the way I decided what I didn't want to be . . . I was determined not to spend my life on some set pattern," and partly because of the death of his father, when Merle was just nine, which seemed to trigger off open hostility to authority and a hatred of school and institutions. He served time at California's notorious San Quentin jail, but during a spell in solitary confinement (in the cell next to convicted murderer Caryl Chessman, who was famous for a long but ultimately unsuccessful fight against execution), he took stock of his situation and decided to follow a new direction with his life. Music provided the key for escaping the poverty trap and his bad ways. He'd loved country music since childhood and had shown promise as a singer during his teens, but didn't seriously consider it as a career until he left prison. He found fame and fortune, though, as his remarkably frank autobiography, *Sing Me Back Home* reveals, the path his life has taken since has rarely been smooth.

1954 Dottsy (Brodt) born in Seguin, Texas. Her first public performance was at a firemen's convention when she was 12. Spotted by Johnny Rodriguez's manager when she was 20, Dottsy won an RCA recording contract and scored her first hit with 'Storms Never Last' in 1975.

7th APRIL

1920 Jimmie Rodgers married Carrie Williamson. At about the same time he contracted pneumonia, an illness from which he never properly recovered. Jimmie suffered from poor health throughout his short but very successful career.

1932 Cal Smith born Calvin Grant Shofner in Gans, Oklahoma. Raised on the West Coast, he became a regular on the TV show California

Hayride, worked with Ernest Tubb as MC and sang with the Texas Troubadours for several years, then launched a solo career on Kapp Records with the 1967 hit 'The Only Thing I Want'. Subsequent number one country hits for Cal Smith have included 'The Lord Knows I'm Drinking', 'Country Bumpkin' and 'It's Time To Pay The Fiddler'.

Bobby Bare

1935 Bobby Bare born on a farm in Ironton, Ohio. A long established, highly respected country performer whose help and encouragement to the up-and-coming Waylon Jennings, Kris Kristofferson, Townes Van Zandt, Guy Clark, Billy Joe Shaver and Tompall Glaser, has been of vital importance to the progress of modern country music. An original Nashville "outlaw", Bobby was the first to demand — and get — complete creative control over his career and music, inspiring others, like Waylon and Willie, to do the same. "I left home when I was sixteen and put a band together, mostly to meet girls and to get out of manual work!" Bare remembers. In 1958 he recorded a song called 'All American Boy' for Fraternity Records, using the name Billy Parsons, but was then drafted into the US Army. The record company hired someone else to go on the road as "Billy Parsons" and the song became a hit — though Bobby says he never received more than $50. Returning from the army, Bobby's career proper started when he recorded in Nashville with Chet Atkins and scored pop hits with 'Detroit City', 'Four Strong Winds' and 'Five Hundred Miles'. His music became more country-oriented in the seventies and he made several well received albums including *Bobby Bare Sings Lullabies, Legends and Lies,* the result of his collaborations with songwriter Shel Silverstein.

8th APRIL

1954 John Schneider born in New York. He came to prominence as Bo Duke in the popular TV series "The Dukes Of Hazzard", then found success as a country singer, scoring his first hit in 1981 with a version of 'It's Now Or Never'. His career had combined music and acting before he found fame — while in Atlanta he wrote the score for a musical titled *Under Odin's Eye,* and in 1977 he made his first record, a children's LP called *Small One.*

1961 Elvis Presley topped the British charts with 'Wooden Heart', which he sang partly in German. The song, based on a Bavarian folk tune, came from the soundtrack of the movie *G.I. Blues.* When RCA in America didn't release the track as a single, Joe Dowell made a cover version for Smash Records and went to number one. When RCA did finally release the Elvis version as a single, in their Gold Standard Series in 1974, it was not a hit.

1973 Kris Kristofferson's first big country hit 'Why Me', entered the country charts. It reached number one on July 7.

9th APRIL

1932 Carl Perkins, the definitive rockabilly performer and writer, born near Tiptonville, Tennessee. Brought up on a plantation farm where his family were the only whites, his musical influences were the blues of the black workers, gospel music, and the country songs he heard on the radio. Carl made a guitar out of a cigar box and a broom handle and won a talent contest at the age of 13, plucking his homemade contraption and singing the self-penned 'Movie Magg' (which he recorded years later as his first disc). Suitably encouraged by his success in the competition, he formed a band with his two brothers Jay and Clayton. They played country music but Carl's guitar and vocals had a distinctive sound that combined country with rhythm and blues. Then he heard Elvis Presley's first record 'That's All Right': "It was identical to what our band was doing," he recalls, "and I just knew that we could make it in the record business". Initially signed to Flip (a subsidiary of Sun), Carl Perkins became Sam Phillips' most successful artist in the period after Elvis' departure, scoring a major hit with 'Blue Suede Shoes', but a serious car accident in 1956 put paid to his efforts to become a big star. Carl's recordings for Sam Phillips, rockabilly classics like 'Dixie Fried', 'Matchbox' and 'Boppin' The Blues', are the personification of the Sun sound.

194? Con Hunley (Conrad Logan Hunley), country music's blue-eyed soul man, born in Fountain City, a satellite community of Knoxville, Tennessee. As a youngster, Con devoted himself to the guitar, patterning himself after country heroes like Chet Atkins and Merle Travis. He grew up listening to the honky-tonk sounds of Lefty Frizzell, George Jones and Ernest Tubb, and his youth was spent in imitation of their music. But he switched to piano and a soul-country sound after hearing Ray Charles sing 'What I'd Say'. Hunley worked at a Knoxville nightspot for nearly a decade, then made some records for Prairie Dust, a label set up for him by a Tennessee businessman, and was offered contracts by several Nashville-based companies. He signed with Warner Brothers, had a modest hit with his first release 'Cry, Cry Darling', in 1978, followed by 'Week-End Friend' which began his run of Top 20 successes.

10th APRIL

1890 Grace Wilson born in Owesso, Michigan. A popular contralto singer, she was featured on the Chicago-based WLS Barn Dance, which became the National Barn Dance. According to country music historian Bill Malone, "From 1926 until her retirement in 1960 Grace Wilson remained one of the best loved Barn Dance stars, and her most popular rendition was 'Bringing Home The Bacon'. During her 36-year career on the Barn Dance (the longest of any performer) she received over one million fan letters and was generally billed as 'The Girl with a Million Friends'.

1898 Fiddlin' Arthur Smith, one of the great early fiddle players, born in Humphries County, Tennessee. He toured extensively with Opry favourites Sam and Kirk McGee as The Dixieliners, and recorded for Bluebird with the Delmore Brothers and the Arthur Smith Trio.

Sheb Wooley

1921 Sheb (Shelby) Wooley, singer and actor, born in Erick, Oklahoma. As a teenager he sang western songs and was a rodeo rider. Signed to MGM in the late forties, he recorded for them with little success for a decade, then scored a huge novelty pop hit with 'The Purple People Eater' in 1958; he subsequently had country success in the sixties, including the chart-topping 'That's My Pa' in 1962.

11th APRIL

1905 Hartford Taylor, half of Karl and Harty, one of the earliest guitar-mandolin duos, born in Mt. Vernon, Kentucky. Karl and Harty were regulars on the WLS National Barn Dance show for over 20 years.

1913 Millie (Mildred Fern) Good, one of the singing sisters who comprised the Girls of the Golden West duo, born in Muleshoe, Texas. Millie and Dolly were two of the earliest female country singers; they began their radio careers in St Louis in 1930, became regulars on the WLS National Barn Dance, then moved to the Cincinnati-based Boone County Jamboree and Midwestern Hayride shows. The Girls of the Golden West recorded prolifically throughout the thirties and forties for several labels including RCA, Columbia and Conqueror.

12th APRIL

1924 Radio station WLS began broadcasting in Chicago. It was initially owned by Sears Roebuck, the mail-order company; and the call-letters stood for "world's largest store". The long-running country music show, WLS Barn Dance, began a week after the station opened.

1925 Ned Miller born in Raines, Utah. He began recording country material in 1956 for Fabor, but had his biggest success with country-pop, most notably 'From A Jack To A King', which was a huge international hit in 1962.

1936 Jimmy Payne, country songwriter and singer, born in Leachville, Arkansas. His "lucky break" came in the army when he was befriended by Chuck Glaser and when his tour of duty was completed, Jimmy moved to Nashville where he signed up with the Glaser Brothers' publishing company.

13th APRIL

1963 California-based singer Buck Owens entered the country charts with 'Act Naturally'. The record rose to number one and was the first of 19 consecutive country chart-toppers for Buck, including 'Together Again', 'Buckaroo' and 'I've Got A Tiger By The Tail'. 'Act Naturally' was later covered by The Beatles, with Ringo Starr, a long-time country fan, handling the vocals.

Sleepy LaBeef

1968 Rockabilly favourite Sleepy LaBeef made his country chart debut with 'Every Day'.

1981 Guy Willis, guitarist and MC with the Willis Brothers, died.

14th APRIL

1933 Buddy Knox born in the small Texas town of Happy. He moved from a country music background to become a successful rock 'n' roll star and scored his biggest hit in 1957 with 'Party Doll', which he recorded at Norman Petty's studio in Clovis, New Mexico. In the sixties Buddy was back singing country music, though with only limited success.

1935 Loretta Lynn born in Butcher Hollow, Kentucky, the second of eight children. She grew up in poverty, married at the age of 13, had her first child a year later and was a grandmother by the time she was 29. Loretta was the first country music millionairess and told her remarkable story in the best-selling *Coal Miner's Daughter*. The book reveals that she was very sick as a child — "I had an ear infection called mastoiditis. The only way they could cure it was by drilling holes in my head to clean out the infection. They done this every day, then put cotton right into the holes. I've still got the scars from the drilling around my ears, which is why I wear my hair so long. Mommy got a letter from a woman a few years ago that said, 'Whatever happened to that little girl that was gonna die?'"

15th APRIL

1900 J. L. (Joe) Frank, pioneering country music promoter, agent and songwriter, born in Rossal, Alabama. While working in Chicago in the twenties and thirties he produced an influential country radio show on WLS and can take some of the credit for inventing the concept of the singing cowboy, playing a key role in launching the successful career of Gene Autry. He moved to Nashville in the late thirties and helped rising stars like Roy Acuff, Eddy Arnold and Pee Wee King. Frank died in 1952 but his achievements were recognised by the Country Music Association when he was elected to the Hall of Fame in 1967.

1933 Roy Clark, accomplished guitarist, singer and comedian, born in Meherrin, Virginia. A multi-talented teenager, he showed great promise in sport by trying out for a St Louis baseball team and boxing in the light-heavyweight division in the Washington D.C. area, and in music by winning the National Music Banjo Championship for two years in succession and working in his father's band. In the sixties Roy Clark proved to be a musical pacesetter; he was one of the first country stars to headline a major hotel showroom in Las Vegas, to break through as a guest on primetime network TV shows, and to sell out at the prestigious New York venues Madison Square Gardens and Carnegie Hall. A regular star of the TV show "Hee Haw" and frequent performer in Las Vegas, Roy is one of country music's highest paid entertainers.

1937 Bob Luman born in Nacogdoches, Texas. His father was a talented country musician who encouraged his son to play guitar and form a group. Bob built a reputation in Texas and Louisiana and became a regular on the Louisiana Hayride show in the late forties. He signed to Warner Brothers and scored a major hit with the million-selling 'Let's Think About Living'.

1944 Welsh rock 'n' roller Dave Edmunds, who frequently flavours his music with country, born in Cardiff. He made a string of fine albums for Swansong, had British hits with 'I Knew The Bride', 'Girl Talk' and 'Queen Of Hearts', was a member of the band Rockpile and has worked with "new country" musicians like Rodney Crowell, Albert Lee and Carlene Carter.

16th APRIL

1977 Waylon Jennings entered the country charts with 'Luckenbach, Texas (Back To The Basics Of Love)', a song written by Bobby Emmons and Chips Moman. Neither Waylon nor the songwriters had ever been to the tiny Texas town celebrated in the song, but had heard about it from Texas writer-singers Guy Clark and Jerry Jeff Walker. Luckenbach was bought in 1970 by Hondo Crouch, a well known storyteller of Texas folk-lore and a unique humorist, and he spread the word about the place by holding an extraordinary series of events like the "Hell Hath No Fury" annual state chili cook-off for women, and the "Mud Daubers Festival". The town is very small, has a handful of tiny stone buildings, a general store and an old ballroom. When the song hit the charts the population consisted of three humans, a flock of chickens and an alcoholic pig named Mona Lisa! Waylon's hit (it was one of the biggest selling country records of the year) made the town a tourist attraction, though it became impossibly difficult to find because souvenir hunters stole all the signs!

17th APRIL

1928 James Garner (Baumgarner), the actor who came to prominence as Bret Maverick on TV screens in the late fifties, born in Norman, Oklahoma. Twenty years after leaving the series and making a name for himself in other shows like "The Rockford Files", Jim was back in the tongue-in-cheek western, recreating the Maverick role. His sidekick was played by country singer Ed Bruce.

1960 Rock 'n' roller Eddie Cochran killed in a car accident near Chippenham, Wiltshire while on a tour of the UK. He was just 21. Co-star and friend Gene Vincent was badly injured in the crash. Ironically, Cochran's last record was called 'Three Steps To Heaven'.

1970 Johnny Cash played the White House for President Nixon, who requested that he play 'Okie from Muskogee', 'A Boy Named Sue' and 'Welfare Cadillac'.

18th APRIL

1924 Clarence "Gatemouth" Brown, blues guitarist, singer and hot-swing fiddler, born in Orange, Texas. A musical chameleon, he's adept at many styles and his multi-faceted albums include a duet set with Roy Clark. To quote John D. and Susan Loudermilk: "Gatemouth's stuff is white-hot, red neck, bluegrass music from a red-hot, blue collar black man from Orange, named Brown!"

1936 Milton Brown, western swing vocalist and leader of the Brownies, died in Forth Worth, Texas. He'd been badly injured in an automobile accident and then caught pneumonia. According to Tony Russell, "If Brown hadn't died at the peak of his fame, the Brownies might have fought Bob Wills and the Texas Playboys all the way to the top of the western swing ladder — and maybe reached it first." Without the spark provided by Milton's leadership the Brownies broke up, in early 1938, and the members scattered to other bands.

19th APRIL

1924 The first broadcast of WLS Chicago Barn Dance, introduced as a show "planned to remind you folks of the good fun and fellowship of the barn warmings, the husking bees and the square dances in our farm communities of yesteryear and even today". As most of the listeners were city-dwellers, the music was a curious mixture of old-fashioned pop songs like 'Down By The Old Mill Stream', and more authentic country sounds from string bands and folk singers. The originator of the show was George D. Hay, who went on to WSM in Nashville a year later and started the Grand Ole Opry. In 1928 the show became the National Barn Dance and had a huge Saturday night audience across much of the USA, making stars of such performers as Gene Autry, Homer and Jethro, Patsy Montana and Red Foley.

1980 For the first time in the history of the *Billboard* country charts, women held the top five positions: 1. Crystal Gayle, 2. Dottie West, 3. Debbie Boone, 4 Emmylou Harris, 5. Tammy Wynette (with George Jones).

20th APRIL

1957 'All Shook Up' begins an eight week stay at the top of the *Billboard* Hot 100 — the longest for any Elvis Presley hit.

1974 Mickey Gilley on the threshold of becoming a major country star after many years as a local favourite in the Houston suburb of Pasadena: his 'Roomful Of Roses' entered the country charts. Mickey had been asked to record a favourite song for a jukebox owner on a limited-edition single, and despairing of what to put on the b-side quickly recorded 'Roomful Of Roses', a song he remembered singing with Jerry Lee Lewis as a teenager. "That was about the only song from the early days that Jerry Lee hadn't recorded. As I played it I thought how much it would sound like Jerry Lee." The song was quickly picked up by DJ's and Playboy Records bought the rights for their short-lived country label. It rose to number one.

21st APRIL

1907 Wade Mainer born in North Carolina. He was a banjoist and one of the brothers who led Mainer's Mountaineers, an important transitional group in country music history — they bridged the gap between traditional music and bluegrass.

1924 Ira Louvin born in Rainesville, Alabama. Charlie and Ira, the Louvin Brothers, began playing and singing together in their pre-teen years and developed to become one of the finest and most respected duos in country music. They joined the Opry in 1955 and were regulars for the next decade, at the same time recording prolifically for Capitol. In 1964 they decided to go their separate ways; a year later Ira and his wife Florence were killed in an horrific road accident. Emmylou Harris and Ricky Skaggs are two contemporary artists who have continued to keep the Louvin Brothers' name and music in the public eye.

1974 Porter Wagoner and Dolly Parton's last live show together, at Salinas, Kansas. Their split was more than a little fraught; Porter didn't want her to leave but Dolly wanted to be free to develop her own career, though she knew that she owed Wagoner a great deal. Alanna Nash, who wrote the fascinating *Intimate Biography Of Dolly Parton,* says, "Neither Porter nor Dolly will talk much about exactly why they broke up, but in many ways Dolly felt that she had outgrown Porter — that she had learned as much from him as she could. With her uncanny knack of knowing exactly when to move on, Dolly knew she was ready to become the big star she had always wanted to be."

22nd APRIL

1936 Glen Campbell born in the tiny town of Delight, Arkansas. The seventh son of a seventh son, he was brought up on a farm and his older brothers and sisters and parents all played guitar and sang. Glen got his first guitar (a $5 Sears and Roebuck model) when he was just four. "I spent the early part of my life looking at the north end of a southbound mule and it didn't take me long to figure out that a guitar was a lot lighter than a plough handle." He left Arkansas in the early fifties and toured with his uncle, playing "dancin' and fightin' clubs in the southwest". At 22 he settled in Los Angeles where he built a reputation as session man, working with the biggest names, including Sinatra and Elvis and cut the hit 'Tequila' with some other session musicians, using the name The Champs. He began a lengthy association with Capitol Records in 1962 and scored his first chart success with 'Kentucky Means Paradise' the same year. After several singles and albums as a solo artist (and six months as a Beach Boy) he scored a huge international hit in 1967 with a version of John Hartford's 'Gentle On My Mind'. More million-selling singles followed, including 'By The Time I Get To Phoenix', 'Whichita Lineman' and 'Galveston', followed by his own TV show, "The Glen Campbell Goodtime Hour" on CBS. Though very popular with C&W fans, Glen has always said "I'm not a country singer, I'm a country boy who sings."

1968 Steve Sholes, influential producer and record company executive, died of a heart attack while driving from Nashville airport to the RCA studios.

23rd APRIL

1900 First use of the expression "hillbilly" in the *New York Journal* — "A hill-billie is a free and untrammelled white citizen of Alabama, who lives in the hills, has no means to speak of, dresses as he can, talks as he pleases, drinks whiskey when he gets it, and fires off his revolver as the fancy takes him."

1936 Roy Orbison, popular singer with the trademark dark glasses and black clothes, born in Vernon, Texas, though his family moved to nearby Wink soon afterwards. "At an early age I played and listened to popular songs," Roy remembers; his first public performance was at the age of eight, co-hosting a radio talent show. "By the time I was thirteen or fourteen I had my own group, The Wink Westerners, and we toured around West Texas playing at jamborees." They played country, then switched to rockabilly after Elvis came through town in 1954. Roy was signed to Sun Records in 1956, but the studio's hard rocking sound didn't suit him and he didn't make a significant impact on the national music scene until he linked up with Fred Foster at Monument in Nashville and began recording pop hits like 'Only the Lonely', 'Running Scared' and

'Oh Pretty Woman'. Though closely involved with country music for many years and author of several hits, he didn't make the country music charts as a performer until 1980, with 'That Lovin' You Feelin' Again', a stylish duet with Emmylou Harris that won a Grammy award.

24th APRIL

1944 Richard Sterban, the booming bass voice of the Oak Ridge Boys, born in Camden, New Jersey. His first public performance came singing a soprano solo in Sunday School at the age of seven and his first paid job as a musician was as a member of the Keystone Quartet in Bristol, Pennsylvania. Richard studied music at Trenton State College and can play trumpet, baritone horn, French horn, E-flat tube and sousaphone. He joined the Oaks in 1972 when they were a gospel group; but they made a transition to country music in the mid-seventies, then scored a huge hit with 'Elvira' in 1981 which took them to the pop audience. According to Richard — "I think that the music we do is really mass-appeal music. When you look at our audience, the grandmas and the grandpas are out there singing 'Elvira' alongside the kids. Our music is structured in such a way that it doesn't really offend or alienate any part of our audience. We feel very strongly about that, and everything that we do is done in a calculated way: our image, the lyrics to our songs and everything else. We try not to offend any portion of our audience, and I think that as long as we maintain that philosophy, the adults will always be there." The Oaks avoid politics and religion, but are very involved with charitable causes. "We turned down a chance to do a beer commercial because we thought it might offend some members of our audience. But we did accept a Dr Pepper commercial!"

1976 Emmylou Harris' first country chart-topper with 'Together Again'.

25th APRIL

1928 Vassar Clements, top-notch fiddler, born near Kinard, North Carolina. He worked with Jim and Jesse as one of their Virginia Boys, also with Faron Young, the Earl Scruggs Review and Bill Monroe, then established a strong reputation as one of Nashville's leading session men. He has subsequently made solo albums and toured with his own band.

1978 Willie Nelson played the White House for President (and country fan) Jimmy Carter.

26th APRIL

1938 Duane Eddy born in Corning, New York, though his hometown became Phoenix, Arizona. With producer Lee Hazelwood, Duane discovered the "twangy" sound of an electric guitar by playing melody lines on the bottom, rather than top strings, and adding echo. He utilised this new sound for a series of instrumental hits including 'Peter Gunn' and 'Rebel Rouser' in the late fifties/early sixties. Duane was married for a time to singer-writer Jessi Colter and he produced her early records. They were divorced in 1968 and Jessi married Waylon Jennings.

1941 Ernest Tubb recorded 'Walking The Floor Over You' for the first time, at Biggs' Studio in Dallas.

194? Phil Kaufman, Road Mangler Deluxe for Emmylou Harris, Rodney Crowell and Rosanne Cash, born. One of the most charismatic backstage figures in new country, Phil gained a notoriety for his Executive Nanny Service, in which capacity he was employed by the Rolling Stones, and with whom he first met country-rock pioneer Gram Parsons. Phil and Gram became close friends; they formed a pact at Clarence White's funeral that if either should die the other would cremate his body at Joshua Tree National Park in California. Gram died a few months later, so Phil stole his body and completed the pact. The bizarre incident won widespread publicity and Kaufman subsequently became a legend in his own crime; he even re-told the story on British television.

27th APRIL

1944 Herb Pederson born in Berkeley, California. He came from a bluegrass background, worked with Flatt and Scruggs in the sixties, then became a key musician in the California country-rock scene, playing with the Dillards, Linda Ronstadt, Emmylou Harris, John Denver and others.

1972 Opryland USA opened to the public, a musical theme park some nine miles from Nashville which today houses the Opry Theatre (the purpose built home of the Grand Ole Opry which opened in 1974), the Opryland Hotel and TV studios where numerous country-oriented programmes are produced each week. Opryland USA spreads over 120 acres of rolling Tennessee countryside, calls itself "the home of American music" and can have as many as 15 fully-staged musical shows in simultaneous production. Admission to the park covers all the shows and the rides, like the cork-screw roller coaster "The Wabash Cannonball" and the carousel "The Tennessee Waltz". The musical shows are slick presentations of various American styles, including *Showboat,* a tribute to the old river boat shows and used as a backdrop for some scenes in the movie *Nashville.*

28th APRIL

1973 'Behind Closed Doors' by Charlie Rich top of the country charts. It became an enormously successful pop hit around the world and was the most important country performance of the year, winning Charlie CMA awards for Best Male Vocalist, Best Single and Best Album (Kenny O'Dell additionally winning the Best Song award for writing the hit). Rich had experienced spasmodic success as a bluesy rock 'n' roller, but was really down on his luck when he was signed to Epic Records in 1967 by successful producer Billy Sherrill (who knew Charlie from the days both had worked at Sun). "I owe a lot to Billy," he says. "He picked me up when it seemed my career was all washed up, and put me on the right road. It didn't happen overnight, and at times we thought it wouldn't happen at all, but we sure got there in the end. The success of 'Behind Closed Doors' certainly changed things for me. It took me out of the bar-rooms to the large supper clubs and concert halls and gave me a faith in my music that I sometimes had lacked." The Sherrill/Rich combination has been seen as the start of the "countrypolitan", easy-on-the-ear sound which made country popular with the middle-of-the-road audiences who had previously shunned it.

29th APRIL

1925 Danny Davis (George Nowlan) born in Randolph, Massachusetts. Originally a swing jazzman, he became involved in pop music as vocalist and record producer (including Connie Frances' hits) before moving to Nashville as Chet Atkins' production assistant. He devised and led The Nashville Brass and they had country oriented pop hits with reworkings of tunes like 'I Saw The Light' and 'The Wabash Cannonball'. The band won the CMA Instrumental Group of the Year award six times between 1969 and 1974.

1927 The first steel guitar recording made for Okeh by Frank Hutchinson, a singer and musician from West Virginia.

1944 Duane Allen of the Oak Ridge Boys, born in Taylortown, Texas. He was four when he made his first public performance, in a family group at church. The Oaks' press release gives Duane's previous occupations as "raising a prize hog which he sold at a country fair" and also an ad. salesman for a radio station in Paris, Texas, though most of his adult life has been spent as a member of the Oak Ridge Boys; he joined in 1966, two years after Bill Golden. Keeping step with the group's deliberately "clean" image, Duane notes: "We try to stay away from material that has a negative message. We like songs that are fun and represent good times."

30th APRIL

1900 Casey Jones (Jonathan Luther Jones), the engineer on the Illinois Central No. 1, killed when his train ran into the back of another near the Vaughan, Mississippi railroad station. Casey and the accident were immortalised in 'Casey Jones' a folk ballad that has become a classic.

1933 Willie Nelson born in Abbott, Texas. His parents divorced when he was a baby, so Willie and his sister Bobbie were brought up by grandparents. After leaving school, Nelson had all manner of menial day jobs and by night worked in bands in some of the roughest and toughest honky-tonks in Texas. After a spell in the air force when he saw active service in Korea, Willie became a disc jockey, writing songs in his spare time. He sold some of them for a pittance — 'Family Bible' went for $50 and 'Night Life' for $150. Realising that he could make money from writing, he moved to Nashville in the early sixties and had numerous successes, including 'Funny How Time Slips Away', 'Hello Walls' and 'Crazy'. Everyone knew that Nelson was a great songwriter, but he wanted recognition as a performer, and that was very hard to come by. "You know, I always thought that I could sing pretty good," he recalled later, "and I guess it kinda bothered me that nobody else thought so". He was signed to Liberty, then RCA and had a few small hits, but little effort was made to promote him. In the seventies Willie moved to Austin, Texas and discovered a new, young audience who were enthusiastic about his singing. He adapted his image; grew his hair long and wore denims, and built a strong and loyal following. He worked his way out of the RCA contract and signed to Atlantic, who treated him with much more sympathy. The two LP's he made for the New York-based company, *Shotgun Willie* and *Phases And Stages* are among his best. Then he switched to CBS and had a huge success with the album *Red Headed Stranger,* which included the million-selling single, 'Blue Eyes Crying In The Rain'. After a decade and a half he'd finally won mass acceptance as a performer. Since then his popularity has grown and he's become a very wealthy man. His songwriting has dried to a trickle, and many of his records now feature re-workings from his 800-song back catalogue, or pop and country standards. Nelson tours frequently with his band, which includes his sister Bobbie, and has begun a promising career in films.

MAY

1st MAY

1894 Sam McGee born in Franklin, Tennessee. He was one of the McGee Brothers, who were Grand Ole Opry favourites for many years, making their debut in 1926 with Uncle Dave Macon, though not appearing as a separate act until the fifties. Sam and Kirk McGee grew up on a farm and learned music from their fiddle-playing father. As part of Uncle Dave Macon's musical troupe they toured the US in the twenties, then teamed up with Fiddlin' Arthur Smith in the thirties and were very successful as the Dixieliners. In the forties they had a lengthy spell with the comedy outfit Sara and Sally, then were key members of Bill Monroe's band.

Sonny James

1929 Sonny James (Jimmie Loden) born Hackleburg, Alabama. He came from a family of musicians, made his stage debut at the tender age of four and was a seasoned performer by the time he'd reached his teens. After a spell in the army during the Korean War, he signed to Capitol and scored a huge hit with 'Young Love' in 1957. His career faltered after this record and for seven years he had only small hits. Then, in 1964 he suddenly went into top gear and began a quite astonishing run of hit records that included 16 consecutive number one's — from 'Need You' in 1967 to 'Here Comes Honey Again' in 1971. The hits continued through the seventies, and to date he's achieved 23 chart-topping country singles. Sonny has also appeared in several films, including *Second Fiddle To A Steel Guitar, Nashville Rebel* (which also featured Waylon Jennings), *Las Vegas Hillbillies* and *Hillbilly In A Haunted House*.

1945 Rita Coolidge born in Nashville, Tennessee. The daughter of a Baptist minister, she was singing in the church choir at the age of two. Her family moved to Florida and at the State University she formed a group called R.C. and the Moon Pies. After working in Memphis she headed west and became a popular back-up singer for California rock acts like Delaney and Bonnie. Her solo career began while touring with Joe Cocker and Leon Russell (who wrote 'Delta Lady' about her). Rita married Kris Kristofferson in the early seventies and they toured and recorded together. More recently she's had pop success as a solo artist with hits like 'We're All Alone' and 'One Fine Day'. Rita and Kris were divorced in 1980.

2nd MAY

1944 John Ware, co-manager of Emmylou Harris, also drummer and driving force behind her Hot Band, born in Tulsa, Oklahoma.

1945 R.C.Bannon born in Dallas, Texas. He began singing at four, in his father's Pentacostal Church. All through high school he sang in rock 'n' roll and soul bands, then moved to Seattle where he was a DJ and professional entertainer. R.C. toured with Marty Robbins in 1973 and the singer advised him to "come to Nashville." He eventually took his advice in 1976, became a staff writer for Warner Brothers (his successes include 'Only One Love In My Life' for Ronnie

Milsap and 'Women Get Lonely' for Charly McClain), briefly signed as performer with CBS then switched to RCA. In 1977 he met Louise Mandrell (sister of Barbara) and they were married two years later. They've been successful as solo artists and duet team — exposure on the network TV show "Barbara Mandrell and the Mandrell Sisters" (R.C. was additionally the programme's writer/arranger/sound mixer and all-round musical technician) gave a substantial boost to their respective and joint careers.

1948 Larry Gatlin born in Seminole, Texas, the son of an oil driller. The eldest of the three Gatlin Brothers, he was singing at church events and writing religious lyrics to pop songs by the age of seven. Larry, Steve and Rudy sang together throughout their school years, winning talent contests and eventually performing on a weekly TV show in Abilene for two years. After graduating from the University of Houston, Larry began studying for a law degree, but music interceded. While touring with gospel group, the Imperials, he met Dottie West who showed an interest in his songs. She recorded several, then sent him a plane ticket to Nashville. "If it weren't for Dottie West, I'd probably be a lawyer in Houston right now!" he laughs. Success as a songwriter (Elvis, Tammy Wynette, Johnny Cash, the Oak Ridge Boys and many others recorded his material) was followed by success as a singer. He recorded with his brothers but most of his early live shows were as a solo performer, because Rudy and Steve were still at college. Today they're very much a group and though Larry inevitably gets top-billing, he has made determined efforts to push them forward and to have the three seen as an integral unit.

3rd MAY

1928 Dave Dudley born in Spencer, Wisconsin. After an injury halted a promising career in baseball, Dave became a DJ and singer in Wisconsin in 1950. Three years later he formed the Dave Dudley Trio who played the clubs and bars of middle America for the rest of the decade. No-one seemed particularly interested in recording Dave, so he hired a studio in 1961 and cut the song 'Six Days On The Road', which he'd learned from a friend. It passed from record company to record company and eventually became a huge hit in 1963, launching a thousand subsequent songs about truck driving. The 18-wheeler replaced the railroad train as the most popular lyrical theme for country songs about travelling. Dave Dudley signed to Mercury and began a long and successful recording career; his other well known hits include 'Truck Drivin' Son Of A Gun', 'Pool Shark' and 'What We're Fighting For'.

1980 Debbie Boone's first country chart-topper 'Are You On The Road To Lovin' Me Again'. This wasn't her first big hit though; in 1977 she had topped the pop charts for several weeks with 'You Light Up My Life,' one of the biggest selling singles of all time.

4th MAY

1902 Al Dexter (Albert Poindexter) born in Jacksonville, Texas. Originally a house painter, Al sang and wrote songs (including several hymns) in his spare time. Music became his career in the thirties when he formed the Texas

Troupers and they recorded for Vocalion and Okeh. In the forties he signed to Columbia Records and was responsible for 'Pistol Packin' Mama', one of the biggest hits of the decade.

194? Stella Parton born in Sevier County, Tennessee, the sixth of 12 children that included sister Dolly and brother Randy. For several years Stella performed around the southeast and Texas. She recorded for small Nashville labels like Royal American and Music City and formed a gospel group, the Stella Parton Singers that worked the gospel music circuit. Returning to popular country music in 1975, she met Bob Dean, a Nashville drummer and trumpet player. They recorded a song she'd written called 'Ode to Olivia', which was a defence of Olivia Newton-John who'd won numerous country music awards amidst protests that she wasn't really country. "I felt we had no right to say who was country and who wasn't," Stella explained "I figured, let her sing her songs and do her thing." The tune was recorded on their own label and sold well enough to draw new attention to Stella. She followed it with 'I Want To Hold You With My Dreams Tonight'. The success of that single finally established Stella as a country performer.

1957 Rock 'n' roller Gene Vincent recorded 'Be Bop A Lula', his best known song, in Nashville.

5th MAY

1942 Tammy Wynette (Virginia Wynette Pugh) born on her grandfather's farm in Itwamba County, Mississippi. When she was eight months old her father, a local musician, died. "The only legacy he left me was his love of music," Tammy recalls. "He made my mother promise him over and over again that she would encourage me to take an interest in music if I had any talent at all. She kept her promise — until I wanted to make a career of it — then she (along with everyone else in my family) thought I'd lost my mind!" Despite her strong ambitions to be a singer, she gave them up when she married and had three children, but the marriage broke up and she began singing to pay the bills. She worked hard and began auditioning for record companies, eventually signing to Epic Records where producer Billy Sherrill was impressed with her vocal ability but told her she should change her name — "You look like a Tammy to me". She cut her first single 'Apartment Number 9' with Billy in 1966 and has gone on to sell over 18 million records, including 'Stand By Your Man', one of the biggest selling country singles of all time. Today, "The First Lady Of Country Music" divides her time between home outside Nashville and a ten-room French Regency beach house in Jupiter, Florida. Much of the rest of the time (an average 15 days a month) is spent criss-crossing America in a luxurious $200,000 custom-designed tour bus. Tammy has married five times (once, for a stormy six years with singer George Jones), and has had several well-publicised relationships with other partners including film star Burt Reynolds and singer Rudy Gatlin.

1962 'Wolverton Mountain' by Claude King entered the country charts. It rose to number one and stayed in the listings for 26 weeks.

6th MAY

1904 Cliff Carlisle born near Taylorsville, Kentucky. Best known as a member of the Carlisle Brothers with younger brother Bill — they mixed country and comedy with considerable success — Cliff is also important for his pioneering use of the dobro. The Carlisle Brothers began performing in the late twenties and their reputation spread with numerous radio shows in the American midwest. The pair went their separate ways in the forties, Bill starting a new group called The Carlisles who joined the Opry and had hits in the country charts, but the brothers did come together for occasional performances over the years.

1949 The Delmore Brothers record 'Blues Stay Away from Me' with Lonnie Glosson and Wayne Raney. It became one of the biggest country hits of the year. According to Wayne —"About four o'clock one morning in Cincinnati's Gibson Hotel, Alton and Rabon Delmore and I were getting ready for a recording session the next day. Alton knew a guitar riff he had learned from Henry Glover, a black songwriter on the King Records staff at the time. We decided to put words to it and a song was born. We recorded it the next day."

7th MAY

1894 (George) Riley Puckett born in Alpharetta, Georgia. He attended a blind school at Macon, Georgia and began playing guitar and banjo as a teenager. He made a living playing at dances, parties and on radio shows — his radio debut was in 1922 on WSB. Riley was the first hillbilly performer to yodel on record, was popular as a singer and guitarist in the twenties and thirties, and was one of the three best known members of the Skillet Lickers (the other two were Gid Tanner and Clayton McMichen), the most famous of the old-time string bands; he was featured vocalist and took part in the historic recording session of March 7, 1924.

1942 Lorrie (Lawrencine Mary) Collins born in Tahlequah, Oklahoma. With her brother Larry, one of the Collins Kids, they sang and played guitar together at junior school, were featured on California in radio shows in their early teens and signed to Columbia in 1955, with whom they made classic rockabilly recordings including 'Hoy Hoy' and 'Beetle-Bug-Bop'. The Collins Kids' career lasted a decade and ended when Lorrie married country promoter Stew Carnall and started a family. She now lives at Reno, where Stew books country acts into night clubs and drives around with a lifesized Willie Nelson mannequin in the back of his car!

1943 Terry Allen, songwriter and singer associated with the new country scene in Lubbock, Texas, born in Wichita, Kansas. His songs, including 'New Delhi Freight Train' and 'Amarillo Highway', have been recorded by Bobby Bare, Little Feat and others, while his idiosyncratic albums and occasional performances with the Panhandle Mystery Band have won him a cult following, particularly in England and Italy.

1969 Roger Miller entered the country charts with 'Me and Bobby McGee'. It only rose to number 12, but is important as Kris Kristofferson's first success as a writer. It became a million-selling rock record for Janis Joplin in 1971. The song was one of the first Kris wrote as staff-writer at Combine Music. "Fred Foster, the owner, called me and said, 'I've got a title for you: 'Me and Bobby McKee'. Bobby was a secretary in Boudleaux Bryant's office, but I thought he said 'McGee'. I thought there was no way I could ever write that, and it took me months of hiding from him, because I can't write on assignment. But it must have stuck in the back of my head. One day I was driving between Morgan City and New Orleans. It was raining and the windshield wipers were going. I started coming out with Baton Rouge and the places I was working at the time. I took an old experience with another girl in another country. I had finished by the time I got to Nashville. That song probably turned over more audience to me than any song I ever had."

8th MAY

1940 Ricky Nelson (Eric Hilliard Nelson) born in Los Angeles, California. His parents were stars in a radio series called "The Adventures of Ozzie and Harriet" and Ricky was featured from the age of eight. The show switched to television in 1952 and ran until the mid-sixties. Ricky kicked off a career as pop star in 1957 and scored with his first release, the million-selling 'I'm Walking'. After two more singles for Verve, he switched to Imperial Records and was teamed with an excellent band that had previously backed Bob Luman and included James Burton on lead guitar. Ricky had numerous hits including 'It's Late', 'Hello Mary Lou' and 'Never Be Anyone Else But You'. He was a big star, a success in TV, records and then in film with *Rio Brave* in 1958, but the rise of The Beatles spelled the end of regular chart appearances for many pop stars, including Nelson. He resurfaced in 1967 as one of the first country rockers, with the LPs *Bright Lights And Country Music* and *Country Fever*; in 1969 he began touring with the Stone Canyon Band, now calling himself Rick Nelson. He took little part in the rock 'n' roll revival shows that were so popular in the early seventies, except for a large-scale event at Madison Square Garden when he sang his old hits and was surprised to be booed off. He wrote the song 'Garden Party' about his experience and it was a multi-million selling hit.

1976 Reba McEntire made her chart debut with 'I Don't Want To Be A One Night Stand'.

9th MAY

1914 Hank Snow (Clarence Eugene Snow) born in Liverpool, Nova Scotia, Canada. One of the best known Canadian country singers, Hank became interested in country music through his enthusiasm for Western movies. In his teens he worked as fisherman, insurance salesman and newspaper boy, then began singing in Nova Scotia clubs for a living. He began using the persona of "Hank, the Singing Ranger" for a radio series in 1934 and was signed to RCA Victor two years later. He stayed with the record company for a remarkable length of time — 45 years. Hank scored several Canadian hits but didn't have any American releases until 1949. He became a regular on the Opry and was a very consistent chart maker — 61 country hits between 1950 and 1970. Among his best known records — 'I've Been Everywhere', 'Rhumba Boogie' and 'I'm Movin' On'.

1968 George D. Hay, the self-styled Solemn Old Judge of the Grand Ole Opry, died at his home in Virginia Beach, Virginia. He'd retired from the Opry in 1951 but remained "on call" and still received regular payment from WSM until his death.

10th MAY

1909 Maybelle Carter (Maybelle Addington), member of the original Carter Family, born in Nickelsville, Virginia. Music was a very important part of family life and she played and sang from an early age. It was while on a visit to see A.P. and Sara that Maybelle met one of A.P.'s brothers, Ezra J. Carter, whom she married in March 1926, bringing together the historic Carter Family trio which would have such a profound effect on country music history. Maybelle sang alto-harmony and played guitar, banjo and autoharp. When the original Carter Family disbanded in the late forties, she became the most active of the three, and performed with her daughters Helen, June (who married Johnny Cash) and Anita — as Mother Maybelle and the Carter Sisters. In the sixties she began touring with Johnny Cash and his road show, performing Carter Family material at concerts and on TV. In 1971 Mother Maybelle was one of the featured artists on the Nitty Gritty Dirt Band's ambitious *Will The Circle Be Unbroken* triple LP project, which introduced her music to a rock audience. She died in 1978.

1980 Eddy Arnold's first Top Ten country hit in a decade, 'Let's Get It While The Gettin's Good'. Between 1949 and 1971, Eddy was the most frequently charted country performer, notching up an amazing 87 entries.

11th MAY

1914 Bob Atcher, very popular star of Chicago folk and country scene for over two decades, born in Hardin County, Kentucky. His family had a strong Kentucky musical heritage and Bob learned from his grandparents and his father, who was a popular local fiddler. He sang on local radio shows, then was lured to Chicago in 1938 by WBBM and signed to Columbia Records. Atcher made the successful transition from radio to TV in the late forties and recorded LP's which drew on the whole range of folk and country, including *Early American Folk Songs* and *Songs Of The Saddle*.

Jimmy C. Newman

1954 Cajun country star Jimmy C. Newman made his chart debut with 'Cry, Cry, Darling'.

1979 Lester Flatt, the bluegrass guitarist whose very successful partnership with Earl Scruggs lasted for over 20 years, died.

12th MAY

1901 Whitey Ford, "The Duke of Paducah", born Benjamin Francis Ford in DeSoto, Missouri. He was a comedian and instrumentalist whose career involved a great deal of radio work and spanned several decades. He began with the Dixieland Jazz Band in 1922, was part of a banjo act that toured the vaudeville circuit, then became a member of Otto Gray's Oklahoma Cowboys. Gene Autry hired him for his radio show, which led to the WLS Barn Dance programme in Chicago; it was during this period that he acquired his famous nickname. In the thirties The Duke hosted the Plantation Party from WLW Cincinnati, and then in the forties started 16 years of regular appearances on the Grand Ole Opry. His famous catchphrase was "I'm going back to the wagon, these shoes are killin' me!"

1921 Joe Maphis (Otto W. Maphis), half of the popular country music husband and wife team Joe and Rose Lee Maphis, born in Suffolk, Virginia. Music was part of his life from an early age; he played local dances when he was ten and made his radio debut as a teenager. Joe was featured on numerous barn dance shows in the forties. He met and married Rose Lee and they moved to California, appearing on Cliffie Stone's "Hometown Jamboree" for several years and then performing regularly on "Town Hall Party" from Compton.

Billy Swan

1942 Billy Swan, singer, writer and producer, born in Cape Giradeau, Missouri. He loved the music of Hank Williams and Lefty Frizzell as a child, but the rock 'n' roll era found him equally attracted to Fats Domino, the Everly Brothers and Jerry Lee Lewis. Billy formed a band when he left school, then went to Memphis to record for Bill Black, though without success. He worked as a gate-guard at Elvis' Graceland mansion, then a song he'd written called 'Lover Please' became a hit for Clyde McPhatter and he moved to Nashville confident of success. It didn't come immediately and he had to take odd jobs, including janitor at the CBS studio, then produced Tony Joe White's big-selling 'Polk Salad Annie', toured with Kris Kristofferson, and finally had a million-selling hit of his own with 'I Can Help' — in 1974. Billy still records and is a member of Kristofferson's band.

13th MAY

1914 Johnny Wright, member of the popular Johnny and Jack duo and husband of Kitty Wells "The Queen Of Country Music", born in Mt. Juliet, Tennessee. Music was an important part of his family's heritage — his grandfather was a champion fiddler and his father played the banjo. Johnny's first radio work came in 1936 on WSIX Nashville, which brought him into contact with singer Muriel Deason; they married two years later, by which time he'd persuaded her to adopt the stage name Kitty Wells. The same year, 1938, he teamed up with Jack Anglin and they performed on numerous radio shows and toured extensively with the Tennessee Mountain Boys, joining the Louisiana Hayride in the mid-forties and the Grand Ole Opry in 1953. Kitty performed with Johnny and Jack as a complete road show unit from 1952 until Jack's tragic death in 1963. Today they have a family show; Johnny, Kitty and their son Bobby work over 200 dates a year.

1916 Johnny Wright's partner, Jack Anglin, born in Columbia, Tennessee. Like Johnny, Jack came from a family with strong traditional music roots. He was brought up on a farm and was playing the guitar as a schoolboy. He moved to Nashville and met Johnny Wright at WSIX in 1936. They built up a joint career and by the fifties were one of the top country music acts in the US. They scored numerous hits including 'Goodnight, Sweetheart, Goodnight', 'Poison Love' and 'Stop The World'. In March 1963, on his way to a prayer service for Patsy Cline, Jack was killed in a car accident.

1960 Tex-Mex country and rockabilly performer Freddy Fender arrested "May, Friday the 13th, 1960 I was busted for 'grass' in Baton Rouge, Louisiana. I'm not bitter, but if friends ask I still say that the three years I had to spend in Angola State Prison was a long time for a little mistake. My time in prison was hard, but the music made it better. I can remember when my bass player and I (we were busted together) walked into Angola, carrying our guitar and bass instead of our clothes. Then every Saturday and Sunday we would play on the 'walk' for all our fellow convicts. I even recorded an album of Chicano songs on a portable tape recorder at the prison" (from Freddy's sleeve notes on his *Before The Next Teardrop Falls* LP).

1975 Bob Wills, "The King of Western Swing" died. He had been unconscious for 17 months since suffering a stroke after a recording session.

14th MAY

1936 Charlie Gracie (Graci) born in Philadelphia, Pennsylvania. A singer who began recording rockabilly in 1953, he had hits for a year with the newly formed Cameo label in 1957, including 'Fabulous', 'Butterfly' and 'Wandering Eyes', and then disappeared into obscurity. On a British visit in his successful year he won rare praise from the normally staid London *Times,* whose critic confessed that Gracie had converted him to the "delights of rock 'n' roll's intoxicating effects".

1972 Thirteen-year-old Tanya Tucker made her debut in the charts with 'Delta Dawn', the first of a series of successful country singles produced by Billy Sherrill. "Everybody says I started in the business so young, 'cos I was only twelve," Tanya told writer Joan Dew. "Well, to me, that was late. I knew what I wanted to do from the time I was eight, and by the time I was nine I had started making plans and working toward my goals."

15th MAY

1918 Eddy Arnold (Richard Edward Arnold) born on a farm near Henderson, Tennessee. From the late forties until the end of the sixties, Eddy was the most successful country singer in America, the first real crossover artist, his smooth ballads appealing to a broad audience, bringing him dozens of hits including 'Make The World Go Away', 'Bouquet of Roses', 'Cattle Call', 'Then You Can Tell Me Goodbye', 'Kentucky Waltz' and 'Eddy's Song'. His father was a fiddle player who encouraged Eddy's early enthusiasm for guitar playing, though country music was a part-time occupation for several years because he was working on the family farm. In 1936, he debuted on radio in Jackson, Tennessee; six years later he earned a permanent spot on station WTJS, then moved to another radio outlet in Memphis. Eddy came to Nashville during the middle forties as a member of Pee Wee King's Golden West Cowboys, joined the Opry and signed a solo record contract with RCA Victor, beginning a career as "The Tennessee Plowboy" that would propel him to legendary status. He was one of the first country stars to appear on network TV and eventually had his own show. Eddy was elected to the Country Music Hall of Fame in 1966, and though the big hits stopped in 1969, he continued to record and was rewarded with a return to the country Top Ten in 1980, a decade after his last big success, 'Please Don't Go'. Approaching his fifth decade with RCA Victor, his latest press release observes — "At an age when many of his old friends and peers have retired to a life of fishing, hunting and spinning yarns, Arnold still records and performs 60-70 concerts a year to capacity audiences in the finest halls and theatres."

1957 'Bye Bye Love' the first hit for the Everly Brothers entered the charts. It reached number one and stayed on the listings for half the year.

16th MAY

1980 In a boom year for movies that had anything to do with country music, the unlikely combination of singer Merle Haggard and actor Clint Eastwood entered the country charts with 'Bar Room Buddies', from the Eastwood-directed film, *Bronco Billy.* The song rose steadily up the listings and reached number one on July 26.

1981 George Strait made his chart debut with 'Unwound'. He was born in 1952 in Pearsall, Texas and brought up on his family's cattle ranch. "For three years I worked the ranch during the day and played music at night," he recalls. But gradually music took over, and with the Ace In The Hole band, he built up a strong following on the southwest Texas honky-tonk circuit, playing music that was rooted in the tradition of his heroes Bob Wills and the Texas Playboys, Merle Haggard and George Jones. MCA executive Erv Woolsey heard Strait in San Marcos, brought him to Nashville and teamed him with producer Blake Mevis. 'Unwound' was one of the first songs they recorded together.

17th MAY

1912 Grant Turner, the "Dean of the Opry Announcers" born in Abilene, Texas. His first radio job was at KFYO in Abilene in 1928. He subsequently moved to stations in Longview, Sherman and Knoxville, before settling in Nashville, Tennessee and joining WSM in June, 1944. After the departure of George D. Hay, he became the most familiar voice for the millions of listeners. Though semi-retired, Grant still handles some of the announcing duties at the Opry, introducing performers and reading commercials. In 1981 he was elected to the Country Music Hall of Fame.

18th MAY

1942 Rodney Dillard, leader of The Dillards, the popular modern bluegrass/country rock outfit, born in Salem, Missouri. He learned to play the guitar at school while his brother Doug practised the banjo. Their bluegrass performances as teenagers were well received and encouraged them to become professional musicians. Forming The Dillards, they headed west for California, won a recording contract with Elektra and began appearing on the "Andy Griffith" TV show. Doug left the band in 1967, but Rodney has continued at the helm and the group has continued to flourish.

Joe Bonsall

1944 Joe Bonsall, tenor voice and resident comedian in the Oak Ridge Boys, born in Philadelphia, Pennsylvania. He made his debut at the age of six on an amateur hour TV show, and sang in a Philadelphia group called The Faith Four, before joining the Oaks. Despite their clean-cut image today, the four-piece were known as rebels on the gospel circuit — "We were controversial," says Joe. "We wore our hair long and dressed more modern. We were also the first gospel group to hire a band."

1980 British rock singer Elvis Costello began recording country songs with producer Billy Sherrill at CBS Studio A in Nashville. The results appeared on an album called *Almost Blue*, which won an enthusiastic response from British critics and modest sales to rock fans, but was snubbed by the American country establishment.

19th MAY

1940 Mickey Newbury born in Houston, Texas. A highly respected singer and songwriter, he has long eluded easy categorization; as Kris Kristofferson said — "Mickey deliberately defies labels. He is neither country nor soul... Behind the deceptive simplicity of some of his lyrics, there are levels of mental landscape that can take you in some strange directions, past the edges of understanding . . . Johnny Cash has probably come closest by calling Mickey Newbury a 'poet'." After a tour of duty in the air force and a spell working on shrimp boats in the Gulf of Mexico, Mickey settled in Nashville and made several records — carefully crafted works that have won high critical praise but not large sales. It's as a writer that he has had considerable success, with hits like 'Just Dropped In To See What Condition My Condition Was In' for Kenny Rodgers and the First Edition; 'She Even Woke Me Up To Say Goodbye' for Jerry Lee Lewis and 'American Trilogy' for Elvis Presley.

1979 The Bellamy Brothers topped the charts with 'If I Said You Had A Beautiful Body, Would You Hold It Against Me'. It was the most successful country song of the year in England, where it reached number three in the pop chart.

20th MAY

1919 George Gobel born in Chicago, Illinois. A star of WLS Barn Dance from 1932, at the age of 13 when he was "The Little Cowboy" to the outbreak of World War II when he left to join the air force. But for the intervention of the war he might have become a successful recording artist, but he changed direction in the services and became a comedian. In 1945 he began playing nightspots as a comic and was so successful that he had his own TV series by the fifties.

1967 Jerry Reed made his chart debut with 'Guitar Man', later a huge hit for Elvis Presley.

21st MAY

1931 Charlie Poole, the banjo player and singer with the North Carolina Ramblers, died. Poole and his string band were greatly admired in Virginia and North Carolina and are still held in very high regard by old time music enthusiasts, though Charlie's career was surprisingly short. According to Norm Cohen, "As Charlie Poole's fame grew, so did his penchant for rambling, and also, apparently, his craving for hard liquor. When the Depression forced his recording career to a close, he seemed to lose interest in music . . . An extensive drinking binge with old friends evidently brought on a heart attack and he died, at the age of thirty-nine."

1977 Waylon Jennings top of the country chart with 'Luckenbach, Texas (Back To The Basics Of Love)'. The record stayed at the top for six weeks.

22nd MAY

1892 Ralph Peer born in Kansas City, Missouri. He was the first record company person to present country music to the American people, and was the man who "discovered" both Jimmie Rodgers and the Carter Family — the two most important acts in the early days of country. His father was a phonograph dealer in

Kansas City, and helping in the shop exposed Ralph to a variety of music and prepared him for a long and varied career. In 1920 he recorded a black blues singer named Mamie Smith, which led to the discovery that there was a huge audience for black music — thereby launching the "race records" industry. Ralph began scouting the American south looking for more black singers and realised there was also considerable potential in recording the folk music of poor whites. His motives were commercial, but he also acted as a folklorist, recording a lot of traditional and old-time string band music which might otherwise have been lost once the musicians died. He advertised in local newspapers and set up temporary studios in hotel rooms to record the acts that came forward. It was in this way that he found both Jimmie Rodgers and the Carter Family during a ten day stay in Bristol, a town on the Tennessee/Virginia border, in the summer of 1927. Peer formed Southern Music in 1928, which became one of the biggest publishing companies involved with country music — owning classics like 'Wabash Cannonball', 'Mule Skinner Blues' and 'You Are My Sunshine' — and has done much subsequently to promote country music worldwide.

23rd MAY

1925 Mac (Malcolm) Wiseman, popular bluegrass banjo picker and singer, born near Waynesboro, Virginia. He was brought up in a traditional music environment in the Shenendoah Valley, learning songs that he later performed throughout his career. He worked as a DJ on WSVA in Harrisburg, Virginia and in the evenings sang and played in clubs, subsequently devoting himself full-time to performing, playing with various artists including Molly O'Day, Bill Monroe and Flatt and Scruggs, and appearing on the Louisiana Hayride and other radio barn dance shows.

1958 Shelly West, daughter of Dottie West — one of the best known country writers and entertainers — born. She toured with her mother in 1975-77, then teamed up with band member Allen Frizzell (baby brother of the great Lefty Frizzell). Through a one-off demo tape made with another Frizzell brother, David, Shelly found herself making her first record 'You're The Reason God Made Oklahoma' which reached the Top Ten. David Frizzell and Shelly West have become one of the most popular new country music duos of the eighties.

24th MAY

1933 Despite being very ill, Jimmie Rodgers completed his last recording session, in New York City. A bed had been set up in the studio so that he could rest between songs. He knew he was dying and that he wouldn't return home alive, but had come to make the recordings so that his wife and daughter would be provided for.

1941 Bob Dylan (Robert Allen Zimmerman) born in Duluth, Minnesota. He is one of the most influential writers and performers in contemporary music. Bob visited Nashville several times to record LP's including *Blonde On Blonde, John Wesley Hardin* and in 1969, his most country-oriented album, *Nashville Skyline,* which features Johnny Cash on one track.

1955 Rosanne Cash, the daughter of Johnny Cash and Vivian Liberto, born in Memphis Tennessee at the time her father was making musical history at the Sun studio with the likes of Elvis Presley, Jerry Lee Lewis and Carl Perkins. In the eighties, Rosanne is breaking musical ground of her own, as one of the leading "new country" singers and writers, along with her husband/producer Rodney Crowell. When she was 11 her parents divorced and she was raised in California by her mother, but retained a close relationship with her father and moved to Nashville after graduating from high school. She toured with Cash's road show, working initially with the wardrobe department. After a period training to be an actress, Rosanne decided to make music her career. She married Rodney in early 1979, the same year that she signed to her father's record company, CBS. Her album, *Right Or Wrong* delivered three hit singles, including the duet with Bobby Bare, 'No Memories Hangin' Round'. The next LP, *Seven Year Ache* was even more successful, including two number one singles, and established Rosanne as one of the leading ladies of country music.

25th MAY

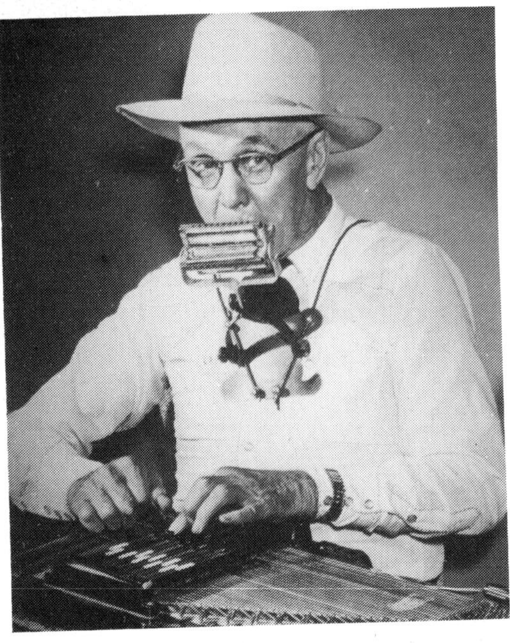

1893 Ernest V. "Pop" Stoneman, country music pioneer, born in a log cabin near Monarat, Carroll County in the Blue Ridge Mountains of Virginia. Brought up in a musical family, he learned to play harmonica, autoharp, banjo and guitar. When he heard Henry Whitter's early hillbilly recordings, he decided that he could do much better and wrote to several New York companies requesting auditions. He then saved up for a train trip north, and recorded songs for Ralph Peer at Okeh in 1924, the first of some 200 selections he cut, often with his wife and family friends, during the twenties. The Depression had a destructive effect on the careers of several hillbilly entertainers, including the Stonemans', and Pop had to take other work, including carpentry and a job in a naval gun factory. He had 13 children who all became musicians. In the forties he formed a family band, and in 1957 his recording career was revived with a Folkways LP, which featured most of his 13 children. They became favourites at folk revival concerts and appeared on TV. Ernest died in Nashville, in 1968, after an illness, but some of his children continued to work in country music including his fiddle-playing son Scotty Wiseman.

1936 Tom T. Hall, "the Nashville Story Teller", born in Olive Hill, East Kentucky. "The home of my boyhood," wrote Tom, "was a frame house of pale grey boards and a porch from which to view the dusty road and the promise of elsewhere beyond the hills. The birthplace of a dreamer . . . In that house eight of us children lived, parented by Virgil L. Hall and Della Henderson Hall. Dad worked ten to twelve hours a day, sometimes six days a week, in a brick plant. His income kept us in food, clothes, and just-barely-enoughs to help ten people survive more than their share of bitter experiences, scandals and death." He started playing the guitar when he was ten, had his first band, the Kentucky Travellers, at 16 and appeared on a local radio station as a DJ. He'd already begun writing songs and during a tour of duty in Europe in the army tried them out over AFN (the Armed Forces Network). Country artists began recording his songs, and he had his first success when Jimmy C. Newman had a hit with his 'DJ For A Day'. In 1963, Tom moved to Nashville and began recording for Mercury. His first hit was 'I Washed My Face In the Morning Dew' in 1967, but his big breakthrough came as the composer of the million-selling 'Harper Valley PTA', a hit for Jeannie C. Riley in 1968. He scored numerous hits as a performer in the seventies including 'Watermelon Wine', 'Faster Horses' and 'The Year That Clayton Delaney Died'.

1947 Jessi Colter (Miriam Johnson) born in Phoenix, Arizona. She took her stage name from the outlaw and counterfeiter Jesse Colter, who was her great-great-great uncle, but her own outlaw status has come through her musical and marital association with Waylon Jennings. Her mother ran a hotel, then had a religious experience and became a minister. Jessi was the church pianist at 11, and at that age decided to centre her life on music. While a teenager she auditioned for rock 'n' roll guitarist Duane Eddy and he recorded her, they toured and then married. After eight years they were divorced, Jessi returned to Phoenix, met Waylon Jennings at J.D.'s club and they began working together. Less than a year later they were married. Jessi recorded an album for RCA and some singles, then concentrated on raising her child, but returned to recording with a Capitol contract, made several LP's and had a huge country and pop hit with 'I'm Not Lisa'.

26th MAY

1933 Jimmie Rodgers died in his New York hotel room, after a massive tubercular haemorrhage. He was just 35 years old. "The Mississippi Blue Yodeller" was buried in his home town of Meridian, where he's remembered each year with a special concert. When the Country Music Hall of Fame began, there was a total agreement that Jimmie should be the first person honoured.

1949 Hank Williams Jnr born in Shreveport, Louisiana. When Hank Snr died, Audrey Williams was determined that her son should follow in her husband's footsteps. By the time he'd reached his teens he was a seasoned performer and by 16 was a country star, had already debuted on the Opry, had a million-selling album and become the youngest winner of a BMI Songwriter's Award. Then, at the height of his career, he decided that success really didn't mean a whole lot to him. In the face of overwhelming criticism and a collapsing personal life, he left Nashville in 1974 and moved to Alabama, where he linked up with an old friend named James R. Smith. Together they set to re-arranging Hank's career to suit Hank instead of Nashville. He recorded the landmark album, *Hank Williams Jnr And Friends* which featured country-rock musicians including Charlie Daniels. Then came disaster; Hank fell 500 feet down a Montana mountain. The accident, on August 8, 1975, caused appalling injuries to his head, and it was a miracle that he lived. Doctors were sceptical about him making a full recovery, but after two years of recuperation, involving several operations, he was fit again. He emerged with an even stronger sense of purpose and the determination to make his own music and to break away from the shadow of his famous father; he succeeded, with a string of gritty, rough-edged, best-selling country albums.

1962 Willie Nelson made his very first appearance on the country charts, with 'Touch Me'.

27th MAY

1931 Kenny Price, now at 300 lbs one of the "biggest" stars in country music, born near Florence, Kentucky. He became established with regular appearances on the Midwestern Hayride radio show in the fifties, and began a run of chart hits in the sixties with 'Walking On New Grass'.

1939 Don Williams, the country superstar with the easy-going manner and the ultra-low profile, born near Plainview, Texas. His first public performance was at the age of three in a talent contest — he won first prize, an alarm clock! Don began playing guitar as a teenager, learning songs from the radio. While in Corpus Christi in 1964 he formed the Pozo Seco Singers with Susan Taylor and Lofton Cline, and they sang a mix of folk, pop and country, scoring a Top Ten hit with 'Time'. The trio disbanded in 1971 and Don pursued a solo career, recording for JMI, then switching to ABC/Dot. His hits began with 'We Should Be Together' in 1974 and a year later he had his first number one with 'You're My Best Friend'. Don became very popular in England after the success of 'I Recall A Gypsy Woman', was the number one album seller in the UK in 1978 (outselling every rock, country and pop act) and was voted "Country Artist of the Decade" by British fans in a 1980 poll.

1978 Newcomer John Conlee entered the country charts with 'Rose Colored Glasses'. One of the biggest hits of the year, it established the Nashville DJ as a new country star.

28th MAY

1945 Gary Stewart, one of the best modern honky-tonk singers, born in Letcher County, Kentucky. He was exposed to country music early in life, but his family moved to Florida when he was 12 and he found a broader range of musical influences. During his teen years he toured with a rock 'n' roll band but the excitement of the road soon dulled and he took a regular gig at a nightclub in Okeechobee. He was "spotted" by Mel Tillis, who gave him the encouragement he needed to work harder on his writing and singing and move to Nashville. Within two years he had written hits for Billy Walker, Jack Greene, Jim Ed Brown and Nat Stuckey. Gary retained strong ambitions as a performer and working with Charley Pride gave him the chance to perform his own songs to large audiences. He was signed to RCA and two of his first three singles 'Drinkin' Thing' and 'Out of Hand' rose into the Top Ten in 1974. Several more hits followed, but then Gary became disillusioned with Nashville and moved back to Florida and the small coastal town of Fort Pierce. Instead of going onto bigger venues or venturing onto the rock circuit, he has stuck almost religiously to playing the honky-tonk clubs where he feels more comfortable.

JERRY LEE LEWIS TAUNTED WITH 'BABY SNATCHER' BY THEATRE AUDIENCE

1958 Jerry Lee Lewis returned to America after a British tour (due to last until the end of June) was cancelled after just four shows. The British press had expressed their horror on discovering that Lewis' companion, his third wife Myra Gail, was also his 13-year-old cousin. Jerry's response to accusations that he was still married to his second wife didn't improve matters — "Myra and I are legally married. It was my second marriage that wasn't legal. I was a bigamist when I was sixteen. I was fourteen when I was first married. That lasted a year, then I met Jane. One day she said she was going to have a baby. I was real worried, her father threatened me, and her brothers were hunting with hide whips. So I married her just a week before my divorce from Dorothy. It was a shotgun wedding." The scandal spread to American newspapers and Jerry Lee Lewis' career slumped.

29th MAY

1952 Hank and Audrey Williams were divorced. Hank paid $4,000 worth of Audrey's legal fees and she got a house, a Cadillac and one half of all royalties due him for songs and records. According to Chet Flippo's controversial biography of the singer—*Your Cheatin' Heart*— "The terms were meaningless to Hank. Money didn't matter. He hadn't challenged Audrey on any of her demands; she could have anything she wanted (he knew she'd come back eventually). . . He just wasn't interested."

1965 Jody Miller's 'Queen Of The House' which was an answer record to the Roger Miller (no relation) hit 'King Of The Road', entered the country charts. The song launched Jody's successful country music career.

30th MAY

1926 Johnny Gimble born on a farm in Tyler, Texas. He began playing fiddle at local dates when he was just 12. In the forties he worked with Bob and Joe Shelton, then joined Bob Wills and his Texas Playboys. Johnny left the music business in the fifties and became a barber in Waco, but returned to performing and recording in 1968, moved to Nashville and was soon very much in demand as a fiddle player for sessions and tours with major country names.

1956 Johnny Cash entered the charts with 'I Walk The Line'. The record stayed on the listings for a remarkable run of 43 weeks, but it never reached number one, stopping short at two.

1966 Dolly Parton and Carl Dean married at Ringgold in Catoosa County, Georgia, just across the Tennessee state line. No-one other than their families knew of the wedding for over a year because Dolly kept her private and public lives totally separate. When she finally announced that she had a husband, several people in Nashville thought he was a figment of her imagination! Carl Dean, an almost total recluse, has rarely been photographed, with or without his wife.

31st MAY

1922 Vic Willis, youngest of the three Willis Brothers — a pioneering country group — born in Schulter, Oklahoma. With the death of brother Skeeter and Guy's retirement in the mid-seventies, he decided to try a new sound and formed the Vic Willis Trio, which performed modern country favourites in close harmony, with Vic's accordion as lead instrument. "It's a sound people say they find unusual, especially the accordion," says Vic. "We've been getting encores at the Opry, and that's the hardest place in the world to get an encore."

1930 Clint Eastwood, the actor who came to prominence as Rowdy Yates in the TV western *Rawhide* and now a top box-office draw with movies like *Every Which Way But Loose*, born in San Francisco, California.

1941 Johnny Paycheck (Donald Lytle) born in Greenfield, Ohio. He dropped out of school, rode freight trains and hitch-hiked around America. "All I did was exist for about 20 years," he recalls. "Eating green apples, sleeping under trucks: it was a hard, exciting time." Many of his experiences were later translated into songs that were frequently fierce and boisterous. His first recording contract was in 1959 when he used the name Donnie Young, but had no success. He worked with Faron Young, Ray Price and then had a long stint with George Jones' band. "I guess we were much alike," says Johnny. "You know, I had a terrible drinking problem most of my life, but during those years I drank all the time and roared and had a big time. George was that way then, and we were like two peas in a pod. He'd fire me one night and hire me back the next day, that kind of stuff!" Drink problem notwithstanding, he began writing hit songs in the mid-sixties, then launched his solo career with the name Johnny Paycheck, which had once belonged to a prizefighter. He had hits, but also innumerable legal problems. "Those were my big years, but I didn't know how to handle it," he recalls. "I was drinking like crazy and wasn't taking care of business." He left Nashville and spent "two and a half years in the gutter". Billy Sherrill helped him solve his problems and produced him for Epic Records in the seventies, a decade that brought his biggest hits.

JUNE

1st JUNE

1915 Johnny Bond (Cyrus Whitfield Bond), western singer, guitarist, actor and songwriter, born in Enville, Oklahoma. His musical career began on Oklahoma radio, then he joined the Jim Wakely Trio in 1937, later becoming a mainstay of Gene Autry's California radio show. He was with Autry for over a decade, simultaneously recording western-style songs for Columbia and appearing as sidekick to Gene and other cowboy stars, in numerous movies. Johnny wrote over 400 songs including 'Cimarron'.

1934 Pat Boone (Charles Eugene Boone) born in Jacksonville, Florida. He had great success in the fifties singing watered-down versions of black rock 'n' roll songs, suffered a decline in popularity in the sixties, but found fame again in the seventies as a country singer.

1954 Johnny Horton's 'Battle Of New Orleans' the number one pop song in America.

1964 Dolly Parton's first day in Nashville, 24 hours after graduating from high school in Sevierville, when she'd told friends, "I'm going to Nashville tomorrow and not coming back until I make it!" Dolly took her belongings from the Greyhound bus station to the apartment of her Uncle Bill and Aunt Cathy, then went to the nearby Wishy-Washy launderette, where she met her future husband, Carl Dean, for the first time.

2nd JUNE

1927 Carl Butler born in Knoxville, Tennessee. After performing on radio stations in Tennessee and North Carolina, Carl joined the Grand Ole Opry in 1948 and in the fifties was established as a Columbia recording artist and a successful song writer. He had a number one hit in 1962 with 'Don't Let Me Cross Over', which featured his wife, Pearl Butler, on harmony vocals. The success encouraged them to perform as a duo and they scored several more hits during the sixties.

1969 Leona Williams made her chart debut with 'Once More', on Hickory Records.

3rd JUNE

19?? Boots Randolph born. A leading Nashville session man in the late fifties/early sixties, his saxophone playing can be heard on numerous country-pop recordings. He had a hit in his own right in 1963 with 'Yakety Sax' on the Monument label.

1949 Ernest Tubb married Olene Adams. They had five children, including Justin who subsequently became a country star.

1972 Donna Fargo top of the country charts with 'The Happiest Girl In The Whole USA';

the longest running hit of the year, it stayed on the charts for 23 weeks. Donna wrote the song with Stan Silver, who's now her husband, producer and manager.

4th JUNE

1903 Charlie Monroe born in Rosine, Kentucky. From the mid-twenties he performed with his younger brother Bill in the pioneering bluegrass group, The Monroe Brothers. They went their separate ways in 1938, Charlie forming the Kentucky Pardners while Bill went on to far greater fame with his Bluegrass Boys. Charlie continued to perform and record with his group until the early fifties, then retired to his farm in Kentucky.

Freddy Fender

1937 Freddy Fender born in the south Texas valley border town of San Benito. According to his own sleeve notes for the *Before The Next Teardrop Falls* LP — "My real name is Baldemar G. Huerta... I'm a Mexican-American, better yet, a Tex-Mex. I just picked up my stage name, Freddy Fender, in the late fifties as a name that would help my music sell better with 'gringos'... Music was part of me, even in my childhood. I can still remember sitting on the street corner facing Pancho Galvan's grocery store, plunking at my three-string guitar. It didn't have a back on it, but it sure sounded pretty good to me and the crowd of little kids listening. Music kept a lot of us happy, even when it was hard for Mama to put beans on the table." He quit school at 16, joined the US Marines, then began playing Texas honky-tonks and started what seemed like a promising recording career, but was busted for "grass" and spent three years in jail. On his release he worked in New Orleans for several years, then returned to Texas. In 1974 he recorded for Huey P. Meaux. One of the songs, 'Before The Next Teardrop Falls', became a huge country and pop hit and Freddy became a very popular performer and TV chat show guest.

5th JUNE

1945 Don Reid, lead vocalist, MC, chief spokesperson and youngest member of the Statler Brothers, born in Staunton, Virginia. The group had its origins with the gospel Four Star Quartet, though Don didn't join until five years later when they were The Kingsmen, still a gospel outfit. "Our greatest influence was the Blackwood Brothers," says Don. "They typified what a gospel quartet should sound like. In other words, what all gospel groups — whether big, small or whatever — thought they sounded like. It's like every country singer in the world reckons he sounds like Merle Haggard. The Blackwoods were a part of our past, they had so much influence on us . . . their harmony and style of singing gospel music is what we adopted for singing country."

1980 *Urban Cowboy* premiered in Houston, Texas. The movie, which starred John Travolta, Debra Winger, Gilley's nightclub and a mechanical bull, wasn't an enormous success though the soundtrack album was a very big seller.

6th JUNE

1885 Gid Tanner (James Gideon Tanner), leader of the unique Skillet Lickers, the popular Atlanta-based old-time string band in the twenties and thirties, born in Thomas Bridge, Georgia. Gid was a charismatic and successful figure on the Atlanta music scene, and a regular winner of fiddling contests. In 1920 a local paper said, "Gid is a husky chap with a complexion of deep crimson hue, and he rejoices in the possession of a vocal range which Caruso might envy." When the Columbia Phonograph Company came to Georgia looking for artists to record for the newly discovered "hillbilly market", they chose Gid. He travelled to New York with his friend

Riley Puckett and they made what are generally regarded as the first commercial string band recordings in March 1924. Gid, Riley, Clayton McMichen and other musicians began recording as the Skillet Lickers in 1926 and became one of Columbia's best-selling acts.

1906 Asher Sizemore, father of Little Jimmy, born in Manchester, Kentucky. Asher and Little Jimmy Sizemore were a very popular act on the Grand Ole Opry in the thirties, with their selection of sentimental "heart songs" like 'The Dying Girl's Farewell' and 'How Beautiful Heaven Must Be'.

1924 Rosalie Allen (Julie Marlene Bedra), the yodelling "Prairie Star", born in Old Forge, Pennsylvania. She was a popular radio star in the American north east between the thirties and fifties.

1943 Joe Stampley born in Springhill, Louisiana. A music enthusiast from a very early age, Joe's first hero was Hank Williams. His musical horizons expanded with the arrival of stars like Elvis and when he began making records in 1958, at the age of 15, they were rock 'n' roll. He had singles released on the famous Imperial and Chess labels, but they sank without trace. He enjoyed a short burst of success in 1966 with The Uniques, but a switch to country music in the early seventies brought him long-lasting popularity. A consistent chart-maker throughout the decade, his biggest hits came after teaming up with another honky-tonk singer from the south west, Moe Bandy.

7th JUNE

1934 Wynn Stewart born in Morrisville, Missouri. His family moved to California and he made his first record there when he was just 15. Wynn recorded for Capitol in the mid-fifties, but with little success, then switched to Challenge where he scored his first hit in 1959. Four years later he was back with Capitol, and this time his California honky-tonk sounds were well received and he had a long run of hits including the number one 'It's Such A Pretty World Today' in 1967. He performed regularly at his Nashville-Nevada club in Las Vegas for a few years, and had his own TV show.

1940 Tom Jones born in Pontypridd, a mining town in Wales. After a string of international pop successes like 'Green, Green Grass Of Home' and 'It's Not Unusual', Tom became very popular on the US concert trail. He's now based in California and has had success in the country music market, most notably with 'Say You'll Stay Until Tonight', which reached number one in March 1977.

Tom Jones

1944 Clarence White born in Lewiston, Maine. One of the important musicians who introduced country and bluegrass to young rock audiences in the late sixties/early seventies, he began playing at the age of ten with the Country Boys, a group that developed into the respected Kentucky Colonels in 1962. Clarence left in 1965 and worked as a session guitarist with Wynn Stewart, the Everly Brothers, Rick Nelson and others, then joined The Byrds. His promising career ended tragically when he was killed by a drunken driver in 1973.

1966 Claudette, wife of Roy Orbison, killed in a motor cycle accident. In 1958, the Everly Brothers had a number one hit with 'Claudette', the song Roy had written about his wife.

1969 The Johnny Cash and Bob Dylan TV Special shown on American television.

8th JUNE

1941 Vernon Oxford, singer and fiddler whose hard-core country sound has made him popular in Europe, born in Benton County, Arkansas. Vernon was brought up in a musical family and his father was a prize-winning fiddler. He had a brief association with RCA in the mid-sixties and was then dropped, but British sales and demands for more records encouraged the label to re-sign him. He had several hits in the seventies, including 'Redneck (The Redneck National Anthem)' and 'Clean Your Own Tables'.

Vernon Oxford

1945 Steve Fromholz, a leading light in the Austin progressive country scene, born in Temple, Texas. He began writing songs when he was 18 and was a member of the Dallas County Jug Band with another country-rocker of the future, Michael Murphey. Steve joined Dan McCrimmon in the duo Frummox and made the album *From Here To There* in 1968, which included his classic 'Texas Trilogy'. He met Stephen Stills and joined his country-rock band Manassas, then worked with Michael Nesmith. In 1974 he moved to Austin where he was befriended by Willie Nelson, who recorded his 'I'd Have To Be Crazy' and then helped out on Steve's debut album *A Rumor In My Own Time* (Capitol), which was acclaimed by the critics.

9th JUNE

1915 Guitarist Les Paul (Lester William Polfus) born in Waukesham, Wisconsin. His early professional musical experiences included working as a country instrumentalist and comedian in the thirties, when he used names like Hot Rod Red and Rhubarb Red. He became interested in jazz and was running his country career side by side with a jazz trio for a time. In the forties he moved to California and did session work, then teamed up with singer Mary Ford, whom he subsequently married. In the fifties they had several big hits in the pop charts, including 'How High The Moon' and 'Vaya Con Dios'. He designed the Les Paul guitar for Gibson, which became a firm favourite with rock guitarists, immortalising his name for generations of musicians. Les went into semi-retirement in the sixties, after his divorce from Mary Ford, but made occasional forays into the studios for various projects, including the successful duo LP with Chet Atkins, *Chester and Lester,* in the mid-seventies.

1939 Stoney Cooper and Wilma Lee Leary married. They'd met in the Leary Family band, and continued to play and sing with the group until the mid-forties, when they began their career as a duo.

1958 With his career in ruins after the scandal surrounding his short visit to Britain, Jerry Lee Lewis wrote "an open letter to the industry", which appeared in the trade magazine *Billboard* .

Dear Friends:

I have in recent weeks been the apparent center of a fantastic amount of publicity and of which none has been good.

But there must be a little good even in the worst people, and according to the press releases originating in London, I am the worst and am not even deserving of one decent press release.

Now this whole thing started because I tried and did tell the truth. I told the story of my past life, as I thought it had been straightened out and that I would not hurt anybody in being man enough to tell the truth.

I confess that my life has been stormy. I confess further that since I have become a public figure I sincerely wanted to be worthy of the decent admiration of all the people, young and old, that admired or liked what talent (if any) I have. That is, after all, all that I have in a professional way to offer.

If you don't believe that the accuracy of things can get mixed up when you are in the public's eye, then I hope you never have to travel this road I'm on.

There were some legal misunderstandings in this matter that inadvertently made me look as though I invented the word indecency. I feel I, if nothing else, should be given credit for the fact that I have at least a little common sense and that if I had not thought the legal aspects of this matter were not completely straight, I certainly would not have made a move until they were.

I did not want to hurt Jane Mitcham, nor did I want to hurt my family and children. I went to court and did not contest Jane's divorce actions, and she was awarded $750.00 a month for child support and alimony. Jane and I parted from the courtroom as friends and as a matter of fact, chatted before, during and after the trial with no animosity whatsoever.

In the belief that for once my life was straightened out, I invited my mother and daddy and little sister to make the trip to England. Unfortunately, mother and daddy felt that the trip would be too long and hard for them and didn'tgo, but sister did go along with Myra's little brother and mother.

I hope that if I am washed up as an entertainer it won't be because of this bad publicity, because I can cry and wish all I want to, but I can't control the press or the sensationalism that these people will go to to get a scandal started to sell papers. If you don't believe me, please ask any of the other people that have been victims of the same.

Sincerely,

Jerry Lee Lewis

10th JUNE

1931 Jimmie Rodgers and the Carter Family recorded together at a session organised by Ralph Peer in Louisville, Kentucky. Though both had been "discovered" in Bristol in early August 1927, this session was the first occasion that they'd met. According to country music historian John Atkins, "Rodgers by now was a star. He was also very sick, and at the Louisville session it took him from June 10 through 17 to record just eleven songs, with three or four takes of each." There were two duets with Sara, including 'The Wonderful City', the only sacred song Rodgers ever recorded, plus a couple of the humorous skits that were considered essential for the repertoire of hillbilly performers in those days.

1978 Willie Nelson had the best-selling LP, *Stardust,* and single, 'Georgia On My Mind'. The *Stardust* album remained at the top for 11 weeks and is still in the charts (enjoying its 220th week!) at the time of writing. It features Willie singing pop standards to country instrumentation and is undoubtedly one of the biggest critical and popular successes among LPs recorded in the seventies.

11th JUNE

1939 Wilma Burgess, who had country hits in the sixties including 'Misty Blue' and 'Baby', born in Orlando, Florida. Hers is not a typical country singer's biography; she was a city girl with little or no knowledge of country music until she attended an Eddy Arnold concert while a high school student and she had no plans for a musical career, though sometimes she sang at social events. When she left college in 1960, Wilma went to Nashville to demo songs for a country songwriter friend, but her voice attracted more attention than the songs and she was signed to Decca Records. TV appearances and hit singles followed soon afterwards.

1949 Hank Williams finally made his debut at the Grand Ole Opry. The show had a clean and wholesome image and the Opry had delayed inviting him for as long as possible. Hank sang 'Lovesick Blues' and won six encores, an unprecedented feat in the long history of the Opry. Even after this success there was still some hesitation about booking him regularly on the show. According to his biographer Roger M. Williams — "Although Hank had kept out of trouble with liquor for about a year, the stories of his earlier antics were still fresh in the memories of promoters and other business types in the country music field. Could he be counted on to honour his commitments, in sober fashion?"

12th JUNE

1932 Charlie Feathers born in Myrtle, near Holly Springs, Mississippi. He is one of the most revered of all rockabilly singers, due to records made for the Meteor, King, Kay, Memphis and Redneck labels, though he's never had even a whisper of a hit. Charlie also recorded hillbilly material for Sun and co-authored one of Elvis Presley's hits on the label, 'I Forgot To Remember To Forget'. Most other rockabilly performers have become country singers, but Charlie Feathers has continued to perform authentic-sounding fifties rockabilly in Memphis nightspots.

1957 Jerry Lee Lewis' second record, 'Whole Lotta Shakin' Goin' On' entered the charts.

Thanks to a carefully planned sales campaign by Judd Phillips of Sun, and an appearance on the networked Steve Allen TV show, the song rose to number one and Jerry Lee Lewis became a major star. His concert price increased from $50 to $10,000, and the record eventually sold over six million copies worldwide.

13th JUNE

1922 Radio station WSB in Atlanta boosted to 500 watts. The audience increased, and so did the popularity of programmes featuring local musicians like Fiddlin' John Carson and the Reverend Andrew Jenkins. WSB played a key role in making Atlanta an important centre in the early days of country music.

1923 Okeh's first out-of-town recording session, in Atlanta. Ralph Peer supervised the session and Fiddlin' John Carson performed 'The Little Old Log Cabin In The Lane', a pop song, and 'The Old Hen Cackled And The Rooster's Gonna Crow', a minstrelly fiddle tune. Peer said he thought Carson's singing was "pluperfect awful", but was persuaded to release the songs on a record and was suitably surprised by its success.

1924 Vernon Dalhart recorded 'The Wreck Of The Old '97' and 'The Prisoner's Song' for Victor. The resulting record became country music's very first million-seller.

1949 Dennis Locorriere, lead vocalist with Dr Hook, born in New Jersey. In the mid-seventies they appeared on the Grand Ole Opry and, although they had cut some good country tracks (the LP *A Little Bit More* was recorded in Nashville with Waylon Jennings playing and singing background on one of the songs), they are one of the few rock-oriented groups, and probably the most outrageous act, to appear on the Opry stage.

Dr Hook

14th JUNE

1909 Burl Ives (Burl Icle Ivanhoe Ives) born in Hunt City, Illinois. Singer, actor, author and song collector — he's committed over 500 American folk songs to memory — Burl had success in the sixties with several songs which made both pop and country charts, most notably 'A Little Bitty Tear' and 'Call Me Mr In-Between', both of which were written by Harlan Howard.

1968 Ernest "Pop" Stoneman, leader of the Stoneman Family, died in Nashville.

Alabama

1980 Alabama made their debut in the *Billboard* country LP chart with *My Home's In Alabama*. The record rose to number one and was still in the charts at the time of writing, two years later. In the seventies Alabama (then known as Wild Country) could expect to earn $1,100 between them in a good week, but as the first new superstar country group of the eighties, they earn over $50,000 — for a night! The roots of Alabama can be traced to Fort Payne, Alabama, where Jeff Cook was working for Western Electric, his cousin Randy Owen was still at school, and Teddy Gentry was laying carpets. They began jamming together around Christmas 1969, then played weekend gigs at the nearby Canyonland tourist park. In 1973 they quit their day jobs and became the house band at a club in Myrtle Beach, South Carolina, where they began incorporating original material into the show. Stage success with their own songs encouraged them to record and press their own discs, which they distributed to local radio stations. After being turned down by nearly every label in Nashville, they were signed to GRT in 1977, and released the single 'I Want To Be With You', which bottomed out at 77. In 1979 they signed to the Dallas-based MDJ Records and Nashville producer Harold Shedd began working with them. Their drummer quit, but after months of searching they found Mark Herndon who proved to be the catalyst the group needed to put them into high gear. The Alabama-Shedd collaboration resulted in the single 'I Wanna Come Over' which reached 32 and led to the Top 20 hit 'My Home's In Alabama' in early 1980. They signed to RCA Records in April and their first two singles 'Tennessee River' and 'Why Lady Why' (both from the *My Home's In Alabama* LP) went to number one.

15th JUNE

1880 Blind Alfred Reed born. A West Virginia mountain fiddler and songwriter, his best known compositions are 'How Can A Poor Man Stand Such Times And Live' and 'Always Lift Him Up'.

1917 Leon Payne born in Alba, Texas. Blind from childhood, he was a student at the Texas School for the Blind for 11 years, where he learned to play several musical instruments. Leon began performing with various Texas-based western bands in the mid-thirties and was with Bob Wills for several years, at the time the Texas Playboys were at their peak. He began writing songs and by the sixties had composed over a thousand, many proving successful for other artists. Leon's own recording career covered several decades with labels including Decca, Bullet, MGM, Starday and Capitol. His best known song, 'I Love You Because' gave him one of the big hits of 1949 and was later an international success for Jim Reeves. Leon formed his own band, the Lone Star Buddies, in 1949; they became popular performers on the Grand Ole Opry and Louisiana Hayride.

Waylon Jennings

1939 Waylon Jennings born in Littlefield, Texas. Both his parents played guitar and his father was in a country dance band. Young Waylon took an early interest in music and was a DJ at the age of 12. In 1958 he moved to Lubbock where he worked on a radio station and played bass with rock 'n' roller Buddy Holly. After the singer's tragic death in a 'plane crash, Waylon moved to Phoenix, Arizona and became a mainstay at J.D.'s club with his band The Waylors, who played a popular mix of rock and country. In the mid-sixties, Waylon was "discovered" by Bobby Bare, who tipped off Chet Atkins in Nashville; this led to an RCA recording contract. Jennings had success as a country singer but became increasingly unhappy with the material he was expected to record; in the early seventies he upset his Nashville bosses by going over their heads to the RCA office in New York and getting a new deal whereby he had control over the musicians and songs on his albums. From 1972 there was a noticeable change in Waylon's sound and the LPs *Ladies Love Outlaws, Lonesome On'ry And Mean* and *Honky Tonk Heroes* featured new songs by contemporary writers like Steve Young, Lee Clayton and Billy Joe Shaver. Waylon was an "outlaw" in the eyes of many Nashville establishment figures, but the image was developed by a creative RCA man who devised the very successful *The Outlaws* compilation LP, pushing Jennings into the superstar league.

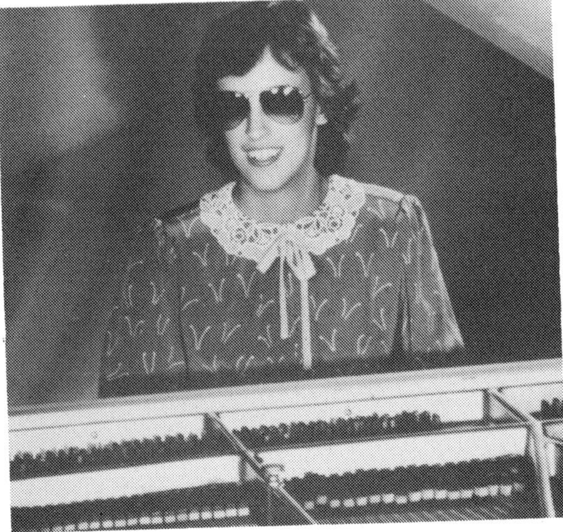

1954 Terri Gibbs, the blind girl singer with the low, husky voice, born in Augusta, Georgia. Her musical gifts transcended her handicap almost from the beginning — at three she astounded relatives with her piano playing. She made her singing debut with gospel music before she was a teenager, won talent contests at high school, and had her first band, Sound Dimension, at 20. In 1975 Terri began a five year gig at Augusta's Steak and Ale Restaurant, where she "paid her dues" with three sets and 50 songs a night, all the while sending demo tapes to Nashville. In 1979 one reached producer Ed Penney, who was very impressed with her voice. She was signed to MCA and the Penney-produced debut album, *Somebody's Knockin'* was an immediate success with critics, while DJs picked up on the title track. The 'Somebody's Knockin' single became one of the biggest pop and country hits of 1981 and Terri was lauded with several "New Female Vocalist of the Year" awards.

1961 Patsy Cline, high in the charts with 'I Fall To Pieces', badly injured in a road accident while being driven back from a shopping trip to Madison, Tennessee. Patsy went through the windscreen after the head-on collision, suffered multiple injuries and was hospitalised for a long time. According to a WSM/Grand Ole Opry newsletter of the time: "One of the reasons Patsy had such a long pull was that she insisted on the police and ambulance people taking care of the other people first — and she lost a lot of blood in the process — so it is taking her longer to build up her strength".

16th JUNE

1939 Billy "Crash" Craddock born in Greensboro, North Carolina. After playing with his brother in the Four Riddles, Billy kicked off a solo career as Columbia recording artist in 1959, but quit over disagreements about the musical direction he should take. After several different jobs he returned to music and developed a popular country-rock sound. He had hits on Cartwheel Records in 1971, then with ABC/Dot including number one's 'It's Broken Down In Pieces' and 'Rub It In', and more recently with Capitol.

1939 The Rouse Brothers, Gordie and Ervin, recorded the first version of the classic fiddle breakdown 'Orange Blossom Special' for RCA Victor in New York. According to Ervin Rouse, "About 1936 or 1937 we played a little ol' fiddlin' piece we thought was a little crazy — me and my brothers Gordie and Earl." Their manager named the tune after the powerful steam locomotive that ran from Miami to New York, and Ervin added appropriate words in 1938. 'Orange Blossom Special' is one of the most frequently performed tunes in country music.

17th JUNE

1910 Red Foley (Clyde Julian Foley) born in Berea, Kentucky. He was fascinated by music from an early age and impressed relatives and friends with his singing. Red was "spotted" by a talent scout while at college and signed to the Chicago-based WLS National Barn Dance in 1932. Five years later he started the Renfro Valley show and in 1939 had his own radio programme with Red Skelton. Signed to a lifetime contract with Decca Records, he had numerous hits including 'Old Shep' (which Elvis Presley heard on the radio as a child, copied and sang at a talent contest — winning second prize), 'Chattanooga Shoeshine Boy' and several hymns, like 'There'll Be Peace In The Valley' and 'Take My Hand, Oh Precious Lord'. A regular on the Opry in the forties, Red had one of the first country-oriented TV shows with "The Ozark Jubilee", on ABC.

1915 Stringbean (David Akeman), popular comic and banjo picker on the Grand Ole Opry and the "Hee Haw" TV show, born in Annville, Kentucky. His father played the banjo and David's own enthusiasm for the instrument was encouraged. A professional musician at 18, he played with numerous country stars including Ernest Tubb and Bill Monroe, was featured on Red Foley's radio show for many years, and became a close friend of Uncle Dave Macon, another banjo picker who taught him a great deal. A tall, thin man (hence the nickname) he was an Opry favourite from 1942 until November 10 1973, when he was murdered at his home after returning from the Ryman Auditorium. His brutal killing cast a long shadow over the Nashville music scene.

18th JUNE

1915 A. P. Carter and Sara Dougherty married. A.P. lived in Maces Spring, Scott County, Virginia, and Sara lived nearby in Copper Creek, near Nickelsville. The couple had met when A.P. was on a fruit tree selling trip. According to John Atkins, "They naturally began singing and playing music together and were in fact offered a recording contract with Brunswick Records, for whom they auditioned, singing 'Log Cabin By The Sea' and 'Poor Orphan Boy', with a few fiddle tunes thrown in by A.P. The record company wanted to dub A.P. 'Fiddlin' Doc' and get them to record mostly square dance tunes, which A.P. refused to do, in the knowledge he would offend his parents' religious beliefs". The couple were joined by Maybelle Carter in 1926, and began singing and playing together as the Carter Family, making their first record in August 1927.

19th JUNE

1903 Howard Dixon, one of the Dixon Brothers, who were popular RCA recording artists in the thirties, born in Darlington, South Carolina.

Flatt and Scruggs

1914 Lester Flatt born in the Appalachian foothills of Overton County, Tennessee. He came from a musical family, showed an early enthusiasm for the banjo (which both his parents played), then switched to the guitar. He worked as a textile worker in the Depression days when few people could earn a living as a musician, then began his country career with the Happy-Go-Lucky-Boys. In 1943 Lester and his wife Gladys were hired by Charlie Monroe, though their membership of his Kentucky Pardners group was short lived. A year later Lester joined Charlie's brother Bill Monroe as guitarist and lead singer with the Bluegrass Boys. His future partner Earl Scruggs joined the line-up in 1945 as banjo player. Lester and Earl quit in 1948 and within a month had decided to work together. With their band, the Foggy Mountain Boys, they began an association that was long, successful and very busy. They toured extensively, had TV and radio shows sponsoring Martha White Flour and Biscuits and were regular members of the Grand Ole Opry. In the late fifties they found themselves hailed as folk musicians, appeared at the Newport Folk Festival and on TV shows, and in the sixties were among the most profitable acts in popular music. The partnership came to an end in 1969; Lester led a new group, Nashville Grass, still selling Martha White Flour on the radio and still playing traditional music, while Earl became involved with country-rock.

1926 Forty years before Charley Pride's debut on the Grand Ole Opry, Deford Bailey, a black harmonica player, made his first appearance. Born in Carthage, Smith County, Tennessee in 1899, he had infantile paralysis, which stunted his growth and limited his job opportunities. The handicap led him to a musical career in the same way that blindness led several amateur old-time musicians into careers as performers. According to the historian Charles K. Wolfe, "Much of the music Deford was exposed to during his formative years was not blues as such but, to use his own phrase, 'black hillbilly music'. Deford is quick to acknowledge that in his youth he knew many blacks playing forms of old-time music; his father played 'black hillbilly music' on the fiddle, and his uncle was the best black banjo player he ever knew." Deford performed frequently on the Opry show in the late twenties, amplifying his harmonica playing through a megaphone, but his contributions grew shorter and shorter until he was eventually dropped, in 1941, whereupon he went into voluntary musical exile and began to operate a Nashville shoe-shine business. He died in 1982.

1960 Loretta Lynn's debut in the country charts with her first single 'Honky Tonk Girl'. Loretta and her husband Doolittle worked hard on promoting the single — "We didn't know anything about releasing a record, but we tried our best. Doolittle had a hobby of photography at the time, so he made up a picture of me. We mailed out 3,500 copies of the record and my picture and sent them to every radio station we could find." The couple followed this by driving in their old Mercury car from station to station to promote the record. One of the DJs impressed by this technique was the young Waylon Jennings.

1976 Eddy Arnold entered the charts with 'Cowboy', his 100th country hit.

20th JUNE

1916 T. Texas Tyler (David Luke Myrick), popular singer and western band leader in the forties and fifties, born near Mena, Arkansas. He spent his early years in Texas (hence the nickname), worked for several years on the East Coast, but found fame and fortune when he chose California as a base of operations in 1940. His big hits include the self-penned 'Deck Of Cards' and

'Bumming Around'. T. Texas Tyler was a popular TV performer in the fifties and sixties, having begun a small screen career with his own "Range Round Up" on a local Los Angeles station.

1924 Chet Atkins, guitar picker and RCA supremo, born in Luttrell, Tennessee. He was a shy child and found music an ideal way of self-expression; he got his first guitar in exchange for a rusty old pistol! After graduating from high school, Chet played with the Dixieland Swingers on a Knoxville radio show, then had numerous other jobs before arriving in Nashville in 1950, while playing with Maybelle Carter. Chet's career and reputation grew side-by-side with the fledgling Nashville music industry. He was organising RCA sessions in 1953 and when the company upgraded their Nashville operation, he was placed in charge. Under his sophisticated production guidance the sound of country music changed to the full, orchestrated music that is now known as "The Nashville Sound". He was named RCA Vice President in 1968 and held the post until he retired in 1979. During his long and distinguished career he produced such artists as Jim Reeves, Don Gibson, Charley Pride, Waylon Jennings, Jerry Reed, Dottie West, Trini Lopez and Perry Como. He's won numerous awards, was named "Outstanding Instrumentalist" by *Cash Box* magazine 14 years in a row and was elected to the Country Music Hall of Fame in 1973. Chet claims he rarely listens to his own records, but lists the *Chester and Lester* duet album with Les Paul and the *Me and Jerry* LP recorded with Jerry Reed as two of his favourite works.

1946 Anne Murray born in Springhill, Nova Scotia, Canada. Music came second to sport for several years in Anne's life, but producer Brian Ahern (now Emmylou Harris' husband and producer) persuaded her to give serious thought to a singing career. He produced her debut LP *What About Me* in 1968, which led to a contract with Canadian Capitol and the hit 'Snowbird', which sold over a million copies in 1970. More hits followed, including 'Danny's Song', which were certainly helped by appearances on the Glen Campbell TV show. Anne was away from the music scene for a couple of years when she married and had a son, but on her return she began a second, and considerably more successful, run of hit singles and albums including 'You Needed Me' (which won a Grammy award), 'I Just Fall In Love Again' and 'Daydream Believer'. She's won numerous gold discs and is a best-seller in the pop, country and easy-listening markets.

21st JUNE

1955 Johnny Cash's first single released by Sun Records in Memphis. Johnny and the Tennessee Two (Luther Perkins and Marshall Grant) had auditioned for Sam Phillips with the song 'Hey Porter'. He was very impressed and told them he would release it if they could come up with another original song. Legend has it that Cash wrote 'Cry, Cry, Cry' overnight. The single (Sun 221), spent one week on the *Billboard* country charts at number 14, in November 1955.

1975 Don Williams top of the charts with 'You're My Best Friend'. A year later the record was a pop hit in Britain.

22nd JUNE

1930 Roy Drusky born in Atlanta, Georgia. He had little interest in music as a youngster, but became interested in country during a spell in the US Navy, bought a guitar and started singing. His first professional band was The Southern Ranch Boys, formed in 1950, and his recording career began soon afterwards for Starday. His biggest hits came in the sixties, for Decca and then Mercury, and include 'From Now On All My Friends Are Gonna Be Strangers', 'Another', 'Anymore' and the chart-topping duet with Priscilla Mitchell, 'Yes, Mr Peters'. Roy has recently experienced a welcome career boost in England, where his Jim Reeves-style vocals have made him very popular. He has been a member of the Grand Ole Opry since the sixties.

1936 Kris Kristofferson born in Brownsville, Texas. As the son of a two-star general he spent much of his youth travelling from base to base before settling in California. He won a Rhodes Scholarship which took him to England, where he studied William Blake, still his favourite poet. After college he joined the army and while in Germany put together his first band. A meeting with Johnny Cash in Nashville, while he was on vacation, seems to have provided the motivation for giving up his army commission, leaving his wife and trying his luck as a country songwriter. He arrived in 1965 and worked his way up from the bottom; his first job was as a $58 a week janitor at Columbia Studios (Bob Dylan was the first singer he emptied ashtrays for), then he flew helicopters to off-shore oil rigs. His breakthrough came when Roger Miller recorded his song 'Me And Bobby McGee'. His songs, including such classics as 'Help Me Make It Through The Night', 'Sunday Morning Coming Down', and 'For the Good Times' have

subsequently been recorded by over 450 artists and won him numerous awards. His success had a radical effect on Nashville — he opened the door for all manner of changes, made long hair, beards and denim acceptable, and liberated country songwriting from some of its previous restrictions. Writers like Billy Joe Shaver, Guy Clark and David Allan Coe have much to thank him for — after his breakthrough, their own thoughtful and intelligent songs became much more acceptable to the Nashville establishment. Kris has also found success as a singer and film star. He won a Golden Globe award for his performance in *A Star Is Born,* the film which vaulted him to Hollywood stardom. Other film credits include *Pat Garrett and Billy The Kid* and *Convoy.*

23rd JUNE

1929 June Carter, one of Maybelle Carter's three daughters, born in Maces Spring, Virginia. Her whole life was steeped in country music and she was singing as soon as she could talk. June began performing with her sisters Helen and Anita in 1943, as the Carter Sisters; they then toured frequently with their famous mother. In 1950 they joined the Opry, but June went solo soon afterwards and combined a singing career with a new interest — acting. She made records and had success as a songwriter: 'Ring of Fire', which she co-authored with Merle Kilgore, was a huge hit for her future husband Johnny Cash in 1963. June began touring with Cash in 1967, they had a hit with 'Jackson', and were married a year later. She's been a vital part of the Johnny Cash Show ever since.

1970 Beatle Ringo Starr arrived in Nashville to make a solo album of country songs. Titled

Beaucoup Of Blues, it was produced by steel guitarist Pete Drake and featured several top session men including harmonica player Charlie McCoy.

24th JUNE

1929 Connie Hall, a popular country songstress of the fifties and early sixties, born in Walden, Kentucky. She scored her biggest hits for Decca Records, including 'It's Not Wrong' and 'Fool Me Once'.

1978 Joe Sun made his chart debut with 'Old Flames Can't Hold A Candle To You'. He was a radio promotion man at Ovation Records and was given the chance to make his own single after he'd broken The Kendalls' 'Heaven's Just A Sin Away', one of the biggest country hits of the previous year. Sun worked similar magic on his own record, then left the job to concentrate on a full-time career as a performer. He was brought up on a farm near Minnesota, then worked in a variety of jobs including a spell as DJ. He sang with a variety of semi-pro bands and was Jack Daniels (his real name is James Paulson) for a time in Chicago. Joe moved to Nashville in the early seventies and went through the time-honoured process of pitching songs and "hanging out", before landing the promotion job at Ovation. He made a trio of well received LPs for the label, including another hit 'On Business For The King', then switched to Elektra Records.

25th JUNE

1876 The Battle of Little Big Horn, also known as Custer's Last Stand. Little Big Horn is a valley in Montana and the site of an attack on Sioux Indians by a command of the Seventh Cavalry led by Lieutenant Colonel George Custer. The battle lasted just an hour and all of Custer's men were wiped out; only a cavalry horse survived the battle and is now stuffed in a museum. There were conflicting reports about the disaster, which led to a controversy that has continued for over 100 years.

1925 Clifton Chenier, the King of Zydeco music, born near Opelousas, Louisiana. Like Cajun music, Zydeco songs frequently feature patois French lyrics and the accordion as the lead instrument.

Billy Sherrill (right) with Johnny Rodriguez

1966 David Houston entered the country charts with 'Almost Persuaded', a future number one. The song was the first country hit written and produced by Billy Sherrill, now Vice President and Executive Producer of CBS in Nashville.

The son of a travelling preacher, Billy was born in Alabama in 1939; his early musical experience came playing piano at his father's meetings. After high school he took to the road, playing sax with honky-tonk bands in the South. Arriving in Nashville, he worked for Sam Phillips at his Nashville studios, then moved to Epic in 1963. His hit songs include 'Stand By Your Man', 'The Most Beautiful Girl' and 'Too Far Gone'; artists that he has helped to stardom include Tammy Wynette, Tanya Tucker, Lacy J. Dalton, Charlie Rich, Johnny Rodriguez, Barbara Mandrell and Janie Fricke.

26th JUNE

1976 The chart debut of the Oak Ridge Boys, with their first secular recording 'Family Reunion', for Columbia. The Oaks had been very successful in the gospel field for many years, but had decided to change their style to try and break into the country music market. Though they made the charts, the record climbed no higher than 85 and they were dropped by Columbia. Encouragement came from Johnny Cash, who invited them to open for him in Las Vegas, and successful manager and talent booker Jim Halsey, who signed them up, saying "You guys are only three minutes away from being superstars. Your stage act is there, all you need is a hit single." They began recording for ABC/Dot, and within a year had their first hit, 'Y'all Come Back Saloon'.

1977 Elvis Presley's final concert, at the Market Square Arena, Indianapolis, Indiana. It was the last date of a ten day tour. In Presley's later years he did numerous short tours like this, and each show followed a similar format: opening with Richard Strauss' 'Also Sprach Zarathusa' (which had become very popular as the theme to the movie *2001 — A Space Odyssey*) songs from the early days, 'Hound Dog', 'Jailhouse Rock', 'Don't Be Cruel' and 'Teddy Bear', were all sung on this evening; dramatic renditions of popular standards like 'I Can't Stop Loving You' and 'Bridge Over Troubled Water'; a couple of songs spotlighting his band and gospel singers, The Stamps; plus a lot of joking and talking with the audience. From the stage Elvis introduced his father Vernon Presley (who went along to most of his shows), his girl friend Ginger Alden, her mother and sister, RCA producer Felton Jarvis and some of his cousins. The last song he performed was 'Can't Help Falling In Love'. That night he flew home to his Memphis mansion, Graceland.

27th JUNE

1913 Nathan Abshire, foremost exponent of the accordion in traditional Cajun music, born in Gueydan, Louisiana. His parents and two brothers played the accordion and Nathan began playing in public when he was just eight. He made his first record in the early thirties with Happy Fats and the Rainbow Ramblers, appeared frequently with the Balfa Brothers — they made several trips outside Louisiana for special events like the Newport Folk Festival — and wrote songs, including the classic 'Pine Grove Blues'. Abshire's music, an invigorating blend of French lyrics and rapid, rhythmic bursts on the accordion, punctuated by cries and hollars, epitomised the good-time Cajun spirit of the Saturday night 'Fais Do Do' (party). He died in 1981.

Paul Kennerley (right) with Johnny Cash

1948 Paul Kennerley, singer and writer, born in Hoylake, Cheshire, England. Paul has authored two remarkable concept albums *White Mansions*, a story in song about the American Civil War, which featured Waylon Jennings and Jessie Colter, and *The Legend Of Jesse James* with Johnny Cash, Emmylou Harris, Charlie Daniels and Levon Helm.

28th JUNE

1925 George Morgan, country singer and writer whose run of hit singles began in the late forties and continued until the seventies, born in Waverly, Tennessee. His parents moved to Ohio and George made his radio debut as a teenager in the "Rubber City" of Akron. Later he became a regular on WWVA Jamboree in Wheeling, West Virginia and joined the Opry in 1948. His first hit was also his biggest: 'Candy Kisses', in 1949.

Roy Orbison

1980 Twenty-four years after making his first record, Roy Orbison finally cracked the country charts — as part of a duo with Emmylou Harris, singing 'That Lovin' You Feelin' Again' (from the soundtrack of the movie *Roadie*), which subsequently won both artists a Grammy award. Roy's late arrival in the country listings is surprising when one considers his close association with Nashville throughout his career: his pop successes were recorded at Monument with Fred Foster, he was an early supporter of the CMA, and he's had country hits as a composer over four decades!

29th JUNE

1973 The first Luckenbach World's Fair. According to Becky Crouch Patterson's book, *Hondo, My Father,* "Ten thousand came. Freaks, straights, businessmen, the whole spectrum of humanity was represented. . . Hondo won the tobacco spitting contest with a spit of 23 feet. Other contests included chicken flying, cow-chip throwing (a semi-skill) and armadillo racing." The tiny town's facilities were hopelessly stretched and the following year the Fair was held in Fredericksburg.

1980 George Jones top of the country charts with 'He Stopped Loving Her Today'. The song, written by Bobby Braddock and Curly Putman, won a Grammy, was voted "Song of the Year" by the Nashville Songwriters Association, "Single Of The Year" by the Academy of Country Music, and "Song of the Year" by the Country Music Association for two years in succession — 1980 and 1981. "That song lay around here for about three years," said Curly Putman. "We couldn't get anybody to cut it. I think it was because of the down-type of song it was. But we kept believing it and pitching it."

Curly Putman

30th JUNE

1922 The first country music recording session. Eck Robertson and Henry Gilliland performed six traditional fiddle tunes at the Victor studio in New York City. The couple had turned up at the Victor offices, dressed in full Confederate Army uniform and demanded to make a record. Robertson (who was actually born 20 years after the Civil War) was a champion fiddler in Texas and had teamed up with 74-year-old Gilliland at a Confederate Veterans Reunion in Virginia, then travelled to New York by train. Two tracks were released — 'Sallie Goodin' and 'Arkansas Traveler'. As writer Nick Tosches has pointed out — "This may be the first country record by authentic country artists, but there were many earlier recordings of country songs by artists who probably had their roots in pop . . . Len Spenser had recorded 'Arkansas Traveler' for Edison in 1902 . . . The Victor Military Band cut 'Soldier's Joy', a traditional rural fiddling tune before 1920."

1973 Ronnie Milsap's chart debut with 'I Hate You' c/w 'All Together Now'. The double-sided record made the Top Ten.

J U L Y

1st JULY

1894 John Lair, country radio pioneer, born in Livingstone, Kentucky. John was the producer and announcer of WLS National Barn Dance from 1927, then founded the Renfro Valley Barn Dance from radio station WLW in Cincinnati. The popular and long running radio show, which began in 1937, was named after Renfro Valley in Kentucky, an area that produced several fine country musicians, including Red Foley, Doc Hopkins and Karl and Harty.

1969 A year after the demise of Sun Records, Nashville businessman Shelby Singleton bought an 80 per cent controlling interest in the Sun catalogue from Sam Phillips. Classic fifties singles by Jerry Lee Lewis, Carl Perkins, Roy Orbison and Johnny Cash were re-issued on the new Sun International label, while the Sun label was re-activated with country-oriented material from artists like Sleepy LaBeef, Jimmy Ellis and Billy Lee Riley.

1978 Margo Smith top of the country charts with 'It Only Hurts For A Little While'. A native of Dayton, Ohio, Margo's other chart successes include 'Don't Break The Heart That Loves You' and 'Little Things Mean A Lot'.

2nd JULY

1925 Marvin Rainwater (Marvin Percy), the country singer who is part Indian, born in Wichita, Kansas. Like several other performers, he first realised that he had talents as an entertainer while serving in the armed forces — for Marvin it was a spell in the Navy during World War II. He played in night clubs and at country fairs for several years after his discharge, then made a successful appearance on the Arthur Godfrey TV talent show which led to regular work on the WWVA Jamboree and Red Foley's Jubilee USA. Marvin began recording for MGM in the fifties, and they made great play of his Indian ancestry. He scored hits with 'Gonna Find Me A Bluebird' and 'Half Breed', and had a number one in England with 'Whole Lotta Woman'. Though his popularity dipped in the US, he remained a firm favourite with British country fans for many years.

1982 Deford Bailey, the black harmonica player who was one of the earliest members of the Grand Ole Opry, died in Nashville.

3rd JULY

1946 Johnny Lee, singer with the house band at Gilley's club for several years before his "overnight success" with the song 'Looking For Love', born in Texas City, Texas. Johnny grew up on a farm and listened to his idols Jerry Lee Lewis, Elvis, Chuck Berry and Fats Domino while helping to milk the cows. "Rock 'n' roll was my favourite," he remembers, "I thought country music was too twangy then." He got his start as a musician in a Future Farmers of America group while at the Sante Fe High School, then led Johnny Lee and the Road Runners. After a tour of duty in the Navy, he "bummed around California", then returned to Texas and started working with Mickey Gilley. Johnny told Mickey that they'd worked together on a Galveston TV show years before and reminded him of a job offer he'd once made. It was an outright lie, they'd never worked together, but it got him a job! Through his regular appearances at Gilley's, the huge Pasadena nightspot, Johnny Lee became a local celebrity and had several hits in the Houston area with country singles, but 'Looking For Love', which was featured on the soundtrack of the movie *Urban Cowboy,* provided him with a monster hit and suddenly he was a national country star. He's subsequently had more big hits including 'Bet Your Heart On Me' and 'Picking Up Strangers'; he now has his own Pasadena club, Johnny Lee's, which is just a few miles down Spencer Highway from Gilley's.

4th JULY

1883 The first ever rodeo, held at Pecos, Texas. The idea was borrowed from the Spaniards and Mexicans, but American rodeo has been a distinct and unique sport ever since.

1972 A Willie Nelson sponsored festival at Dripping Springs near Austin, Texas featured the best of old and new country — Tex Ritter, Roy Acuff, Bill Monroe, Tom T. Hall, Waylon Jennings, Billy Joe Shaver, Kris Kristofferson, Charlie Rich and Sammi Smith. It was a financial disaster for the promoters, an uncomfortable experience for the audience (due to heat and excessive policing), but was a watershed event for the progressive country movement and was, as Willie Nelson said afterwards, "The first time that anyone had seen all types of people together listening to country music. It was actually the first time the hippie and the redneck had got together."

1973 The first Willie Nelson 4th of July Picnic, held at Dripping Springs. It was a financial and musical success.

1974 Willie Nelson's Picnic held at a new venue, in Bryan, Texas. The annual events were getting bigger, there were fewer cowboys and red-necks in the audience and the bill of musical fare was changing, modern rock replacing the traditional country artists of previous years.

1976 Willie Nelson announced from the stage that this was the last 4th of July Picnic. The music was still good, but the events had become, to quote writer Charles Wolfe, "mismanaged, brain-frying, counterculture extravaganzas". Willie later changed his mind, and the Picnics continued for four more years.

1980 The last annual Willie Nelson Picnic, held at his country club in Perdernales, Texas. The star-studded bill included Merle Haggard, Ray Price, Asleep At The Wheel, Hank Cochran and Delbert McClinton. 30,000 people turned up.

1981 Gilley's 4th of July Picnic. After Willie had stopped his annual concerts, the Pasadena honky-tonk held their own. The history of the club has been one of consistent growth and success, but the Picnic was a disaster. The organisers had to change the outdoor venue at the last moment because of protests from local residents and the event attracted only a few hundred customers.

5th JULY

1938 Thomas "Snuff" Garrett, successful record producer, born in Dallas, Texas. He's worked with artists as diverse as Frank Sinatra and Bobby Vee, as well as numerous country acts. Snuff Garrett put together the successful soundtrack for the *Every Which Way But Loose* movie, which led to a spate of films using country themes and soundtracks.

1954 Elvis Presley recorded with Scotty Moore and Bill Black for the first time. According to Scotty: "We had gone through several songs and put them on tape. During a break Elvis started singing, 'That's All Right' and was clowning and jumping around the studio. Bill picked up his bass and started slapping it and, not to be left out, I grabbed my guitar and started trying to find something to play along with it. Sam (Phillips) came to the studio door and asked, 'What are you doing?' and we said, 'We don't know,' so he said, 'Go back to the microphone and see if you can do it again.' We struggled around for a minute, worked out a format, ran through it a couple of times and recorded it." 'That's All Right' (Sun 209) was Elvis Presley's first record release — a rocking combination of country and blues, bursting with youthful energy and life. Rock 'n' roll records had been made before, but this was the important one; it started a musical and social revolution.

Jeannie Seely

1975 The Amazing Rhythm Aces debuted on the country charts with 'Third Rate Romance'. The Memphis-based band made a series of critically acclaimed albums in the seventies that synthesised country, R&B, gospel and rock, though their popular success was limited. They broke up in 1980, explaining that "the cost of living exceeded the living we were making". The lead singer and composer of 'Third Rate Romance', Russell Smith, went on to a solo career with Capitol Records.

6th JULY

1925 Bill Haley born near Detroit, Michigan. His family moved to Pennsylvania when he was four and he developed a keen interest for music. He formed a hillbilly band and travelled the length and breadth of the USA, hearing several musical styles, from blues to dixieland, which he eventually incorporated into rock 'n' roll. Bill Haley's Saddlemen changed musical direction and became Bill Haley and the Comets. Their first release was the Haley original 'Crazy Man Crazy', then they signed to Decca and recorded 'Rock Around The Clock'. It sold only moderately at first, but the follow-up, 'Shake, Rattle and Roll' became a Top Ten hit in Britain and the US. 'Rock Around The Clock' was re-released in 1955, used in the opening sequences of a movie called *Blackboard Jungle,* and shot to the top of the charts. It became an anthem for teenagers everywhere and made Haley the first rock 'n' roll star.

1940 Jeannie Seely born in Pennsylvania. She made her radio debut at 11 and appeared on the Midwestern Hayride while still at high school. She moved to California where she recorded for Challenge, then met and married songwriter Hank Cochran. Jeannie moved to Nashville and had success as a writer and performer, scoring hits on Monument Records in the mid-sixties including 'It's Only Love' and 'Don't Touch Me'. She then worked with Porter Wagoner and toured with Jack Greene.

1963 Bobby Bare entered the country charts with 'Detroit City', a song that remains one of his best known. It was written by Danny Dill and Mel Tillis. "I played this little club in Detroit and saw these people that are in the song," Dill told Dorothy Horstman, "They were from Alabama, West Tennessee, Kentucky, and they'd go to Detroit and work in the car factories. Now, they had more cash money in their pockets than they'd ever seen in their lives, but they were homesick. And to keep from being so lonely, they'd go sit in a bar and drink. And

when they did get home, they'd get home with no money. They wasted literally ten or fifteen years of their lives, and they wanted to go home all the time."

1978 Tammy Wynette married to George Richey, her fifth husband.

7th JULY

1917 Elton Britt (James Britt Baker), one of the major country stars of the forties, born in Marshall, Arkansas. His parents came from musical backgrounds and encouraged their son's enthusiasm for singing and guitar playing. He was "discovered" in 1932 by talent scouts from a Los Angeles radio station, who'd come to Oklahoma looking for a genuine country boy who could yodel. The 14-year-old Elton fitted both requirements and made the trip west, where he worked and recorded with the Beverly Hillbillies, then started a solo career and a long association with RCA Records in 1937. He scored numerous hits in the forties, including the million-selling 'There's A Star Spangled Banner' (which was originally a b-side), 'Chime Bells' and 'Candy Kisses'. The latter was one of several duets with Rosalie Allen. In the late forties he began appearing in films and on TV. Elton died in June 1972.

Charlie Louvin

1927 Charlie Louvin born in Rainesville, Alabama. He had two careers in country music: first he was half of the renowned Louvin Brothers, one of the best loved country duos of all time (their harmony style has influenced contemporary performers like Emmylou Harris and The Kendalls), then after his brother Ira died in 1965, Charlie continued to achieve hits as a solo artist. Charlie and Ira were raised in a small Alabama town nestled in the southern cotton belt. When Charlie was 16 they won an amateur contest in Chattanooga, Tennessee and the first prize was a radio show on WDAF. It wasn't long before the brothers were able to quit their jobs in the cotton mill and devote themselves full time to music. The Louvin brothers recorded together between 1949 and 1963 and became members of the Opry in 1955. In 1964 the brothers decided to go their separate ways professionally, just prior to Ira's tragic death in a car accident. Charlie went on to record over a dozen albums and had solo hits including 'I Don't Love You Anymore'.

1929 Roy Acuff, a promising young baseball player, collapsed at Knoxville's Caswell Park with severe sun-stroke. He suffered three more collapses in the next few weeks, was ill for a long time and had to spend most of 1930 confined to bed until he had properly recovered. Roy realised that his sporting days were over and became a musician. But for the sun-stroke he might never have become a professional musician, let alone earned the title "King of Country Music".

1930 Doyle Wilburn born in Thayer, Missouri. With brother Teddy he was a child performer on the Opry, in 1941, then featured on the Louisiana Hayride. After the Korean War, Teddy and Doyle returned to Nashville as the Wilburn Brothers. Webb Pierce helped them get a recording contract (with Decca) and soon they were back on the Opry, as full members. They also appeared on numerous TV shows, including Arthur Godfrey's "Talent Scouts" programme and had a string of hits during the sixties, including 'Trouble's Back in Town', 'It's Another World' and 'Roll Muddy River'.

8th JULY

1941 Legendary Cajun musician, "Papa" Link Davis, born in Van Zandt County, near Dallas, Texas. He's best known for writing and recording 'Big Mamou', but was also featured as session man on numerous pop hits including the Big Bopper's 'Chantilly Lace', and Johnny Preston's 'Running Bear'. He died in 1972.

1924 Uncle Dave Macon's first recording session, in New York, for Vocalion. Macon was accompanied by Sid Harkreader and recorded 14 songs. According to country historian Charles Wolfe "His first released number was 'Chewing Gum', perhaps his most popular comedy song . . . Another song from this first session was 'Hill Billie Blues'; it was the first tune, and the first record, to bear the term hillbilly, which was soon to become synonymous with early country music."

1978 Gail Davies made her first appearance in the country chart, with 'No Love Have I'. Gail (who will not reveal her birthday) was born in Broken Bow, Oklahoma into a "family full of music". Her father had a jukebox in the front room, which he kept stocked with country singles. The family moved to Seattle, Washington and Gail's musical horizons widened, first through the influence of the Beatles and later, when she married a jazz musician. Her attempts to become a jazz vocalist borrowed heavily from Ella Fitzgerald and Billie Holiday, but the more she learned the more she came to appreciate her country roots. After several years of performing, Gail was advised by doctors to give her voice a rest. She blames her enforced hiatus on "All those nights singing too hard and too much in smoky bars over a bad PA system". The rest gave her the chance to write songs and learn to play the guitar. When she recovered she became a fixture of the Los Angeles music scene and did sessions. She moved to Nashville in the mid-seventies and was briefly signed to CBS Records, then switched to Warner Brothers, with whom she's had Top Ten country hits including 'I'll Be There (If You Ever Want Me)' and 'Blue Heartache'. Gail Davies is one of the very few female country artists who produce their own albums.

9th JULY

1907 Eddie Dean born in Posey, Texas. He began his singing career in gospel groups, then was a featured vocalist on the WLS Barn Dance in Chicago, later heading for California where he worked on Gene Autry's popular radio show and appeared in numerous cowboy B movies. Eddie recorded for several different labels, though his biggest successes came as a song writer; he co-authored 'One Has My Name, The Other Has My Heart', a hit for Jimmy Wakely, and 'I Dreamed Of A Hillbilly Heaven', a 1961 success for Tex Ritter.

1923 Molly O'Day (LaVerne Williamson) born in Pike County, Kentucky. She started singing professionally from the age of 16 with her brother, when she had the first of several stage names, Mountain Fern, later changed to Dixie Lee. She married Lynn Davis (who was in her band) and they spent the forties working for several different radio shows, pausing in 1946 to record for Columbia. Molly O'Day might have become one of the leading female stars of country music, but quit the business in 1952 to become a minister in the Church of God.

1929 Jesse McReynolds, of the popular bluegrass duo Jim and Jesse, born in Coeburn, Virginia.

1947 Bernie Leadon born in Minneapolis, Minnesota. He was a key figure in the Los Angeles country rock movement and was involved with Hearts and Flowers, Dillard and Clark, the Flying Burrito Brothers, Linda Ronstadt's band, and was a founder member of The Eagles.

10th JULY

1937 Hank Williams' family moved from Greensville to the Alabama state capital, Montgomery. According to Hank's biographer Roger Williams, "Lilly (Hank's mother) figured a big city offered better possibilities. She also figured it offered a better chance for her musician son to build a professional career." Lilly turned her new home into a boarding house, while the 13-year-old Hank Williams continued to shine shoes and sell peanuts, though he spent most of his waking hours making music with his cheap guitar.

1965 Roy Acuff injured in a serious road accident. He suffered two pelvic fractures, a broken collarbone and crushed one side of his rib cage. Despite his injuries, Roy was back on stage at the Opry by the end of August.

1971 Tom T. Hall entered the charts with 'The Year That Clayton Delaney Died', a future chart-topper and one of his best-loved songs. "I was thirteen, and that was the year that Clayton Delaney died. You see, Clayton Delaney was my country hero. He could play a guitar better than anyone within walking distance of where I lived. And I don't remember if he sang or not, but I suppose he did, though we didn't then — and still don't now, do we? — require that our country heroes have any great ability to sing. He was just a great picker." Tom T.'s song was the second biggest country hit of the year; the biggest was 'Easy Loving' by Freddie Hart, which also entered the charts on this day. After a decade of small hits, Freddie became a superstar with this one song. "It was with 'Easy Lovin' that I finally learned what the people wanted," says Freddie, "I try and write little episodes in my life, something people have done or want to do. And I try and write something simple. That's a hit song to me . . . Something every man would like to say, and something every woman would like to hear."

11th JULY

1944 Commander Cody (Gordon Frayne) born. He formed Commander Cody and the Lost Planet Airmen in 1968. A crazed but musically versatile band, strongly influenced by country music, they moved to San Francisco in 1969 and built a strong following with the West Coast rock audience. They had success with albums like *Hot Licks, Cold Steel and Truckers' Favourites*, and *Tales From The Ozone* which was produced

by Hoyt Axton. Noted musicians with Cody's band at various times have included Norton Buffalo, harp; Andy Stein, fiddle and Bill Kirchen, guitar.

1960 Cowboy Copas, a popular country star in the late forties/early fifties, returned to the charts after an absence of nine years. The song 'Alabam' rose to number one and was his biggest hit.

1981 Earl Thomas Conley top of the charts with 'Fire and Smoke', one of the hottest hits of the year, and the song that won him an RCA contract. He was born in Portsmouth, Ohio, a river town of steel mills and train yards on the Kentucky border. His father, a railroad man with eight children to support, was laid off when steam engines were replaced with diesels in the forties. "This might seem kind of old-fashioned," says Earl, "but we didn't have toys and stuff, never mind the TV. So I got into carving, painting, drawing and all, just to entertain myself." His early manhood was spent as painter, drifter, sculptor, dreamer and singer. "I never could find a job that interested me, all I knew is I wanted to do something with the arts." He finally found his niche as songwriter; Mel Street scored with his 'Smokey Mountain Memories', and Conway Twitty took 'This Time

I've Hurt Her More Than She Loves Me' to the top of the charts in early 1976. Earl won a recording contract with GRT, had minor success with some singles, then made an LP for Songbird that spawned the hits 'Silent Treatment' and 'Fire and Smoke', leading to press write-ups that described him as one of country music's new heroes for the eighties. Originally just Earl Conley, he added the Thomas because, "With John Conlee, Con Hunley and Earl Conley, everyone was getting confused."

12th JULY

1942 Steve Young born in Alabama. He was a folk singer in Montgomery, then moved to California in the late sixties and became involved with the start of the progressive country movement. He worked alongside Gram Parsons and Gene Clark at A&M in Los Angeles where he made his debut LP, *Rock Salt And Nails,* the first of several solo albums that brought critical accolades but disappointing sales. Young is best known as songwriter — his hit compositions include 'Seven Bridges Road' for The Eagles, and 'Lonesome On'ry and Mean' for Waylon Jennings, but he's highly rated as a singer by fellow musicians.

1945 Butch Hancock born on a farm near Lubbock, Texas. He's one of the leading new songwriters to have emerged from the Texas scene in the late seventies and his material has been recorded by Joe Ely, Jerry Jeff Walker and others. Butch has also made a series of highly praised solo albums, including *Diamond Hill*, on his own Rainlight label.

13th JULY

1895 Bradley Kincaid born in Garrard County, Kentucky in the foothills of the Cumberland Mountains. He learnt folk songs from his family and neighbours and while at college in Chicago was invited to perform a programme of mountain songs. He was well received and became a regular on the WLS National Barn Dance show. His long radio career took him to numerous stations, he also had an association with WSM's Grand Ole Opry in 1944 and part ownership of WWSO in Springfield, Ohio, on which he performed from 1949. In the sixties, Bradley made several LPs of the songs he'd popularised over the radio airwaves in the previous four decades.

195? Louise Mandrell born in Corpus Christi, Texas. She began playing banjo, guitar and fiddle at an early age, and was playing bass with big sister Barbara's Do-Rites Band when she was 15, then worked with Stu Phillips and Merle Haggard before starting a solo career with Epic Records. Louise has featured on her sister's successful NBC TV series and performs as a duo with R.C. Bannon. The couple met at the Nashville Fan Fair in 1977 and were married two years later.

1973 A disastrous Everly Brothers concert at Buena Park, California. Phil smashed his guitar and walked off-stage mid-way through the show. "It's over, " Don is reported to have said afterwards, "I've quit. I'm tired of being an Everly Brother."

14th JULY

1895 Pat Garrett, Sheriff of Lincoln County, New Mexico, caught up with Billy the Kid at Pete Maxwell's ranch, and shot him dead. Billy was on the run, having escaped from jail after his conviction for murdering Sheriff Brady.

1912 Woody Guthrie, the great American folk balladeer, born in Okemah, Oklahama. He wrote hundreds of songs about his country and its people — "When you hear them, you really hear America singing," said folk singer Cisco Houston.

Woody Guthrie

1933 Del Reeves born in Sparta, North Carolina. He sang country songs at social functions as a teenager, moving to the West Coast in the fifties in a successful pursuit of fame and fortune. He appeared on several TV shows and then had his own series for four years. Del moved to Nashville in the sixties and began a long run of hits including 'Be Quiet Mind' and the chart-topping 'Girl On The Billboard'. He joined the Opry in 1966.

1973 Clarence White, one of the finest progressive country musicians, killed by a drunken driver while loading equipment onto a van after a gig. He is remembered for his work with the Kentucky Colonels and The Byrds.

15th JULY

1913 Cowboys Copas (Lloyd Copas) born in Muskogee, Oklahoma — the town later immortalised by Merle Haggard in the redneck anthem, 'Okie From Muskogee'. He was brought up on a ranch, began playing the guitar at 10, won a talent contest at 16, then began touring with a young Indian fiddle player named Natchee. Copas went solo in 1940 and within a few years was a regular on the Boone County Jamboree radio barn dance show from Cincinnati. He signed to King Records (also based in Cincinnati) and had best-selling records like 'Tragic Romance' and 'Signed, Sealed and Delivered', then teamed up with Pee Wee King's band and was featured on the Grand Ole Opry. He had several more big hits, but his career went into a decline during the fifties, only to revive in 1961 with the chart-topping 'Alabam'. Cowboy Copas was killed in a 'plane crash on March 5, 1963, along with Patsy Cline and Hawkshaw Hawkins.

1915 Guy (James) Willis, leader and eldest of the Willis Brothers trio, born in Alex, Arkansas. He grew up on an Oklahoma farm with his brothers Vic and Skeeter; as boys they sang and made music for fun. In the thirties they turned professional and performed on numerous radio stations and at country music shows, at first using the name Oklahoma Wranglers. Guy was front man and guitarist, Vic played the accordion and Skeeter was the fiddler. After war service the brothers re-formed and became a part of Eddy Arnold's touring show, also working in recording studios backing several country singers; they are the musicians on Hank Williams' first recordings for Sterling. Their popularity increased during the fifties and sixties and they made records and toured extensively, at home and abroad.

1946 Linda Ronstadt born in Tucson, Arizona. "It was so boring," she recalls. "All there was were cows and cactus." She fled to Los Angeles when she was 18 and formed a group with Kenny Edwards and Bob Kimmel, called the Stone Poneys, and they had a hit with Michael Nesmith's 'Distant Drum'. The group split two years later, in 1969, and Linda began a solo career. She hung out at the famed Troubadour club in Los Angeles with musicians who became well known as California-based country rockers. The men who'd later be known as The

Eagles played on her third LP *Linda Ronstadt*. Her career blossomed when she linked up with British producer Peter Asher and made *Heart Like A Wheel*, the country-rock album that propelled her into the platinum class of rock stars. By 1975 she was the "Queen of Country Rock" and she remained one of America's top three female stars (behind Barbra Streisand and Diana Ross) until the end of the decade, though her music moved further and further from country. As she explained, "I'm not a country singer, I'm a pop singer with country influences. In pop music you draw on every root source you can; I listened to country and Mexican and blues and gospel and, sporadically, jazz."

1958 The Ash Grove opened on Melrose Avenue, Los Angeles. Top name folk, bluegrass and traditional country acts were featured, but the club also featured up-and-coming young musicians like Ry Cooder and Hoyt Axton.

16th JULY

1976 'Teddy Bear', the sentimental tale of a little crippled boy and the truck drivers who help him after hearing him on the CB radio, topped the country charts. The performer, veteran country star Red Sovine, made several such records, and explained to a journalist that he took his material very seriously — "I'm very sentimental; to do a recitation well, you have to get all wrapped up in it. I still cry sometimes when I do 'Teddy Bear'". The song was a hit in America at the height of the CB craze, and it's interesting to note that five years later, when enthusiasm for CB radio had reached the UK, the song was a hit all over again, reaching number two on the pop charts and selling almost half a million copies.

Red Sovine

1925 Frank Page, announcer on the long-running Louisiana Hayride from its inception in 1948 to the last regular show in 1960, born in Little Rock, Arkansas. The programme, broadcast from KWKH in Shreveport, Louisiana became known as "the cradle of the stars", because of the up-and-coming performers who were helped by appearances on the show, including Hank Williams, Elvis Presley and Jim Reeves, the latter originally hired by Page as an announcer.

17th JULY

1918 Red Sovine (Woodrow Wilson Sovine) born in Charleston, West Virginia. He began performing on local radio shows with Jim Pike and the Carolina Tar Heels, graduating to the prestigious WWVA Jamboree from Wheeling, West Virginia. In 1947 he started his own group, the Echo Valley Boys, and two years later they were hired by the Louisiana Hayride to replace Hank Williams (who'd joined the Opry). Red acquired the curious nickname, Old Syrup Sopper, while on the show; he also became good friends with another performer, Webb Pierce. The two men sang together frequently, and when both were members of the Opry in 1954 they began recording as a duo, notching up big hits with 'Why, Baby Why', and 'Little Rosa'. Red Sovine had several solo successes in the sixties, mostly with truck driving songs and sentimental recitations, but his biggest hit came in the mid-seventies with 'Teddy Bear'.

1951 The death of Harry Choates, 25-year-old composer of the Cajun classic 'Jole Blon'. Choates, who had something of a wild reputation, was said to be an alcoholic. He was found dead in a prison cell at Travis County, Texas, where he was on a contempt of court charge.

18th JULY

1952 'It Wasn't God Who Made Honky Tonk Angels', Kitty Wells' answer record to Hank Thompson's 'Wild Side Of Life', entered the country charts. It rose to number one and was the first in a remarkable run of hits — Kitty charted every year from 1952 until 1972; this earned her the title "Queen of Country Music".

1954 Ricky Skaggs born in Cordell, in the eastern Kentucky hills. He had an old fashioned mountain upbringing, traditional music and religion being a vital and important part of family life. Both his parents were local musicians; he learnt to sing from his mother and learnt to play from his father, who started him on the mandolin at the age of five. Ricky was a child prodigy, appearing on Flatt and Scruggs' Nashville TV show when he was seven. He was very impressed by a local concert given by the Stanley Brothers, and they in turn were amazed by the youngster's potential, and gave him strong encouragement. After Carter Stanley's death, Ralph hired Ricky for his band — he was just 15. The exhausting work, long hours and low pay took their toll, and Ricky left the music business for a time and moved to Washington DC; but that area was rich in bluegrass music and it wasn't long before he was playing again. He worked with various bands, then formed his own — Boone Creek. By the age of 25 he had an awesome reputation among fellow musicians and was hired for Emmylou Harris' Hot Band. Ricky won international recognition for his work with Emmy, and played a key role in her best-selling *Roses In The Snow* LP which was widely acclaimed as a bluegrass masterpiece. In 1981 he was signed to CBS by the far-sighted Rick Blackburn and made *Waitin' For The Sun To Shine,* an album that combined traditional music with some modern influences. Skaggs and CBS were rewarded with good sales and a string of successful singles, including 'Crying My Heart Out Over You', which went to number one and was the most authentic-sounding country record to top the charts in several years.

19th JULY

1937 George Hamilton IV born in Winston Salem, North Carolina. He was a country fan as a youngster, but began his career with a big pop hit 'A Rose And A Baby Ruth', then made the transition back to country music and had numerous best-selling records in the sixties, including 'Abilene', 'Early Morning Rain' and 'Canadian Pacific'. George became very popular in Canada, where he had his own coast-to-coast TV show, and in the UK, where he continues to be one of the most popular American country artists. Over the years George Hamilton IV has earned a reputation as the "International Ambassador of Country Music". His firsts make an impressive list: In March 1974 he became the first American country singer to perform in Czechoslovakia and Russia; he hosted the first country music festivals to be held in Sweden, Finland, Norway, Holland and Germany; he was the first country star to have his own TV series in South Africa, Hong Kong and New Zealand, and the first to have his own summer season at a British seaside resort.

1969 Kenny Rogers (with the First Edition) made his debut on the country charts with the painfully sad song, 'Ruby, Don't Take Your Love To Town'. According to the writer, Mel Tillis, the song, about a man paralysed as a result of a war injury, was based on a true story: "'Ruby' stood by him till she could stand it no longer. Then she started fixing her hair, putting flowers

in it, painting her lips, and walking back and forth in front of the pool room. She was lonesome, needed attention. She was a good girl, actually, but the way I wrote it, I put the blame on her . . . Eventually, he killed her and himself too."

1975 Lefty Frizzell died after suffering a stroke.

20th JULY

1898 J. E. Mainer, leader of J. E. Mainer and his Mountaineers, one of the best country bands of the twenties and thirties, born in a one-room log cabin in Buncombe County, in the Blue Ridge Mountains. He began playing the banjo at nine and the guitar at 17 and later teamed up with some like-minded musicians for a long and busy career. They performed on over 140 radio stations, made innumerable personal appearances throughout the South, and several records for Victor from 1935. J. E. Mainer died in 1971.

1935 Sleepy LaBeef (Thomas Paulsley LaBeef), rockabilly performer with a deep, booming voice, born on a watermelon farm in Smackover, Arkansas. The tenth of ten children, he was called "Sleepy" on account of his drooping, sleepy eyelids. A first generation rockabilly artist, he performed in obscurity for years until being "discovered" by rockabilly enthusiasts in Europe in the seventies.

1944 T. G. Sheppard born in Humbolt, Texas. He moved to Memphis when he was 16 and had a brief career as pop singer with the name Brian Stacy — "This was in the days of Bobby Vee, Brian Hyland and Bobby Vinton, and that name just seemed to fit," says T.G. "People say, 'What's in a name?' but I think there's a lot in a name and the right one is important for a career." His pop career was unsuccessful, so he became Bill Browder (his real name), record promoter. "For many years I lay dormant as an artist, " he explains. "Then in 1974 along came this song called 'Devil In The Bottle', and I was sure it could be a hit, though I couldn't find a

record company who'd take me." But Melodyland, the newly formed country label of the soul company Motown, signed him up and 'Devil In The Bottle' was a number one country smash; so was the follow-up, 'Try To Beat The Morning Home'. T.G. had picked up his new name just prior to these hits: "One night I sat down and made it up. They're just initials really, but I got tagged 'The German Sheppard' and then 'The Good Sheppard', and I've kinda stuck with the last one." After another dormant period, T.G. resurfaced on Warner Brothers in 1977, with whom he's had spectacular success including several number ones and a string of best-selling albums.

21st JULY

1895 Ken Maynard, the man who introduced singing to cowboy films, born. He was a trick rider with Buffalo Bill's Wild West Show, then starred in countless low-budget Westerns, many featuring his horse, Tarzan. Gene Autry made his debut in Maynard's *In Old Sante Fe* in 1934. Ken lost favour with the film makers in the late thirties and was a poverty-stricken alcoholic when he died of malnutrition in 1977.

1898 Sara Carter (Sara Dougherty), a member of the original Carter Family, with her husband A.P. and cousin Maybelle, born at Flat Woods in Wise County, Virginia. When her mother died, Sara moved to Cooper Creek and lived with her uncle and aunt. Uncle Milburn played the fiddle, and helped his niece to learn the banjo, guitar and autoharp. She married A.P. in 1915, and they had three children: Gladys, Janette and Joe. With Maybelle, the trio made their first recordings in 1927. A.P. and Sara were divorced in 1938, but the Carter Family continued to record until 1941. Sara married Coy Bayes in 1939 and lived with him in California. In 1952 Sara, A.P., Joe and Janette recorded together for the small Acme label but, apart from their brief reunion, Sara did very little professional singing after the break-up of the Carter Family. She died on January 8, 1979.

22nd JULY

1874 Obed "Dad" Pickard, leader of the Pickard Family, who were early stars of the Grand Ole Opry, born in Ashland City, Tennessee. He was a commercial traveller but spent much of his spare time making music — he could play almost every instrument. The Family made their Opry debut in 1926. According to Opry folklore, WSM

The Eagles

had broadcast an urgent message for Obed to call home because his daughter had been killed in an accident. He went to the station to thank them, sat through a portion of the Opry, then returned some weeks later with some instruments and offered to play. The Pickard Family became regulars, and then (according to Charles Wolfe) became the first group to use the show as a springboard for a wider national audience. They built up an immense following on the basis of radio appearances in cities around the US, including New York, Chicago, Philadelphia and New Orleans. The Family made some records, of which the most popular was Obed's version of 'Kitty Wells'. He died in 1944 but his family continued to record and perform.

1946 Don Henley of The Eagles, born in the tiny Texas town of Linden.

23rd JULY

1943 Tony Joe White born near the Mississippi River swamplands in Oak Grove, Louisiana. He had a very big hit with the country/soul song 'Polk Salad Annie' in 1969.

Tony was popular with Southern rock audiences but, though his music was deeply rooted in country, he didn't have much success in the country marketplace.

1977 An inauspicious chart debut for Alabama. Their GRT single 'I Wanna Be With You Tonight' only managed to go as high as 78. In the same week, five years later, their fortunes had changed dramatically — they were top of the LP and singles charts with 'Feels So Right', and their debut album *My Home's In Alabama,* was at 54, having celebrated a whole year on the listings.

24th JULY

1926 The Grand Ole Opry debut of the Crook Brothers, the popular hoedown band led by Herman Crook. There were two unusual things about them — where most groups of the time used the fiddle as lead instrument, they used the harmonica — and they weren't brothers, though a banjo player who joined after the band was named was also called Crook.

1941 Seventeen-year-old Chet Atkins landed his very first radio job on WRBL in Columbus, Ohio. He sent a postcard to his mother, Mrs Ida Strevels, announcing the good news and hoping that she'd be able to pick up the radio station in Tennessee. It was the first of many radio jobs, working on stations in North Carolina, Virginia, Missouri and Colorado, before he became established in Nashville as musician and, later, producer.

25th JULY

1948 Steve Goodman born in Chicago, Illinois. He is a folksinger and writer whose work has overlapped with country on several occasions — which isn't surprising, since he lists Hank Williams Sr and Jimmie Rodgers as major influences. Steve wrote the classic train song, 'City Of New Orleans', which was a pop hit for Arlo Guthrie and a country success for Sammi Smith. The song, written at the tail end of the railroad era was inspired by a trip Steve made in the early seventies on the famous locomotive which linked Chicago and New Orleans.

Slim Whitman

1952 Slim Whitman's first chart entry, 'Indian Love Call'. It became a huge hit and stayed on the listings for six months. Three years later it was a best-selling record in England, which helped establish him as a star there for over two decades.

1967 Tommy Duncan, the vocalist with Bob Wills and his Texas Playboys for many years, died.

26th JULY

1964 In a prophetic interview, published just days before his tragic death, Jim Reeves said, "I book one hundred personal appearances a year because I like to perform before people. But what I dislike most is the travelling. The main trouble and danger with tours is getting there and back." On July 31 he was killed flying home to Nashville after a concert.

1969 Elvis Presley's first live concert appearance in eight years, at the Las Vegas International Hotel. His manager, Colonel Tom Parker,

had decided that a change was necessary for Elvis' career. His films were no longer so successful and Parker realised that personal appearances would probably earn much more money. The management had guaranteed him $150,000 a week for the Las Vegas shows (Presley was booked for a month). The first show was a great success, a mixture of old and new hits, with Elvis' new release, 'Suspicious Minds' drawing the biggest applause. Presley was backed by a top-notch band led by guitarist James Burton, two groups of singers — the all-girl Sweet Inspirations, and the male quartet The Imperials, plus a full orchestra. Elvis won unanimous praise from the critics, *Newsweek* observing, "There are several incredible things about Elvis, but the most incredible is his staying power in a world where meteoric careers fade like shooting stars."

27th JULY

1918 Homer (Henry D. Haynes) born in the same town as his partner and friend, Jethro. "Our home town is Knoxville, Tennessee," they once wrote. "We usually don't mention this in our publicity; when we left there, we said we'd keep it quiet. They've been very nice to us through all these years and they have a very big Homer and Jethro club in Knoxville. They use it on us every time we get near the place!" Their corny routines were very popular with country audiences from 1932, when they made their debut on a local radio show, until 1971, when Homer died. They signed to RCA in the forties and had success with a series of parody records, including 'That Hound Dog In The Window', 'Hernando's Hideaway', 'The Battle Of Kookamonga' and 'I Want To Hold Your Hand'. Both were musicians — they made a number of instrumental albums — and Homer was a particularly gifted guitarist.

1925 Charlie Poole and the North Carolina Ramblers made their first recordings. Among the songs was 'Don't Let Your Deal Go Down', which became their best known number.

1927 The *Bristol News Bulletin* carried a news story publicising the arrival of Ralph Peer from the Victor Talking Machine Company in New York, who was in town auditioning local musicians. It was almost certainly the newspaper story which alerted A.P. Carter and led to the first recording of the Carter Family.

1944 Bobbie Gentry (Roberta Streeter) born in Chickasaw County, Mississippi. She spent her childhood in Mississippi and by the time her family had moved to California she was an accomplished singer and guitarist. She took her stage name from the 1953 movie *Ruby Gentry,* signed to Capitol Records in LA, and almost immediately recorded 'Ode To Billy Joe', which became a huge international hit. Several other country-pop hits followed, including two duets with Glen Campbell, 'Let It Be Me' and 'All I Have To Do Is Dream'.

28th JULY

1954 The first interview with Elvis published in the *Memphis Press-Scimitar.* "Interview" wasn't really the right word — Elvis was so nervous that he confined himself to polite "yes sir's" and "no sir's", and Sam Phillips' assistant, Marion Keisker did all the talking. A few days earlier Presley had given his first radio interview to Dewey Phillips at WHBQ. "Mr Phillips, I don't know nothing about getting interviewed," he said, but Dewey explained that it would be easy, "Just don't say nothing dirty". They chatted for 15 minutes, then Phillips thanked Elvis for coming. He was disappointed, thinking that the DJ had changed his mind about the interview, then discovered that the microphone had been open all the time. "He broke into a cold sweat," said Phillips later.

1979 Dolly Parton top of the country charts with 'You're The Only One'.

29th JULY

1949 Ernest Tubb entered the charts with 'Slippin' Around'.

1955 Johnny Cash recorded his second single, 'Folsom Prison Blues'. He was inspired to write the song after seeing Steve Cochran acting in the movie, *Inside The Walls Of Folsom Prison.* Thirteen years later Cash recorded the song again, inside Folsom Prison. It became one of the biggest country singles of 1968, and the album *Johnny Cash At Folsom Prison* was one of the very first million-selling country albums.

1972 'Missing You' by Jim Reeves entered the charts. It was eight years since his tragic death in an air crash, but he was still scoring regular chart hits, with songs that had either been "previously unreleased", or were old recordings given new backing tracks. 'Missing You', which reached the Top Ten, was one of three Jim Reeves hits in 1972.

30th JULY

1954 A country package featuring Webb Pierce, Slim Whitman and Marty Robbins performed at the Overton Park Shell in Memphis. The star of the show turned out to be the up-and-coming local country singer, Elvis Presley, who'd been added to the bill at the last minute. It was the first time that he'd played before a large audience, and the first time he made his famous "wiggling" stage movements. Two years later Elvis explained what had happened, "I came out and I was doing a fast-type tune, one of my first records, and everybody was hollering and I didn't know what they were hollering at. Everybody was screaming and everything and I came off stage and my manager told me they were hollering because I was wiggling. Well, I went back for an encore and I kinda did a little more. And the more I did, the wilder they got." Webb Pierce had a different version; he told author Vince Staten, "Elvis told me that it was the first time he had ever sung before a big crowd and that he was really scared. He said he thought he was gonna faint out there on stage, so he started flapping his legs, just to keep from passing out. Then he noticed that the crowd was reacting to it, so he just kept doing it." There are several other stories about the origin of the wiggle, but everyone seems to agree that it was an accident.

31st JULY

1964 Jim Reeves killed when his single-engine Beechcraft went down over middle Tennessee during a heavy rainstorm. Gentleman Jim was dead, but his velvet vocal-style lived on because of the unusually large backlog of unreleased recordings that had been left behind and were

made available to RCA by his widow, Mary. Modern recording techniques were applied to give those basic cuts a contemporary sound. Fifteen years after his death, the voice of Deborah Allen (who was a small child in 1964) was added to several of his recordings and Jim became part of a successful duo. In 1981, Nashville producer Owen Bradley brought together two versions of 'Have You Ever Been Lonely', by Reeves and Patsy Cline, and combined them as a duet. The experiment worked surprisingly well: Patsy and Jim, who had never recorded together, had a big country hit nearly two decades after both had been killed in 'plane crashes. Jim Reeves is buried in East Texas; a monument by his grave carries the inscription — "If I, a lowly singer, dry one tear or soothe one humble heart in pain, then my homely verse to God is dear, and not one stanza has been sung in vain." Mary Reeves opened a "Jim, Reeves Museum" at Evergreen Place, Nashville in 1981, and the stream of visitors who've been coming to see the exhibits and a film of Jim's last recording session, prove that he's likely to remain a very popular country musician for the forseeable future.

A U G U S T

1st AUGUST

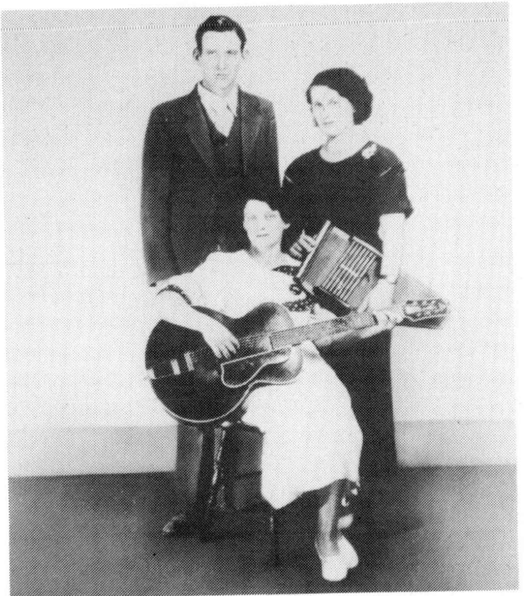

1927 Ralph Peer recorded the Carter Family for the first time, at 410 State Street in the Tennessee/Virginia border town of Bristol. It had taken Alvin Pleasant, Sara and Maybelle the best part of the previous day to make the 25 mile trip from their Maces Spring home near Clinch Mountain to Bristol, down rough dirt roads, in A.P.'s Model A Ford. The trio had met with considerable opposition from their family, particularly Maybelle's husband Ezra, but they were determined to make the journey and audition for the Victor Talking Machine Company. All three had been making music since childhood, knew dozens of traditional songs and had been performing as a group at local social functions for some time. A.P. sang bass, his wife Sara sang lead and played second guitar, while their sister-in-law Maybelle sang alto-harmony and was the main musician, playing guitar. They recorded six songs — 'Bury Me Under The Willow Tree', 'Little Log Cabin By The Sea', 'The Poor Orphan Child,' 'The Storms Are On The Ocean', 'Single Girl, Married Girl' and 'Wandering Boy'. Peer realised that he had made an important discovery, particularly with Sara who had a very appealing voice, and all six songs were released on records. A shrewd businessman as well as an alert talent scout, Peer also arranged the publishing of their songs and suggested that A.P. be credited as composer; even though he hadn't written any of them, he could claim some responsibility as arranger. The Carter Family's discs sold well enough for them to continue to record throughout the Depression years, which few other musicians were able to do. They continued making records until 1941 and their songs are still performed today as an integral part of the repertoire of many bluegrass and folk acts.

1958 Johnny Cash signed a long-term contract with CBS Records.

2nd AUGUST

1876 Wild Bill Hickok, legendary western soldier, scout and lawman, murdered in a saloon at Deadwood, in the Black Hills of Dakota at the age of 39. His final years had included some time with Buffalo Bill's Wild West Show.

1935 Hank Cochran, songwriter and sometime singer, born in Isola, Mississippi. He began singing professionally in the fifties, working for a time with Eddie Cochran, then an up-and-coming hillbilly singer, but soon to be a rock 'n' roll star. The pair weren't related but appeared as the Cochran Brothers. Hank moved to Nashville at the start of the sixties and began an extremely successful career as songwriter. He's won over 75 BMI awards for such country evergreens as 'I Fall To Pieces', 'Make The World Go Away' and 'She's Not You'. As a performer, Cochran has recorded for Liberty, Monument and RCA, and has had some minor hits. He's married to singer Jeannie Seely.

194? Hank DeVito, pedal steel guitarist with Emmylou Harris' Hot Band and Rodney Crowell's Cherry Bombs, born. Hank is also a successful songwriter and his hits include Juice Newton's 'Queen Of Hearts'.

1953 Betty Jack Davis of the Davis Sisters killed in a car accident while returning to Cincinnati after a radio show. Her partner, Skeeter Davis, was seriously injured. After a long break spent recovering physically and emotionally from the tragedy, Skeeter began performing as a solo artist.

3rd AUGUST

193? Gordon Stoker, first tenor with the Jordanaires, born. Probably the best known back-up singers in the world, the Jordanaires came to prominence when they won an Arthur Godfrey Talent Scout TV show in 1956, and through their work with Elvis Presley. Their first session with him was in July 1956 when they provided vocal backing for 'Hound Dog' and 'Don't Be Cruel'. The four-piece have appeared on thousands of records — country, rock 'n' roll and gospel — and have worked with hundreds of singers including Ricky Nelson, Don Gibson, Marty Robbins, Connie Francis and Johnny Horton.

1957 Warner Mack made his chart debut with 'Is It Wrong' on Decca. The record stayed in the best-sellers for 36 weeks, one of the longest running hits of the fifties, yet Warner didn't have another success for seven years. Mack is not his real name but, unlike most other singers, his wasn't changed on purpose. MacPherson was his real name and Mack his nickname, but a record company employee printed it on the label of his first release; once the mistake had been made, Warner decided to keep it.

4th AUGUST

1890 Carson Robison born in Oswego, Kansas. Early hillbilly singers were either amateur performers from the South who were discovered by adventurous talent scouts like Ralph Peer, or they were professional entertainers like Vernon Dalhart, who drew on their southern roots to perform authentic-sounding hillbilly material. Carson was one of the latter; brought up in Kansas where he began singing professionally at 15, he moved to New York in 1920 and was first featured on RCA records as a whistler, later switching to hillbilly songs. In the thirties he led the Buckaroos, and in the forties and fifties fronted the Pleasant Valley Boys, who were named after his home in New York state. From RCA, Carson went to MGM, continuing a recording career which would span four decades and included the best-selling 'Life Gets Tee-Jus Don't It' in 1948, and 'Rockin' With Grandma', a rockabilly cult hit recorded shortly before his death in 1957.

1927 Jimmie Rodgers auditioned for Ralph Peer in Bristol, just a few days after the Carter Family. Both had responded to the same story in the *Bristol News Bulletin*. Peer was instantly taken with Rodgers' voice and recorded him singing 'The Soldier's Sweetheart' and 'Sleep Baby Sleep'.

5th AUGUST

1943 Sammi Smith born in Orange, California. She grew up in Oklahoma and was singing in local clubs at 12. She was spotted by Luther Perkins of the Tennessee Three, who introduced her to Johnny Cash; this was the meeting that led to a contract with CBS and some country hits in the late sixties. In the seventies Sammi was recording for Mega and scored her biggest success with a version of Kris Kristofferson's 'Help Me Make It Through The Night'.

194? Bobby Braddock born. He's a Nashville-based songwriter who has authored numerous Top Ten country hits, including 'D-I-V-O-R-C-E' for Tammy Wynette and 'Golden Ring', which was a successful duet for Tammy and husband George Jones.

Bobby Braddock

1969 Luther Perkins, guitarist with Johnny Cash since the mid-fifties, died in hospital. Two days before, he'd fallen asleep in his living room with a lighted cigarette in his hand. He was severely burned in the resulting fire and never regained consciousness.

6th AUGUST

1961 Wanda Jackson's country chart debut as a solo artist, with 'Right Or Wrong', the first of 20 hits in the sixties. She'd actually first made an appearance in the charts while still a schoolgirl, in 1954, as part of a duet with Billy Gray from Hank Thompson's Band. She completed her schooling, then turned towards rock 'n' roll and was one of the few successful female rockers in the fifties, scoring with the classic 'Let's Have A Party'. With rock 'n' roll on the decline in the early sixties, she switched back to country, for a long and prosperous career.

1964 Loretta Lynn gave birth to twin girls. One was named Patsy, after Patsy Cline, the other Peggy, after Loretta's eldest sister.

1977 The Kendalls, the father and daughter duo from St. Louis, entered the charts with 'Heaven's Just A Sin Away'. It went to number one, stayed there for four weeks and was one of the biggest country hits of the year, winning a Grammy and CMA Single of the Year Award.

7th AUGUST

1925 Felice Bryant, of the Boudleaux and Felice Bryant songwriting partnership, born in Milwaukee, Wisconsin, of Italian parentage. She grew up in the city and was working as an elevator operator at the Sherwood Hotel when she met Boudleaux, who was in town with a jazz band. "When I was eight years old, I dreamed of this man;" recalls Felice, "he and I were dancing to 'our song', and I remembered this man's face. So when I saw Boudleaux, I recognised him!" They were married soon afterwards and began writing country songs for their own enjoyment, Felice writing the words and Boudleaux the melody; they found they could make a living with their compositions and moved to Nashville. One of their most successful songs is 'Rocky Top', which has been recorded over a thousand times, but took only 10 minutes to write!

1950 Rodney Crowell, one of the brightest young writers, producers and performers in Music City, born in Houston, Texas. "I remember growing up," says Rodney. "It was like the ghost of Hank Williams lived in our house. All my relatives referred to him as 'Hank' — they didn't know him but were caught up with his music. That lonesome voice is the first thing I remember." Crowell moved to Nashville in the early seventies, determined to become a songwriter, and

eventually landed a job with Jerry Reed's publishing firm. A chance encounter with producer Brian Ahern took him to California, where he joined Emmylou Harris' Hot Band in 1975. Rodney's talents as a writer were recognised by Emmy and she recorded his classic, 'Till I Gain Control Again'. He left the Hot Band in 1977, intent on launching a solo career, and released his first LP, *Ain't Living Long Like This*. It wasn't a big-seller but won critical acclaim and became a musician's favourite — several established artists picked up on his songs, including the Oak Ridge Boys, Waylon Jennings and the Dirt Band. In 1979 he married singer Rosanne Cash and has subsequently produced her very successful albums *Right Or Wrong, Seven Year Ache* and *Somewhere In The Stars*.

1954 Johnny Cash, recently discharged from the US Air Force, married Vivian Liberto at St. Ann's Catholic Church in San Antonio, Texas. After the ceremony they travelled to Memphis, Tennessee, where Johnny planned to start work as a home appliance salesman.

1970 The opening of the Armadillo World Headquarters, the dance hall/studio complex in Austin, Texas that became the focal point of the progressive country/redneck rock movement in the mid-seventies. It was here that Willie Nelson first discovered his huge following among young Texans. The 'Dillo closed at the end of 1980 and was torn down to make way for an hotel complex, but the name lives on through a mail-order service and the Armadillo Record label.

8th AUGUST

1926 Webb Pierce, one of the most successful singers in the fifties and the man who did more than anyone to popularize the sound of the steel guitar in country music, born in West Monroe, Louisiana. He was an accomplished guitarist as a teenager, joined the Louisiana Hayride in the late forties and built a strong local following. This popularity brought him to the attention of Decca Records, with whom he had a very long and successful career. He scored hits every year between 1952 and 1972, including chart-toppers, 'Back Street Affair', 'It's Been So Long' and 'There Stands The Glass'. He joined the Grand Ole Opry in 1954 with Red Sovine, a close friend from the Louisiana Hayride, and they had a few hits as a duo, including 'Why Baby Why'.

1932 Mel Tillis, gifted songwriter, successful performer and the most famous stutterer in country music, born in Tampa, Florida. He started writing when he was in the Air Force, and returned to civilian life with several songs that would later earn him a lot of money. After a spell as fireman, then milkman, he moved to Nashville and was signed to a publishing house. His attempts to become a recording artist were

not immediately successful; several producers told him that a man who stuttered could never make it in the music industry. But Mel's stuttering, which has since become a comic trademark, didn't interfere with his singing — "With the instruments playing along," he says, "the rhythm and everything moving, my voice just seems to flow with it." He eventually signed to CBS in 1958, and was subsequently on Ric, and then Kapp. He had some moderate hits in the sixties, but his greatest successes in the decade came as a writer, most notably with 'Detroit City' for Bobby Bare and 'Ruby, Don't Take Your Love To Town' for Kenny Rodgers and the First Edition. In the seventies he became better known as a performer: he was with MGM from 1970, scored his first number one, 'I Ain't Never', then moved to MCA in 1976, the year he was named Entertainer of the Year by the Academy of Country Music. By the late seventies, Tillis found himself much in demand for TV, where he's appeared on dozens of talk and drama shows.

1939 Philip Balsley, baritone singer with the Statler Brothers, born in Augusta County, Virginia.

Hank Williams Jnr.

1975 While hiking along the Continental Divide in Montana, Hank Williams Jnr fell 500 feet down a mountain side and was seriously injured. "It was just like falling out of an airplane — straight down," Hank told *New Times* magazine. "So down I went, slidin' headfirst on my back. Emotionally, I just froze inside. No feeling, just shock. And I thought, 'You're dead. You're just gonna splatter on the rocks' . . . Finally I hit the snow like a swan dive. There was a boulder stickin' up through there, and I just hit it straight on, headfirst." His injuries were appalling, but he somehow survived, was airlifted to hospital and spent seven and a half hours in an operating theatre. Reconstructive surgery and recuperation lasted for two years, which gave him time to plan the major career alterations he'd already begun before the accident. He returned to the music scene with a new sense of purpose and a very successful new sound.

9th AUGUST

1934 Merle Kilgore born in Chickasha, Oklahoma. While still a schoolboy he was a DJ, on radio station KENT in Shreveport, Louisiana, had a hillbilly band and was featured on the Louisiana Hayride. He was a regular on a local TV show in 1952 and made some records for Imperial, which were small hits in Louisiana, though some are now prized by rockabilly enthusiasts. He had national country hits in 1960 with 'Dear Mama' and 'Love Has Made You Beautiful', but they represented the peak of his career as a performer. He really made his mark as a writer, with several big hits in the sixties, including 'Woolverton Mountain', which he co-authored with the singer Claude King and 'Ring Of Fire', written with June Carter.

1975 Texas-based Western swing aggregation, Asleep At The Wheel, entered the country charts with 'The Letter That Johnny Walker Wrote'. A favourite band in Texas and with music critics in general, the group never had a big-selling record. This single was their most successful release; it reached number ten.

10th AUGUST

1928 Jimmy Dean, best known for 'Big Bad John', the story of a mine disaster hero, born in Plainview, Texas. He learnt to play guitar, accordion and harmonica as a child and joined his first band while in the Air Force. On his discharge in 1948 he began playing in the Washington D.C. area where he gradually built a reputation, won a recording contract with Four Star and had a hit in 1953 with 'Bumming Around'. In the mid-fifties he had his own local TV show and toured extensively, but had no more hits until he signed with CBS in 1961. His very first recording for them was his own composition 'Big Bad John', an international success that sold over two million copies. Considerable TV exposure, including his own network afternoon show, helped boost his record sales throughout the sixties, and he had several more hits, including 'PT 109' and 'The Last Thing This Morning'. Many observers thought his chart-making career was over in the seventies, but he bounced back to the Top Ten in 1976 with 'I O U'.

1971 An historic recording session at the Woodland Sound Studio in Nashville, featuring Roy Acuff and country-rock outfit, the Nitty Gritty Dirt Band. The session was part of an ambitious project co-ordinated by the band's producer and manager Bill McEuen. He intended to record a triple LP acoustic set with his band and some of the "elder statesmen" of country music, including Merle Travis, Earl Scruggs, Doc Watson, Jimmy Martin, Mother Maybelle Carter and Pete "Oswold" Kirby. Few of them had heard of the young, California-based group before, but seemed very happy to be involved (though Bill Monroe was one musician who reportedly wanted nothing to do with the project). The band were worried before the arrival of Acuff, a conservative who might have been offended by their long hair, but their fears were unnecessary. "They are very nice boys," he told a reporter from *The Tennessean,* "and they certainly knew what they were doing." Roy went on to explain that he'd taken part in the project on the advice of his publishing partner Wesley Rose, who thought, "It might increase the respect between our brand of music and theirs". The sessions produced some superb performances, and the triple album release, *Will The Circle Be Unbroken* received widespread acclaim.

11th AUGUST

1946 John Conlee born in Versailles, Kentucky. He was raised on a tobacco farm; as a child he played the guitar and harboured a strong ambition to work in radio and as a teenager played in a folk trio, but when he graduated from high school his show business aspirations were sidetracked and he worked as a mortician. After six

years he finally got a job in radio at Fort Knox, subsequently worked in other towns, then moved to a Nashville station in 1971. "Music was the ulterior motive for moving to Nashville," recalls John; "it was what I wanted to be involved with all along." His radio job, albeit as a rock disc jockey, helped him to make contacts in the Nashville music business and he began cutting country singles for ABC. The first three were flops, but then he came up with 'Rose Colored Glasses', a song he'd written with a newsreader at the radio station, and it became a big hit. The follow-up, 'Lay Lady Down', went to number one and John was able to give up his radio job and work full time as a country singer. He's been very successful since, has scored several more hits, was voted Best New Male Vocalist by the Academy of Country Music in 1979 and was the first new member of the Opry in five years.

1952 Jim Denny telephoned Hank Williams to tell him that he was fired from the Grand Ole Opry and WSM for frequently failing to turn up for shows. Denny said that if he could straighten himself out and conduct himself properly for a year, he could return.

12th AUGUST

1929 Buck Owens (Alvis Edgar Owens), one of the most successful country stars of the sixties, born in Sherman, Texas. He was a farm labourer in his teens, making music in his spare time, then he moved to Bakersfield, California in the early fifties and found full-time employment in music, joining the house band at a country club. He built up a reputation as a guitarist and began getting regular session work in Los Angeles with artists like Sonny James and Wanda Jackson. He was signed to a solo contract with

Capitol in 1957 and two years later scored his first hit with 'Second Fiddle'. He had fantastic chart success in the sixties — 39 of his records charted and 19 made number one. Buck had a hand in writing many of the hits, including 'Act Naturally', 'I Got A Tiger By The Tail' and 'Together Again'. With his band, the Buckaroos, he played to packed houses wherever he went. Because he didn't move to Nashville, his home town of Bakersfield became an important country music centre, bringing attention to local singers, like Merle Haggard, and several musicians from Buck's band, including Don Rich and Doyle Holly. Owens' chart success in the seventies was less spectacular than in the previous decade, but the hits continued, including some duets with Susan Raye. He became a familiar personality for TV viewers due to regular appearances on the "Hee Haw" show.

1930 Porter Wagoner, popular country music showman and another very successful recording artist of the sixties, born in West Plains, Missouri. He learnt to play the guitar as a child and sang the country songs he heard on the radio. Porter worked in a grocery store and when business was slow, he'd play and sing to anyone who'd listen. His boss enjoyed the impromptu performances and sponsored an early morning radio programme to showcase Wagoner's talents and advertise the store. From such beginnings, Porter landed a weekly spot on KWTO in Springfield, Missouri in 1951 and then, a few months later, the Ozark Jubilee began at the station with Red Foley as director. Red provided valuable advice and Wagoner was soon the featured singer on the nationally televised edition of the show. He signed to RCA in 1955 and had a string of chart successes, including 'The Green Green Grass Of Home' and 'Skid Row Joe'. His long-running syndicated TV series began in 1961, with 18 stations, but by 1967 the number had increased to 86. This was the first year that Dolly Parton was featured. They became very popular as a duo and won three CMA awards. The partnership lasted until 1974, when Dolly left to concentrate on her solo career. Today Porter is a very successful Nashville businessman, though he continues to be active in country music, both recording and performing.

1940 Rod Bernard, swamp-pop singer, born in Opelousas, Louisiana. "Swamp-pop" is a rocking SW Louisiana synthesis of Cajun, rhythm and blues, and country music. Rod had several local hits in the fifties and sixties, plus one national success, 'This Should Go On Forever'. Several country songs have been given the distinctive swamp-pop treatment by singers like Bernard and Johnnie Allan, and are available on the Ville Platte record label, Jin.

13th AUGUST

1978 Razzy Bailey entered the country charts with 'What Time Do You Have To Be Back In Heaven'. After 20 years of struggle, frustration and failure, he finally had a hit record. He had spent years on the honky-tonk circuit of Georgia, Alabama and Florida and had several tries at making a successful record. "I got a pay-for-your-own record deal in Atlanta on the Peach label," he recalls, but nothing came of it, then Freddy Weller produced a single called 'Stolen Moments' for him on ABC. Next he tried producing himself on Capitol's 1-2-3 label. Nothing again. Still undaunted, he formed a label called Aquarian and made a single, 'I Hate Hate', which impressed MGM enough to buy and release it. Nothing once more. Things looked up when he teamed with producer Bob Montgomery on Capricorn Records. Alas, still nothing. Once more he sank his own money into a label — Erastus. The single 'Keepin' Rosie Proud Of Me' actually made the charts, but only to position 99, and he lost his money. By the mid-seventies Bailey's career in records seemed to be practically over. He felt like a complete loser. Then, suddenly, things changed. Dickie Lee had a huge hit on RCA with one of his songs, and Razzy got one more chance to make a record. All at once the struggling paid off. 'What Time Do You Have To Be Back In Heaven' was the first of a string of Top Ten hits all produced by his old mentor, Bob Montgomery.

14th AUGUST

1941 Connie (Constance) Smith born in Elkhart, Indiana. One of 14 children, Connie was a country fan as a teenager but, though she occasionally sang at parties, had no ambitions to make a career in music. However, in 1963 she entered a talent show in Ohio and was heard by Bill Anderson. He was very impressed with her performance and helped get her an RCA contract. Within a year she had a number one hit with Bill's song 'Once A Day'. Many more hits followed and she became a regular member of the Grand Ole Opry. But success took a serious toll on her private life — "I have no foundation," she said. "It was an experience to travel over 100,000 miles a year on the road when you weren't used to leaving your own town. I couldn't face the reality of life, and I became bitter when the people I admired didn't act the way I expected them to off stage." She had two failed marriages and became very depressed, but then recovered, drawing particular strength from a religious awakening. "I don't think I could have lived if I hadn't found God," she said later.

15th AUGUST

1933 Bobby Helms born in Bloomington, Indiana. A country and pop star of the late fifties, he's best known for 'Jingle Bell Rock' and 'Fraulein', a 1957 hit which spent a whole year on the country charts. Bobby was a teenage guitar star on a local Bloomington TV station and built a strong following throughout the mid-west, leading to a debut appearance on the Grand Ole Opry when he was only 17. He began recording for Decca in the mid-fifties and 'Fraulein' was his first hit, followed by 'My Special Angel', whch was also a number one smash. His recording career went into a decline in the sixties, but after a seven year absence from the charts, he returned in 1967 with the first of several small hits on the Little Darlin' label.

1952 Hank Williams entered the country charts with 'Jambalaya', a tribute to Cajun food and good times, which had been inspired by a trip to New Orleans with his wife Audrey.

16th AUGUST

1935 Patsy Montana recorded 'I Wanna Be A Cowboy's Sweetheart', which became the first million-selling country single by a woman. There were no charts and no gold record awards in the thirties, which is why many sources credit 'It Wasn't God Who Made Honky Tonk Angels', a 1952 hit for Kitty Wells, as the first best-selling country record by a woman.

1948 Danny Flowers, long-serving guitarist with Don Williams' band, born in Henderson, North Carolina. A successful songwriter and author of Don's hit 'Tulsa Time' among others, he's also made his own records with fellow band-members, as Danny Flowers and the Scratch Band.

1977 The day Elvis died. Presley had played an energetic game of racket ball at the floodlit court in his home, Graceland, until about 5am, then had gone to bed. In the early afternoon his girlfriend, Ginger Alden, discovered him lying face down in his bathroom. He wasn't breathing. Ginger called for help and Presley's road manager, Joe Esposito, summoned an ambulance. Dr Nichopoulos, Elvis' private physician, accompanied his patient to the Baptist Memorial Hospital in Memphis, reportedly pleading, "Come on, Presley, breathe. Breathe for me," during the seven minute drive. Desperate attempts were made to revive him at the hosptial, but at 3.30pm Elvis Presley was officially pronounced dead. He was just 42.

17th AUGUST

1921 Wayne Raney, old-timey harmonica player, born in Batesville, Arkansas. He had a radio show in the early forties, then worked as a sideman with the Delmore Brothers and is best known through the band's recordings of 'Blues Stay Away From Me', one of the biggest hits of 1949, which he helped to write. Johnny Cash listened to transcriptions of Raney's radio shows and credits them as important in stimulating him to follow a career in music.

1958 Charlie Rich's first recording session for Sun as a solo artist. He had been discovered by Bill Justis at the Sharecropper Club in Memphis. Bill liked his voice, but not his style, "He was just too jazzy for Sun, all thirteenths," Justis recalled, "I gave him a bunch of Jerry Lee Lewis records and told him to come back when he could get that bad." Charlie did as he was told, returning to sing 'Whirlwind' and 'Philadelphia Baby' as Jerry Lee-style rockers.

1977 The shock waves of Elvis Presley's death spread around the world. It had been well known that Presley was unwell and overweight, but few people realised how serious his condition had become. Doctors suggested that Elvis had suffered heart failure. A Baptist Hospital spokesman said, "Elvis had the arteries of an eighty-year-old man; his body was just worn out. His arteries and veins were terribly corroded." Journalists and fans flooded into Memphis; *Rolling Stone* magazine sent Caroline Kennedy, daughter of the late President John F. Kennedy, to interview some of the 75,000-strong crowd outside Graceland. At 3.00pm the gates were opened and fans were allowed into the house to file past Elvis' body, which lay in an open coffin.

18th AUGUST

1918 Hank Penny born in Birmingham, Alabama. He was a western swing musician who was a regular performer on the Midwestern Hayride radio show in Cincinnati during the late thirties and early forties.

1939 Molly Bee (Molly Beachwood), actress and singer, born in Oklahoma City, Oklahoma. She came to prominence in the California area at the age of 11 as vocalist on Cliffie Stone's "Hometown Jubilee" TV programme, later winning national fame through regular appearances in Tennessee Ernie Ford's network shows.

1966 Jim Reeves entered the British pop charts with 'Distant Drums'. It stayed there for 25 weeks and reached number one. Jim Reeves was very popular with the British record buyers in the sixties and had two dozen pop hits.

1973 A live recording in the little town of Luckenbach, Texas (population 3) by Jerry Jeff Walker and his band. Walker was going through a phase where he hated working inside recording studios and the wooden dance hall in Luckenbach seemed the perfect location. The best of the evening's music appeared on the MCA LP *Viva Terlingua*. Jerry Jeff enthusiasts rate it as one of his best.

1977 The funeral of Elvis Presley. There were 150 mourners for the service at Graceland, including his manager, Colonel Tom Parker, his ex-wife, Priscilla and his nine-year-old daughter (and heiress), Lisa Marie. After the service the body was taken to the Forest Hill Cemetery and laid to rest beside the grave of Gladys Presley.

19th AUGUST

1895 John Wesley Hardin, notorious Texan gunfighter, killed. He was shot in the back of the head while drinking in the Acme Bar, El Paso, by a policeman. Hardin had a deadly cross-hand draw which involved grabbing each gun with the opposite hand. He is supposed to have killed 40 people, including a Pinkerton detective, for which crime he served 16 years in jail.

19?? Eddy Raven born in Lafayette, Louisiana. His father was a truck driver, and also a musician, who sometimes took Eddy, his eldest son, to sing with him in honky-tonks. Raven's musical education was balanced by regular singing in church. As a teenager he led several bands (they played a rocking combination of Cajun and rhythm and blues), worked for a time running moonshine liquor and was an avid baseball player, until a broken ankle stopped his dreams of a professional sporting career. Louisiana musician Bobby Charles (author of 'See You Later Alligator') persuaded him that a musical career could be lucrative. Eddy found radio work and then won a recording contract with a local label. He met Cajun-country star Jimmy C. Newman who offered help if he ever went to Nashville. In 1972 he took up the offer and was assisted in getting a publishing deal with Acuff-Rose. Soon afterwards he won a record deal and for several years had small hits with a variety of labels: ABC/Dot, Monument and Dimension (which he formed with his manager), but then broke into the country Top 20 in 1982, after signing to Elektra, with the hit 'Who Do You Know In California'.

1979 Rockabilly singer Dorsey Burnette died. He sang with brother Johnny and their friend Paul Burlison in the Johnny Burnette Trio, from 1956 to 1959, then went solo and had hits in 1960 with 'Hey Little One' and 'Tall Oak Tree'. In the seventies Dorsey recorded some country singles for Capitol.

20th AUGUST

1923 Jim Reeves born in Panola County, Texas. Baseball and music were Jim's great loves as a teenager. He showed promise as a pitcher with the University of Texas baseball team, was signed up by the St. Louis Cardinals, but then a leg injury nipped his professional sporting career in the bud. His show business career began as a DJ on the powerful Shreveport, Louisiana radio station KWKH, but once his singing talents were recognised he became a regular performer on the station's famous Louisiana Hayride show. Jim made some records for local labels and scored a number one country hit with a version of 'Mexican Joe' on the Abbott label in 1953. He signed with RCA and began a long and very successful recording career which lasted well after his tragic death, in an air crash, because of the large amount of unreleased material that he left behind and the hard work of his widow. Reeves was one of the first country cross-over artists, removing the distinctive sound of steel guitar and fiddle parts from his records and scoring huge international pop hits, helping to introduce country music to millions of new listeners. Jim's big record successes include 'He'll Have To Go', 'Four Walls' and 'Welcome To My World'.

19?? James Burton born. One of the great rock guitarists, he began as a musician with rockabilly star Dale Hawkins, played lead on Ricky Nelson hits, became an in-demand session man and worked with several country-rock acts including Gram Parsons. He was with Elvis Presley for the first half of the seventies and then was a central figure in the original line-up of Emmylou Harris' Hot Band.

1952 Rudy Gatlin, youngest of the Gatlin Brothers, born in Texas. After spending much of his childhood singing with elder brothers Steve and Larry, he attended Texas Tech in Lubbock where he graduated with a BA in business administration. "I'm glad I got a college degree," he explains, "but I always knew that I wasn't going to be a banker or an accountant or a lawyer. I always knew that eventually I'd be doing what I'm doing now with my brothers. I firmly believe we're doing exactly what we were put here to do. We've got God-given talent and, hopefully, we're doing what God wants us to do with it: making Gatlin music — making our music."

21st AUGUST

1938 Kenny Rogers, best-selling country singer in the pop market-place, born in Houston, Texas, one of eight children in a family he describes as both "very poor" and "closely knit". Like so many of today's successful country acts, Kenny has "paid his dues" — nearly 20 years of hard work with a variety of musical aggregations before 'Lucille' made him a superstar in 1977. He formed his first band, the Scholars, while at high school, after "discovering that girls were particularly attracted to musicians", and they had a small, local hit with 'Crazy Feelings'. After graduation, Kenny spent several years as bassist and singer with a popular Houston jazz outfit, the Bobby Boyle Trio. They made an LP for CBS in 1966, but it bombed. He then joined the New Christy Minstrels, a folk band that was coming to the end of a successful career which had involved several hit singles. After a year he quit, with three colleagues, and they formed the First Edition. Kenny was lead singer and had a short, but significant, burst of fame, scoring two big hit singles, 'Just Dropped In (To See What Condition My Condition Was In)' and 'Ruby, Don't Take Your Love To Town'. Then came several line-up changes and shifts in musical direction, and the group disbanded. These were difficult days for Kenny Rogers, but he shrugged off his personal and career misfortunes and decided to concentrate all his energies on a solo career. He signed to United Artists in 1975, and began working with producer Larry Butler. After some small hits he broke through with the million-selling 'Lucille', and hasn't looked back since.

1939 Harold Reid, bass vocalist and joker in the Statler Brothers pack, born in Augusta County, Virginia. Harold leads the Statler's alter-ego band, Lester "Roadhog" Moran and his Cadillac Cowboys.

1965 Waylon Jennings made his chart debut with 'That's The Chance I'll Have To Take' on RCA records.

22nd AUGUST

1938 Rockabilly performer Dale Hawkins (Delmar Allen Hawkins) born in Goldmine, Louisiana. 'Susie Q' was his biggest hit, in 1957, but he made several other records, now highly prized by rockabilly enthusiasts, including 'La Do Da Da' and 'Class Cutter', which benefited from classy guitar work by the likes of Scotty Moore, Roy Buchanan and James Burton.

1968 George Jones and Tammy Wynette married, or so the country music reference books will tell you, but as Tammy revealed in her autobiography, *Stand By Your Man* — "We announced we'd gotten married August 22, but actually we weren't married at all." They finally wed on February 16, 1969, but decided not to announce that they'd been married "again".

23rd AUGUST

1917 Tex Williams (Sol Williams) born in Ramsey, in rural Illinois. An accomplished musician before he reached his teens, he had his own one-man radio show at 13, joined his first band, The Reno Racketeers, two years later, then at 17 went to California, teamed up with Tex Ritter and made several cowboy movies and was featured vocalist with Spade Cooley's band.In the mid-forties, Tex formed the Western Caravan band; they signed to Capitol and scored with 'Smoke, Smoke, Smoke (That Cigarette)', a million-selling single and one of the biggest hits of the decade. Tex and his band gained widespread popularity through numerous TV appearances in the fifties and sixties, and continued to record into the seventies.

19?? Rex Allen Jnr, famous son of a famous father, born. He's been familiar with a life "on

the road" since the age of six. Summers were spent travelling with his dad, Rex Allen, "The Arizona Cowboy", playing rhythm guitar, wrangling his father's horse, Koko, and as a rodeo clown. He trained as an actor, then decided to make music his career. He sang and played in LA bars, but with little success, so moved to Nashville where he signed to Shelby Singleton's Plantation Records. "In the two and a half years I was on the label," he recalls, "Shelby taught me more about the record business than I could have learned in ten years. They released seventeen singles and one album on me and nothing reached the charts. Looking back I'm flattered that they believed in me so much." An unsuccessful stint on JMI followed and he was about to give up, "But my agent convinced me to go talk to Larry Butler." Larry could see that Rex had talent and bankrolled a recording session. "I recorded on Monday and by Friday was signed to Warner Brothers," says Allen. His career turned right around, and 'The Great Mail Robbery', a Warner Brothers release in 1973, was the first of several small hits. He cracked the Top Ten for the first time three years later, with 'Two Less Lonely People'.

24th AUGUST

1897 Fred Rose born in St. Louis, Missouri. His long career involved many musical activities — he was a professional pianist at 10, and as a teenager had started writing songs, was singing in clubs, and had made successful records. Fred performed on radio shows in Chicago, then Nashville (before the growth of the country music industry there), and worked with Gene Autry in Hollywood. It was on his return to

Nashville, in the early forties, that he really made his mark. He formed the Acuff-Rose publishing house with singer Roy Acuff, and had songwriting success with country classics including 'Take These Chains From My Heart', 'Kaw Liga' and 'Fire Ball Mail'. Fred "discovered" Hank Williams, one of several up-and-coming country stars that he helped with songwriting and career development. Rose died in 1954; his contributions to country music were recognised when he was one of the first four men elected to the Hall of Fame in 1961.

1968 'Harper Valley PTA', one of the most successful country singles of all time, entered the charts. It kicked off a long run of country hits for the singer, Jeannie C. Riley, and marked a major improvement in the fortunes of the writer, Tom T. Hall. "When I was a small boy, there was a lady in town who had taken on the entire PTA for their indiscretions," wrote Tom in his book, *The Storyteller's Nashville,* "I was always amazed that one very unimportant lady could be so brazen as to take on the aristocracy of the community . . . It was not hard to write, and I don't recall that it took more than an hour or so. But I had had the idea for twenty years in one form or another."

1977 Waylon Jennings arrested on a charge of conspiracy and possession of cocaine. The charges, which were later dropped, came a few months after Waylon had been named an honorary police chief by the Nashville Metropolitan Police Department.

25th AUGUST

1973 British singer Olivia Newton-John made her debut on the American country charts with 'Let Me Be There'. Olivia didn't consider herself a country singer at the time and her background was such that she knew little about the genre. The pedal steel guitar on the record, which helped win acceptance with country DJ's, was added after Olivia had recorded her vocal parts.

1979 The Charlie Daniels Band top of the country and rock charts with 'The Devil Went Down To Georgia'. The big, barrel-chested bandleader, who spends much of each year touring, finds that most of his support comes from working people — "I come from the working class. That's where my heart is and always will be. I sympathize with the old boy who gets out of bed at 5.30 in the morning and goes runnin' a bulldozer all day in the farm — anything working people do. That's the people I think our music appeals to. It does reach into other areas, but we've never exactly been darlin's of the intellectual community. Which suits me fine."

26th AUGUST

1937 Country comedian Don Bowman born in Lubbock, Texas. He's actually proud of his reputation as "the world's greatest guitarist", and is the only guy who's hung around Nashville but can't play 'Wildwood Flower'. Don has scored some novelty hits, like 'Chet Atkins, Make Me A Star' and 'Willon and Waylee', plus several near misses, including 'Folsum Prison Blues No. 2', 'Poor Old Ugly Gladys Jones' and 'Boll Weevil Airlines'.

1955 In America, rock 'n' roll had begun to make a significant impression on the charts — Bill Haley was enjoying his ninth and final week at number one with 'Rock Around The

Clock', but in Britain pop vocalists still dominated the charts. Slim Whitman was enjoying a tremendous run of popularity; 'Rose Marie' was number one for the fifth week, and 'Indian Love Call' was also in the Top Five, along with two Frankie Laine records, and one by Frank Sinatra.

27th AUGUST

1925 Carter Stanley, guitar player and eldest of the Stanley Brothers, born in McClure, Virginia. Ralph and Carter were born into a family, and area, where traditional music was an important part of life. Their mother taught them harmony singing as young children, then encouraged them to play guitar and banjo. They performed at local social functions, were regulars on the Farm And Fun Time programme broadcast from WCYB at Bristol, Virginia in the late forties, and recorded for Sid Nathan's King label in Cincinnati. They came to national prominence in the fifties during the folk boom, and won a deserved reputation as two of the finest bluegrass musicians in the US. Carter died in Bristol in 1961.

1927 Jimmy C. Newman born in Big Mamou, Louisiana. He grew up in Bayou country and developed a musical style which mixed traditional Cajun with contemporary country — the C in his name stands for Cajun. He started his professional career at the Louisiana Hayride, had his first hit in 1954 with 'Cry, Cry Darling' and then became a member of the Grand Ole Opry in 1956. Jimmy and his versatile Cajun Country group are frequent visitors to Europe, where they enjoy considerable popularity.

1963 Death of Jim Denny, talent booker at the Opry and a very successful manager and publisher. One of his few mistakes was telling the young Elvis Presley, after a disappointing Opry debut in 1954, that he should go back to driving trucks!

28th AUGUST

1925 Billy Grammer born in Benton, Illinois. One of 11 children, he came from a poor family and saw music as a way of escaping the poverty trap while still a youngster. He became one of the first great Nashville session guitarists, playing on dozens of hit records, then found success in his own right, scoring a major hit with 'Gotta Travel On', in 1959, which led to him joining the Grand Ole Opry.

1977 Crystal Gayle top of the country charts with 'Don't It Make My Brown Eyes Blue'. It stayed there a month and would earn writer Richard Leigh the CMA Song Of The Year Award in 1978. The single outsold anything Crystal's big sister Loretta Lynn had ever recorded, and established her as a crossover pop star.

29th AUGUST

1900 Buell Kazee born in Magoffin County, Kentucky. Brought up in an area where great emphasis was placed on music and religion, he learnt traditional and gospel songs from his relatives and neighbours and showed a keen affinity for performing, playing a home-made banjo his father had given him when he was just five. Buell was ordained as a Baptist minister when he was 17, and became a very keen folk collector while at college, a hobby he continued for half a century. In the twenties he made some of the first folk recordings, for Brunswick and Vocalion, and gave recitals whenever he could spare the time from preaching. He retired from the ministry in the sixties and became a regular performer at American folk festivals.

1977 Three men arrested at Forest Hill Cemetery in Memphis. There was speculation that they were preparing to steal the body of Elvis Presley and hold it for ransom. Vernon Presley, understandably concerned about security at the cemetery, made arrangements for the remains of both Gladys and Elvis to be moved and reburied at Graceland.

30th AUGUST

1919 Kitty Wells (Muriel Deason), "Queen of Country Music", born in Nashville, Tennessee. Music was her first love and as a teenager she sang on the Old Country Store show, broadcast over Nashville's WSIX radio station, with her three sisters and a cousin. When she was 16 she met singer Johnny Wright and they married two years later. Kitty, who changed her name at Johnny's suggestion after the folk song popularized by the Carter Family, toured with Johnny and Jack during the forties, and appeared on numerous country radio shows. In 1947 Kitty joined the Louisiana Hayride and was one of the show's most popular stars. She left in 1952 to return to her home town of Nashville, joined the Opry and signed with Decca Records. Her recording of 'It Wasn't God Who Made Honky Tonk Angels' was the biggest selling country hit of the year, established her as the leading country female singer, and led to the title "Queen Of Country Music". Kitty Wells remains the most honoured woman in country music; she was voted top female singer for 12 consecutive

years and Record World's Artist of the Decade, then in 1976 was elected to the Country Music Hall of Fame. Kitty continues to tour, working upwards of 200 dates a year, with her husband Jack and son Bobby Wright.

31st AUGUST

1939 Jerry Allison, drummer with The Crickets, born. After the death of Buddy Holly, the band continued to perform and make records. Jerry remained the only constant fixture of The Crickets in two decades, and was joined at various times by musicians including Glen D. Hardin and Englishmen Rick Grech and Albert Lee.

1957 Young super-picker Roy Clark married Barbara Joyce Rupard.

1974 Dolly Parton top of the country charts with 'Love Is Like A Butterfly', completing a hat trick of number one hits during the year. The other two — 'Jolene' and 'I Will Always Love You'.

S E P T E M B E R

1st SEPTEMBER

1931 Boxcar Willie (Lecil Travis Martin) born in Sterratt, Texas in a small wooden house close to the railroad tracks—his father was a railroad worker. He grew up during the Depression years and has strong early memories of the hobos who rode the rails, sometimes stopping at his house and asking for work. Martin sang as a child, made his first radio broadcast at the age of 10 and was playing honky-tonks in his early teens. His professional singing career continued until the arrival of rock 'n' roll limited the opportunities of country acts. He worked in various jobs, including a spell as DJ. In 1975, disillusionment with modern country trends prompted him to return to performing and to adopt the persona of a railroad hobo singing in the style of his hard-core country heroes, Jimmie Rodgers, Lefty Frizzell and Hank Williams. He built a strong base of support in his native Texas but when he visited Nashville he could find few people interested in him, except a Scottish promoter named Drew Taylor. Boxcar Willie became a star in the UK, won the loudest ovation in the history of the Wembley Country Festival and earned gold discs for record sales. News of his success filtered back to the US and in the early eighties he became a star there too; he joined the Grand Ole Opry and had best-selling records.

1933 Conway Twitty (Harold Lloyd Jenkins) born in Friars Point, Mississippi, the son of a Mississippi River boat captain. He learnt to sing and play the guitar when he was five, formed his own band, the Phillips County Ramblers, at ten and they had their own radio show on KFFA in Helena, Arkansas. After army service he found success as a rock 'n' roll star, taking his stage name from two local towns: Conway, Arkansas and Twitty, Texas. The highspot of his rock career came in 1958 with the million-selling success of 'It's Only Make Believe', which he also wrote. Seven years later he returned to making country music, his first love, and began a remarkable run of hits, with over 40 singles topping the country charts, several as part of the award-winning duo with Loretta Lynn. A successful country performer and businessman, Conway owns several music publishing companies, half of United Talent (Loretta is joint owner), and is a major stockholder of the Nashville Sounds baseball team.

2nd SEPTEMBER

1912 Johnnie Lee Wills born in Texas. Younger brother of Bob Wills, he played banjo with the Texas Playboys until 1940, then led his own

band, Johnnie Lee Wills And His Boys, switching to the traditional family instrument, the fiddle. In 1943 Bob and his band relocated to California and Johnnie took over responsibility for Bob's daily radio show, dances at Cain's Ballroom and the annual Tulsa rodeo. The radio show continued until the late fifties and he disbanded his group in the early sixties. Johnnie continued to live in Tulsa, running a western wear store but, with the revival of interest in western swing, began making appearances in local clubs, then in 1978 cut a new record with members of the old band including fiddler Johnny Gimble.

1980 Bill Boling killed in a car accident. He was a promising songwriter and guitarist with Johnny Rodriguez's band and composed hits including 'Fools For Each Other' and 'Mexico Holiday'.

3rd SEPTEMBER

1925 Hank Thompson (Henry William Thompson), leading western swing bandleader of the fifties, born in Waco, Texas. He was a country enthusiast as a child, the harmonica was his first instrument and he made his professional debut as "Hank The Hired Hand" on a local radio show while still a schoolboy. After war service he returned to radio in Waco and led the Brazo Valley Boys. They became very popular in Texas and recorded for Globe. In 1948 Tex Ritter introduced Hank to Capitol; they signed him and he began making best-selling records immediately, notching up 34 chart entries for the label, including 'Wild Side Of Life', 'Waiting In The Lobby Of Your Heart' and 'Rub-A-Dub-Dub'. There were more successes when he switched to Warner Brothers, then ABC/Dot and MCA. The entry of 'Tony's Tank-Up, Drive-In Cafe' into the country charts in February 1980 meant he'd scored hits in five decades.

1933 Tompall Glaser, eldest and best known of the Glaser Brothers, born in Spaulding, Nebraska. His father was a progressive minded farmer who encouraged the Glaser boys to develop their musical gifts. They performed extensively at country fairs and festivals and in small halls and debuted nationally on the popular "Arthur Godfrey Talent Scouts" TV show. The brothers travelled to Nashville in 1957 and managed to persuade Marty Robbins that they were worth supporting; he signed them to his Robbins label and used them as harmony singers for his records,

including the hit version of 'El Paso'. Tompall and the Glasers were signed to Decca in 1959 and had some moderately successful singles, also working on numerous recording sessions and touring with big names like Johnny Cash. Their fortunes improved when they switched labels to MGM; hits included 'California Girl' and 'Ain't It All Worth Living'. They set up the Glaser Studios in Nashville in 1969; this became a focal point for the new breed of singer-songwriters like Kris Kristofferson, Guy Clark and Billy Joe Shaver. Tompall split from his brothers in 1973 and his solo career was boosted when some of his material was featured on the million-selling *Wanted: The Outlaws* compilation alongside Waylon and Willie. Tompall and the Glasers reformed at the start of the eighties and scored their biggest hit, a new version of Kristofferson's 'Lovin' Her Was Easier', in July 1981.

4th SEPTEMBER

19?? Shot Jackson, dobro player and pedal-steel guitarist, born in Wilmington, North Carolina. Shot was one of the first musicians to move to a Nashville base, in 1943. He's worked with the Bailes Brothers, Johnny and Jack and was then a member of Roy Acuff's Smokey Mountain Boys. He's owner of the Sho-Bud Guitar Company Inc. and is a regular performer on the Opry and the syndicated "Hee-Haw" TV show.

1942 Country-rocker Gene Parsons, drummer and vocalist with Nashville West, The Byrds and a late version of the Flying Burrito Brothers, born in Los Angeles, California.

5th SEPTEMBER

1939 John Stewart born in San Diego, California. He is an influential singer/writer who's drawn on country, folk and rock; he was a member of the Kingston Trio, then made a series of highly praised solo LPs including *California Bloodlines,* recorded in Nashville with Nick Venet in 1969, which was a pioneering combination of country and rock. John's best known songs include 'July You're A Woman' and 'Daydream Believer'.

1980 Johnny Lee top of the country charts with 'Lookin' For Love', from the *Urban Cowboy* soundtrack LP, also number one on the album chart. After several years working at Gilley's club in Pasadena, Johnny was suddenly an "over-night sensation". The record stayed at the top of the country singles list for three weeks and was also very successful in the pop charts.

6th SEPTEMBER

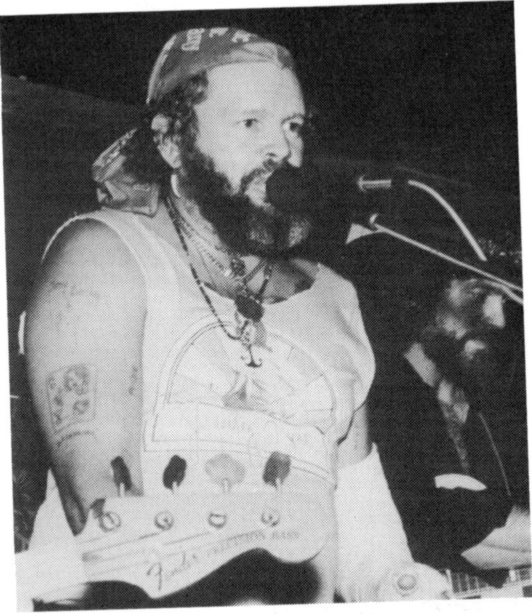

1939 David Allan Coe born in Akron, Ohio. He was an "unmanageable child" and at nine was packed off to reform school by his parents. Later he served time in prison. "For about twenty years," Coe recalls, "I wasn't on the streets for more than sixty days at a time that I can remember". Released from the Ohio State Correction Facility in 1967, he headed for Nashville, determined to be a star. He called himself the Mysterious Rhinestone Cowboy, dressed in a black costume with hat and mask and drove around in a hearse. Despite (or because of) this attention-grabbing act, he had to wait several years for success, which came first as a songwriter, with compositions like 'Would You Lay With Me In A Field Of Stone' for Tanya Tucker, and then through his own unconventional recordings for CBS. His career as a performer has probably suffered because of his dark past and extraordinary self-publicity techniques, but since dropping the Mysterious Rhinestone Cowboy image in July 1978, each of his records has outsold the last, and, while he's yet to have a major hit in his own right, total sales are impressive.

1944 Mel McDaniel, singer and songwriter, born in Checotah, Oklahoma. He started out working in bands in the Tulsa area, then came to Nashville in 1969. Like so many other aspiring writers and singers who arrive in Music City with dreams of landing a recording contract, McDaniel found it wasn't easy getting in front doors and past secretaries. "I pumped gas out at the airport and my brothers sent twenty dollars a week for groceries", says Mel when asked how he survived. After two years he went to Alaska and found steady work in Anchorage clubs. He made occasional return visits to Nashville and got his "lucky break" in the mid-seventies when he was hired to sing on demo records for a publishing company. His singing talents were recognised, he signed to Capitol and had several hits, including 'Countryfied', 'Have A Dream On Me' and 'Soul Of A Honky-Tonk Woman'.

1980 Sylvia, one of the new country stars of the eighties, entered the charts with 'Tumbleweed', her first big hit. Sylvia Kirby Allen was born in Kokomo, Indiana in 1957. She was a country enthusiast as a child and Patsy Cline (who died when she was six) was her idol. "I led a pretty sheltered life. I never even got asked out", she recalls, "music was my escape. I would practise performing in front of a mirror using a deodorant bottle for a microphone". She moved to Nashville in 1976 with big ambitions but little in the way of musical experience; her demo tape featured songs performed acapella, because she didn't know any musicians. She worked as secretary for producer Tom Collins, then auditioned for Dave and Sugar, was runner-up and subsequently signed to RCA as solo artist. Tom Collins produced her, and after some small hits Sylvia broke through with 'Tumbleweed' followed by 'The Matador' and then 'Drifter', her first number one.

7th SEPTEMBER

1935 Buddy Holly (Charles Hardin Holley) born in Lubbock, Texas. A rock 'n' roll star with roots deep in country music, he never scored a country hit though he has proved to be an enormous influence on many up-and-coming musicians, including the young Waylon Jennings, whose first record he produced. Buddy showed an early interest in music and teamed up with schoolfriend Bob Montgomery as a duo. They had their own radio show over KDAV in Lubbock from late 1953 playing "western and bop". Buddy and Bob split in 1955 and Holly formed a band that included Sonny Curtis, now a country singer, and drummer Jerry Allison. With help from Nashville agent Jim Denny, Buddy was signed to Decca Records (who mis-spelled his name "Holly" on the contract) and began recording for them in early 1956. Decca were unsure whether he was a country singer or a rock 'n' roller and failed to promote him successfully as either. After several frustrating recording sessions, Holly started again and worked with producer Norman Petty in Clovis, New Mexico. In 1957, with his band now dubbed The Crickets, he recorded the version of 'That'll Be The Day' which was his first hit, on Coral. In the next 18 months he'd recorded another eight Top Ten pop hits; then, at the height of fame, he was killed in a 'plane crash. Holly's records continue to be very popular in England: in the late seventies, 20 years after his death, a *Greatest Hits* LP topped the charts. A Buddy Holly Week is held each year on the anniversary of his death.

1955 Elvis Presley top of the country charts with 'Mystery Train'/'I Forgot To Remember To Forget', his most successful release on Sun Records. A month later a national convention of country music disc jockeys in Nashville voted him Most Promising Newcomer of the Year.

8th SEPTEMBER

1897 Jimmie Rodgers (James Charles Rodgers), the most revered figure in country music history, born near Meridian, Mississippi. He was frequently sick as a child; his mother had died of tuberculosis when he was four and he seems to have inherited it. Jimmie worked for 14 years on the railroads: various jobs from water carrying to brakeman, and invariably carried a battered string banjo or guitar with him which he used to entertain his fellow workers. Ill health forced him to quit the railroads in the mid-twenties and he tried earning a living as an entertainer, including work as a black-face minstrel in a tent show. He met with mixed fortunes and was at a low ebb (his group the Tenneva Ramblers having just walked out on him) when he recorded for Ralph Peer in Bristol in August 1927. But within days of the release of his first record, later that year, he was a star—he played to packed houses wherever he went and his records sold millions of copies. His career was to be short; he died of TB in 1933, leaving behind a musical legacy of 100 songs that would influence generations of up-and-coming singers. When the Country Music Hall of Fame was instigated in 1961 he was the obvious choice as first person to be honoured.

1903 Milton Brown born in Stephenville, Texas. He is generally credited as co-founder of western swing with Bob Wills; they worked together in the Fort Worth-based Aladdin Laddies in 1931, then formed separate bands and were keen rivals. Milton's Musical Brownies could have been as successful as Bob Wills and his Texas Playboys, but Brown was seriously injured in a car accident in 1935 and died after complications.

1929 Legendary country songwriter Harlan Howard born in Harlan County, Kentucky. Brought up in Detroit, young Harlan loved listening to country music on the radio and started writing songs while listening to his hero Ernest Tubb. He tried to copy down the words as Tubb sang them, and when he couldn't catch them all, he made up his own. Based in Los Angeles in the fifties, he had the first of several big hits as a writer, including 'Heartaches By The Number' a country success for Ray Price and a pop smash for Guy Mitchell. He moved to Nashville in the sixties and wrote hundreds of great songs, including 'I Fall To Pieces', 'No Charge' and 'Pick Me Up On Your Way Down'.

1932 Patsy Cline (Virginia Patterson Hensley) born in Winchester, Virginia. Her first public performance was at age four as a tap dancer in a talent show. She had obvious talent as a singer, and impressed all who heard her during school years, including singer Wally Fowler, who invited her to do a guest slot on the Grand Ole Opry. Her "big break" came in 1957 when she appeared on the "Arthur Godfrey Talent Scouts" TV show and was an easy winner with 'Walkin' After Midnight'. The song became her first hit for Decca and established her as a country star. In the early sixties she was posing a serious threat to Kitty Wells for the Queen of Country Music title, and scored huge hits with 'Crazy', 'I Fall To Pieces' and 'She's Got You'. Then tragedy struck and a brilliant career was cut short when Patsy was killed in a 'plane crash on March 5, 1963.

9th SEPTEMBER

1947 Freddy Weller born in Atlanta, Georgia. He was in the pop band Paul Revere and the Raiders, wrote hits like 'Dizzy' with Tommy Roe and then began a successful career as country singer in 1969. Freddy's hits include versions of 'The Games People Play', 'Down In The Boondocks' and 'Promised Land'.

1972 Faron Young had a surprise Top Five pop success in the British charts with 'Four In The Morning', an American country number one from the previous year. It was his only UK hit and sold half a million copies.

10th SEPTEMBER

1937 Tommy Overstreet born in Oklahoma City, Oklahoma. His cousin, Gene Austin, made successful pop records in the thirties and Tommy toured with him after graduating from university. He moved to Nashville in 1967 and two years later joined Dot Records as office manager and recording artist. Overstreet had a string of chart successes in the seventies, including 'Gwen (Congratulations)', 'Annie (Don't Go Running)' and '(Jeannie Marie) You Were A Lady'.

1960 Ferlin Husky's classic 'Wings Of A Dove' debuted on the country charts. It became one of the biggest hits of the year.

1961 'Walk On By', Leroy Van Dyke's biggest hit, entered the country best-seller list. It rose to number one, stayed in the charts for 37 weeks and was also a Top Five pop hit in the US and UK.

1966 Texan Nat Stuckey made his chart debut with 'Sweet Thang', on the Paula label.

11th SEPTEMBER

1902 Jimmie Davis, singer, songwriter and Governor of Louisiana (twice), born in Quitman, Louisiana. Country music was an important part of his life from childhood but it remained no more than a hobby for many years. After graduating from university he became a history professor, but sang at frequent church and social functions. In the thirties his reputation as a gospel and country singer was spreading and he made several tours, but continued to be employed by the State of Louisiana, working as public service commissioner and criminal court clerk. In the forties he had a major success as a songwriter when Gene Autry recorded 'You Are My Sunshine' and 'It Makes No Difference To Me'. He also served his first term as Governor of Tennessee and made records for RCA Victor. In the fifties and sixties his recording career blossomed, though he had only one *bona fide* hit, 'Where The Old River Flows', in 1962, during his second term at the Governor's residence. Jimmie was elected to the Country Music Hall of Fame in 1972.

1969 Leon Payne, Texan singer who came to prominence with Bob Wills and the Texas Playboys, and scored a big hit with 'I Love You Because', died.

12th SEPTEMBER

1909 Kenneth Threadgill, "The Father of Austin Country Music", born. A club owner and singer, strongly influenced by Jimmie Rodgers, Kenneth got the first beer licence in Travis County, Texas after prohibition finished in 1932; he has been operating honky-tonks ever since. He gave much needed help and encouragement to several generations of young Texas musicians, including Janis Joplin, who left Austin in the late sixties and became a rock star. Threadgill made a cameo appearance in the Willie Nelson film *Honeysuckle Rose* in 1980.

1931 George Jones, a favourite country performer with other singers, born near Saratoga, Texas. "The spiritual heir of Hank Williams" —both have powerful and emotive vocal qualities and led reckless and unpredictable lives — George recalled that, as a child, "I just had no interest in nothing but country music". His musical career began as soon as he left school, in 1947, playing guitar with a duo called Eddie and Pearl. After a spell in the Army he did "nickel and dime" gigs in East Texas honky-tonks, then signed to Pappy Daily's newly formed Starday label in 1952. He made several records but his career didn't take off until three years later when 'Why Baby Why' made the country Top Five. Jones has charted every year since and has scored over 100 hits (including duets) for half a dozen different labels, including Mercury, RCA and Epic. He became a regular on the Louisiana Hayride in 1955, leaving after a year to join the Grand Ole Opry. His popularity led to a hectic touring schedule, which caused the beginnings of the drinking problems and stage fright that have dogged his career since. He married singer Tammy Wynette in 1969 and producer Billy Sherrill teamed them on record. They were country music's favourite couple, but the marriage hit problems and after numerous separations they divorced in 1975. The years that followed marked a particular turmoil for George—his drinking and underlying emotional problems increased, he was a frequent "no show" and went deeply into debt. In late 1979, having gone as far as he could on a downhill swing, he filed for bankruptcy, then volunteered for hospitalisation for treatment of alcoholism, beginning a long rehabilitation process. His friends rallied round; and back in the recording studio he cut *I Am What I Am*, which became his first gold album and included the multi-award winner, 'He Stopped Loving Her Today'.

13th SEPTEMBER

1911 Bill Monroe (William Smith Monroe), "the father of bluegrass", born on a farm in Rosine, Kentucky. His mother, Melissa, and Uncle "Pen" Vandiver were accomplished fiddlers and Bill inherited his love of traditional music from them. As a teenager he played at square dances with his uncle and a black guitarist named Arnold Shultz, whose bluesy style proved to be an important influence on his music. He teamed up with elder brothers Birch and Charlie in the late twenties and they built up a strong following through radio broadcasts as the Monroe Brothers. Charlie and Bill recorded for RCA in 1936 but split up two years later. Bill formed a band, the Blue Grass Boys, and began developing a new style, which he introduced on the Opry in 1939. "Bluegrass is a music that I set out to have as my own", Monroe explained, "I never wanted to be known for copying any man. I wanted a music that had never been played before".Bluegrass evolved over the years as Bill perfected his mandolin style and other musicians made their contributions, most notably with Earl Scruggs' addition of the banjo in 1946. Monroe has been performing with the Blue Grass Boys for over 40 years; it is a line-up that has changed many times and been something of a school for up-and-coming musicians. Bluegrass virtuosos who've passed through his care include Lester Flatt, Earl Scruggs, Vassar Clements, Chubby Wise, Cedric Rainwater, Byron Berline and Peter Rowan. Among the many Bill Monroe classic songs are the autobiographical 'Uncle Pen', 'Blue Moon Of Kentucky', 'I Hear A Sweet Voice Calling' and 'Along About Daybreak'.

1969 Barbara Mandrell made her chart debut with 'I've Been Loving You Too Long', the first in a series of cover versions of rhythm and blues hits. Ten years later she was at the very top of the country music league, and had major successes including the song 'I Was Country When Country Wasn't Cool'.

14th SEPTEMBER

1946 Hank and Audrey Williams travelled by Greyhound bus from Montgomery to Nashville in the hope of auditioning for Fred Rose of Acuff-Rose publishing. They found Fred at the WSM building, playing ping-pong with his son Wesley. "We were on our last game," Wesley told Hank's biographer, Roger Williams, "when a tall, skinny, sharp-featured kid came in with a blond haired woman. They looked like average country folks. The woman said, 'My husband would like to sing you some songs'. It isn't normally done that way. I mean, you don't just walk in cold and say, 'Let me sing you a song'." But the Williams' unconventional technique worked, Fred and Wesley did listen and were impressed by the six songs which included Hank's compositions 'When God Comes And Gathers His Jewels', 'Six More Miles To The Graveyard' and 'My Love For You (Has Turned To Hate)'. Fred Rose signed him to a publishing contract, thinking at the time that his songs would be suitable for singer Molly O'Day. It was undoubtedly the most important meeting in Hank Williams' life, leading to success as writer and as recording artist for MGM.

1948 Vernon Dalhart, who made the first million-selling country record, 'The Prisoner's Song'/'The Wreck Of The Old '97' in 1924 died at Bridgeport Hospital, Bridgeport, Connecticut. Demand for his records had continued during the Depression years, though few companies wanted him to cut new material. Apart from a one-off session in 1938, his recording career had effectively ended in 1933. He spent his latter years teaching "voice placement" and working as an hotel clerk. Dalhart was elected to the Country Music Hall of Fame in 1981.

15th SEPTEMBER

1903 Roy Acuff, "the King of Country Music", born on a farm in Maynardsville, Tennessee. His father was a farmer, lawyer, Baptist minister and sometime fiddle player. As a youngster, Roy sang and played the fiddle, but his first love was sport. The New York Yankees recognized

his baseball talents and invited him to a training camp in Florida, but while on a fishing trip there he suffered severe sunstroke and was ill for a long time. This effectively ended his sporting career. While convalescing he decided to become an entertainer; he began improving his fiddle playing and mastered the art of the yo-yo, which became an Acuff trademark. He joined a medicine show in 1932, then formed a band—the Crazy Tennesseans and was featured on Knoxville radio shows. He set his sights on the Grand Ole Opry and made his debut there in 1938. The performance was extremely well received and he became a regular, starting an association with the famous radio show that would tie up most of his Friday and Saturday evenings for over 40 years. Acuff's arrival marked a significant turning point in the history of the Opry; the string bands who'd previously held sway were replaced in popularity by singing stars of whom Roy, supported by the renamed Smokey Mountain Boys, was the first. His appearance in the 1940 film 'Grand Ole Opry' helped establish him as central figure and most important star of the show. His association with Fred Rose in 1942 to form Nashville's first publishing house, Acuff-Rose, helped him become one of the wealthiest men in country music. Roy's recording career has spanned six decades and includes best-selling versions of 'Great Speckled Bird', 'Wreck On The Highway' and 'Fireball Mail'. He became the first living person to be elected to the Country Music Hall of Fame, in 1962.

1957 Patsy Cline married Charlie Dick (her second husband) at Winchester, Virginia.

1973 Billy Joe Shaver made his debut on the country charts as a performer, with 'Georgia On A Fast Train'. He's best known as a songwriter, notable for *Honky Tonk Heroes*—an album's worth of his songs that were recorded by Waylon Jennings. Billy Joe was born in Corsicana, Texas

in 1941 and started writing by unconsciously filling in the words to songs on the radio whose words he didn't understand. He tried various jobs; he was a bronc buster, worked at a sawmill (where he lost four fingers in an accident) and did a stretch in the Navy. He tried several times to enter the music business, making frequent trips to Nashville, and finally had a lucky break when he met Bobby Bare, who signed him to a publishing contract. Billy Joe has had considerable success as a writer, composing hits like 'I'm Just An Old Chunk Of Coal' and 'Old Five And Dimers Like Me', though his records, for Monument, Capricorn and, most recently, CBS, have brought critical acclaim but generally disappointing sales.

16th SEPTEMBER

1946 Bill Monroe and the Blue Grass Boys, including Earl Scruggs on banjo, recorded 'Will You Be Lovin' Another Man', which some people say marked the birth of bluegrass. Others will argue that the birth was much earlier: 1939, when Bill first worked out the arrangement for 'New Muleskinner Blues', or 1936 when Bill and Charlie Monroe recorded 'What Would You Give In Exchange For Your Soul', while some recall seeing a sign on Bill's old mandolin case that read, "Original bluegrass music since 1927". What is incontestable is that the date marked the first occasion Bill recorded with Earl Scruggs and is therefore the first time that the banjo was used on a bluegrass recording in a position of prominence. The previous banjoist with the Blue Grass Boys, David "Stringbean" Akeman, was only used by Monroe to supply rhythm.

19?? David Bellamy, songwriter and youngest of the two singing Bellamy Brothers, born in North Florida. They began their harmony singing at church: "It was really a rural setting," recalled David. "It wouldn't be anything for the preacher to be preachin' and for a horse to come and stick his head in the window. But we sang every Sunday". They played in local groups but couldn't get any record companies interested in them until one of David's songs, 'Spiders And Snakes', became a million-selling hit for Jim Stafford. Moving to Los Angeles, they signed to Warner Brothers and had a huge country-rock hit with 'Let Your Love Flow'. They returned to Florida in 1978 and their material became more country-orientated, leading to major hits like 'If I Said You Had A Beautiful Body Would You Hold It Against Me', 'Sugar Daddy' and 'Dancing Cowboys'.

1949 Hank Locklin entered the charts with the first hit in his long career, 'The Same Sweet Girl' on the Four Star label.

17th SEPTEMBER

1923 Hank Williams (Hiram King Williams) born on a farm in Georgiana, Alabama. Acknowledged today as the man who provided the key for country music to develop and expand beyond the rural areas of the American South, Hank Williams was a superb songwriter and a classic performer. His influence and importance in country music is equalled only by Jimmie Rodgers —another artist whose life was tragically short and frequently bleak and depressing. Hank was poorly educated, had a limited vocabulary and couldn't read or write, but showed an early gift for music which his mother (who was a church organist) noticed and encouraged; she gave him a guitar when he was eight. Hank became an accomplished guitarist before his teens and by 14 was leading his own band, the Drifting Cowboys, who were featured on WSFA for a decade. His wife, Audrey, encouraged his music making with as much enthusiasm and determination as his mother, travelling with him to Nashville, where he auditioned for Fred Rose the publisher. Hank made a few recordings for the small Sterling label, then Rose got him a contract with MGM, helped him with songwriting and produced his records. Williams was featured on the Louisiana Hayride in 1948, then moved to the Opry in 1949. He was a sensation, and the song that won him six encores, 'Lovesick Blues', became his first country hit. Hank dominated the country charts for the next five years with 27 hits, mostly self-penned, deceptively simple and direct classics, which have influenced generations of songwriters. But his dependence on alcohol and pills made him unreliable, frequently difficult to work with and certainly shortened his life. He died in 1953, aged just 29.

1931 The world's first $33\frac{1}{3}$ rpm record demonstrated by RCA in New York City. It was over 25 years before they were commercially produced in large numbers.

18th SEPTEMBER

1941 Priscilla Mitchell born in Marietta, Georgia. She made her first radio appearance at the age of four, singing Al Dexter's hit, 'Pistol Packin' Mama', and made her recording debut as a female rock 'n' roller named Sadina. In the sixties she became a country singer, for a while maintaining two musical identities. She had solo successes but her biggest hit was the chart-topping duet with Roy Drusky in 1965, 'Yes, Mr Peters'.

1947 The first country music show to be held at New York's Carnegie Hall. Ernest Tubb topped a bill that also included George D. Hay "The Solemn Old Judge" of the Opry, Minnie Pearl, Rosalie Allen and the Short Brothers. It took another 30 years before country music was considered "acceptable" by a significant number of New Yorkers and for there to be regular country shows and permanent country nightspots.

19th SEPTEMBER

1945 David Bromberg born in Tarrytown, New York. A talented multi-instrumentalist whose repertoire ranges through country, bluegrass, folk, jazz and blues, David's popularity is such that he can afford a top-notch "folk orchestra" of quality musicians to tour and record with him.

1968 Red Foley, Grand Ole Opry favourite and originator of the Renfro Valley Barn Dance and The Ozark Jubilee, died in Fort Wayne, Indiana.

1970 Crystal Gayle's chart debut with 'I've Cried (The Blue Right Out Of My Eyes)', a song written for her by big sister Loretta Lynn.

1973 Gram Parsons, country-rock pioneer, died from a heart attack in a motel room at the

Joshua Tree Inn, California, soon after completing his *Grievous Angel* album. He was just 26.

1981 Lee Greenwood made his chart debut with 'It Turns Me Inside Out', his very first country recording. He was born in Los Angeles, raised in Sacramento and began playing saxophone and piano while a child. In his teens he worked in a variety of musical line-ups, including a Dixieland jazz band at Disneyland! Lee's breakthrough into country music came first as a songwriter, Dottie West, T. G. Sheppard and the duet team of Mel Tillis and Nancy Sinatra picking up on his material.

20th SEPTEMBER

1895 Bob Miller, one of the first country music songwriters, born. Most of the early performers either drew on traditional material or wrote their own songs; Bob was one of the few who wrote for other people. He composed several "event" songs, including 'The Life Of Jimmie Rodgers', and 'The Death Of Jimmie Rodgers', which were recorded with success by Gene Autry.

193? Pearl Butler (Pearl Dee Jones) born in Nashville, Tennessee. A country fan and talented amateur singer, Pearl married Carl Butler who was a successful songwriter and rising country star. In 1962 she sang harmony vocals on his 'Don't Let Me Cross Over' and the record was a Top Ten hit. They subsequently worked as a husband and wife duo, had more hits and were regulars on the Grand Ole Opry.

21st SEPTEMBER

1912 Ted Daffan born in Houston, Texas. He worked in several Houston bands, then wrote 'Truck Drivers Blues' (probably the first truck driving song), which was a big hit in 1939 for

both Moon Mullican and Cliff Bruner. This led to Art Satherley signing Ted Daffan and his Texans to a Columbia recording contract. They subsequently had best-selling records, including 'Worried Man' and 'Born To Lose'.

1941 Dickey Lee (Dickey Lipscombe) born in Memphis, Tennessee. He's had success as a pop singer, most notably with the million-selling 'Patches' in 1962, with country hits, including '9,999,999 Tears' and also as a songwriter—Glen Campbell, Don Williams, Brenda Lee and others have recorded his compositions.

1952 Kenny Starr born in Topeka, Kansas. He began singing professionally at the age of five, had his first band at nine and then won a talent contest when he was 16 which led to work with Loretta Lynn and Conway Twitty. Loretta was so taken with the young man's talents that she helped him get a contract with MCA, where he had several hits including 'Blind Man In The Bleachers' and 'Me And The Elephant'.

22nd SEPTEMBER

1922 Old-timey musician Riley Puckett made his radio debut on WSB Atlanta, with Clayton McMichen's Hometown Boys. Puckett, a versatile singer and guitarist, was an immediate favourite with listeners.

1956 Debbie Boone born in Hackensack, New Jersey. The daughter of fifties pop idol, Pat

Boone, she sang back-up vocals behind her father in the early seventies, as part of the Boone Girls with her sisters and mother, Shirley Foley, then branched out on her own and had the biggest-selling pop record of the decade, 'You Light Up My Life', before beginning a run of country hits. Debbie is married to Gabriel Ferrer, son of Jose Ferrer and Rosemary Clooney.

1958 Private Elvis Presley left America for Europe on board the troop ship USS General Randall. The press conference before his departure was recorded and issued as an EP, titled *Elvis Sails*.

1979 The successful combination of honky-tonk stars Moe Bandy and Joe Stampley topped the country charts with 'Just Good Ol' Boys'.

23rd SEPTEMBER

1930 Ray Charles (Ray Charles Robinson) born in Albany, Georgia, a brilliant black musician who blended gospel and blues with great success in the fifties and influenced generations of rock and soul artists. He upset many of his fans in 1962 with a dramatic change of style—he released *Modern Sounds Of Country And Western*, a very commercial, middle-of-the-road collection of country classics, including the best selling single, 'I Can't Stop Loving You'. It subsequently became one of the first albums featuring country songs to sell a million copies.

1935 Bob Wills and his Texas Playboys travelled from their base in Tulsa, Oklahoma to Dallas, Texas to record for Columbia. It was the first in a series of sessions over a 12 year period which produced some of the finest examples of western swing, the combination of country, jazz and blues that Wills and his musicians pioneered and developed. The line-up of the Texas Playboys changed frequently over the years but the core remained much the same, with the significant addition of guitarist Eldon Shamblin. Among the tunes recorded at the Dallas session and produced by Arthur E. Satherley were 'Sittin' On Top Of The World', 'Osage Stomp' and 'Mexicali Rose'. The key musicians, besides Wills on fiddle, were Jesse Ashlock, fiddle; Art Haines, fiddle and trombone; Leon McAuliffe, steel guitar; Sleepy Johnson, guitar and bass; Sonny Lansford, bass; Johnnie Lee Wills, banjo; "Zeb" McNally, saxophone; "Smokey" Dacus, drums; Tommy Duncan, vocals and Al Stricklin, piano.

24th SEPTEMBER

1966 'Distant Drums' by Jim Reeves started a month-long stay at the top of the British pop charts. The song had been specially written for Reeves by Cindy Walker, but though Jim loved it, his producer at RCA, Chet Atkins, didn't think the time was right to record and release it. The singer nevertheless made a demo tape of the song, which he gave to Cindy. After Jim's untimely death, his widow Mary Reeves took the tape to Chet Atkins, who added instrumentation and backing vocals.

1973 'Coal Miner's Daughter', written and recorded by Loretta Lynn, released on Decca. "This is the true story of my early life in Butcher Holler, Kentucky," said Loretta. "My daddy did work in the coal mines and my mamma did wash on the scrub board. The old house is still standing and I go back to see it every now and then."

25th SEPTEMBER

1933 Ian Tyson born in British Columbia, Canada. An authentic singing cowboy—he owns a ranch in Alberta and records for Boot—Ian is best known for his role in the folk duo Ian and Sylvia, and as writer of classics like 'Four Strong Winds', 'Someday Soon' and 'Summer Wages'. He began recording country-oriented material in the early seventies and hosted a long-running Canadian TV series that gave early exposure to the likes of Willie Nelson and Johnny Rodriguez.

1934 Royce Kendall born in St Louis, Missouri. He began singing country songs as a boy, on Arkansas radio stations with his brother Floyce. After a spell in the Army he ran a barbershop, though music continued to be very important to him and he frequently sang with his daughter Jeannie. When she was 15 they travelled to Nashville and made a custom recording. A Music City producer heard the record, liked it, and signed them up. Their first commercial recording, a country version of John Denver's 'Leaving On A Jet Plane' was a small hit in 1970. They subsequently recorded for various labels, then made an album for Ovation which included 'Heaven's Just A Sin Away'. The song became a huge hit for them, led to the CMA 'Single of the Year' award in 1978 and established them as one of the leading country duos.

1954 Elvis Presley made his one and only appearance on the Grand Ole Opry. He sang 'That's All Right' and 'Blue Moon Of Kentucky'. He didn't receive a very warm reception from the crowd and Opry talent co-ordinator Jim Denny suggested that he go back to driving trucks!

1965 The chart debut of the Statler Brothers with 'Flowers On The Wall', which had crossover success on the pop charts. It remains their biggest hit.

Statler Brothers

1975 Bill Monroe's brother Charlie died of cancer. He was 72.

26th SEPTEMBER

1925 Marty Robbins born in Glendale, Arizona. His earliest recollections of music are centred around his father, who played the harmonica, and his grandfather (once a travelling medicine man) who told stories of the old West and taught him cowboy songs. Marty began singing professionally in Phoenix clubs, then graduated to regular work on his local radio and TV station KPHO. Country star Little Jimmy Dickens appeared on a show with Robbins and was so impressed by the youngster's talent and vast repertoire of cowboy songs that he advised his record company, Columbia, to sign Marty. They wisely did as suggested and a long, hit-making career with the label began soon afterwards, in the spring of 1953, with 'I'll Go On Alone'.

Marty's subsequent hits included some pop and country successes like 'White Sports Coat', 'Devil Woman' and his best known recording, 'El Paso' — which became the first country song to win a Grammy Award. An Opry star since the fifties, Marty Robbins has the unique distinction of being the last person to perform at the Opry's former home, the Ryman Auditorium, and the first to play on the stage of the new home at Opryland.

1941 David Frizzell, young brother of the legendary Lefty Frizzell and male half of the successful Frizzell and West duo, born in Texas. David's long career in music began as a teenager when he toured with his famous brother. He had his first record contract in the early sixties, cutting country and rockabilly for Columbia, then had his first taste of chart success in 1970 with 'LA International Airport'. A popular performer at the Golden Nugget in Las Vegas, he also worked for a time with Buck Owens, then teamed up with Dottie West's daughter Shelly and cut 'You're The Reason God Made Oklahoma', which was rejected by every major record company after its intended distributor closed down. Producer Snuff Garrett played the song to Clint Eastwood who asked for it to be used in the movie *Any Which Way You Can.* Once the song was released on the Warner Brothers soundtrack LP, DJ demand prompted its release as a single and "the song nobody wanted" became a smash hit.

1947 Lynn Anderson born in Grand Forks, North Dakota, the daughter of singer and writer Liz Anderson. Her recording career began with the Chart label, for whom she cut over 100 songs and had several hits. Switching to CBS, Lynn scored a huge international hit with 'Rose Garden' in 1970.

1948 Olivia Newton-John, one of the most successful female singers in pop history, born in Cambridge, England. She spent her formative years in Australia, where her family moved when she was young. Olivia had great success in the country market during the first half of the seventies; she had several hits including 'Let Me Be There' and 'If You Love Me (Let Me Know)', and won the CMA "Best Female Vocalist" award in 1974, which caused a storm of protest from several Nashville establishment figures who argued that she was not a genuine country singer.

1955 Carlene Carter, third-generation member from the illustrious Carter Family, born in Tennessee, the daughter of June Carter and Carl Smith. She made her debut performance at five, singing 'Charlie Brown' on her mother's shows. In 1978 she launched a solo career, making the first of several well-received rock albums that had strong country influences. Carlene is married to British musician Nick Lowe and lives in London.

27th SEPTEMBER

1903 The Southern Railroad's mail train crashed, killing engineer Joseph A. Brody and 12 others. The disaster inspired 'The Wreck Of The Old '97', which was featured on the first big-selling country record, by Vernon Dalhart.

1964 Connie Smith made her debut on the charts with 'Once A Day' on RCA. The song had been written by Bill Anderson, the singer who first recognised her potential at an amateur talent contest in Columbus, Ohio.

1976 Hondo Crouch — clown, poet, imagineer, entertainer and artist, also owner, sheriff, chief of police and city manager of the tiny town of Luckenbach, Texas, died. Among the many tributes, one from Willie Nelson, which appeared in the *Luckenbach Monthly Moon*—"Hondo Crouch wasn't just a funny, friendly guy. He was a poet and a good one. His poetry came hard like all good poems do—like the crops in the Hill Country that somehow grow in spite of the cold, the hot sun and the rocks".

28th SEPTEMBER

1926 Humorist Jerry Clower born in Liberty, Mississippi. For 18 years he was employed by a manufacturer of chemical plant foods, where he rose to the position of Director of Field Services. To improve sales he began telling country stories; one about a racoon hunt was so well received that his friends encouraged him to make a record. With the release of *Jerry Clower From Yazoo City, Mississippi, Talkin'* his fame spread rapidly. He's now made several successful albums for MCA, has been voted "Country Comic of the Year" at least eight times, and is a popular TV personality.

1928 The first recording session in Nashville, Tennessee. Victor hired the YMCA hall in the city for a series of recordings that continued until October 6. The Brinkley Brothers with Jack Jackson, and Warmack's Gully Jumpers were recorded on Friday September 28, but the sessions were unsuccessful and the bands returned on the following Monday to repeat their performances. Grand Ole Opry favourites, Deford Bailey, Theron Hale and his Daughters and the Crook Brothers were at later sessions. According to historian Charles Wolfe, they were not particularly successful, only 36 of the 69 sides recorded were released (a very low figure compared to sessions held in Atlanta) and it was a long time before another company came to Nashville to record.

1930 Tommy Collins, one of the musicians who helped put the Californian town of Bakersfield on the country map, born in Oklahoma City, Oklahoma. He had several hits in the mid-fifties, including 'You Better Not Do That', was absent from the charts for a decade, then returned in 1966 with 'If You Can't Bite, Don't Growl' and a second string of hits. He was an early supporter of Merle Haggard, who later wrote a song about him, called 'Leonard', which was a successful country single in 1981.

29th SEPTEMBER

1907 Gene Autry, the most popular singing cowboy of them all, born in Tioga Springs, Texas.

His mother taught him to play the guitar and he began performing while still at high school, as a member of the Fields Brothers Marvelous Medicine Show. After a period working as a telegraph operator, he joined KVOO in Tulsa as "Oklahoma's Singing Cowboy". He made some of the first cowboy song recordings in 1930, including the self-penned best-seller 'Silver Haired Daddy Of Mine' and had his own show on the powerful WLS station in Chicago. Gene moved to California in 1934 and became a film star, eventually appearing in over 100 films as a singing cowboy. He had several million selling records, including 'Rudolf The Red Nosed Reindeer' and 'Here Comes Santa Claus'. His California-based radio show Melody Ranch ran for 17 years—a successful mixture of music, comedy and a playlet, featuring Autry and Champion, his famous horse. Champion went along to many of Gene's live shows, performing tricks between the musical items.

1935 "The Killer", Jerry Lee Lewis, born in Ferriday, Louisiana. He followed Elvis Presley's path to Sun Records in Memphis, Tennessee and became a rock 'n' roll star. His career slumped after the scandal that followed marriage to his 13-year-old second cousin, but he re-emerged as a successful country singer in the late sixties. Jerry Lee's country chart successes have included 'What's Made Milwaukee Famous (Has Made A Loser Out Of Me)', 'She Even Woke Me

Up To Say Goodbye' and 'Another Place, Another Time'.

1950 Alvin Crow, one of the leading young musicians involved in the revival of interest in western swing in the seventies, born in Oklahoma City, Oklahoma. He's been a fixture of the Austin, Texas club scene for over a decade and has made two albums for Polydor with his band, the Pleasant Valley Boys.

1973 Leon Russell's country music alter-ego, Hank Wilson, entered the charts with 'Roll In My Sweet Baby's Arms'.

30th SEPTEMBER

1950 The Grand Ole Opry televised for the first time.

1954 Patsy Cline signed a contract with Four-Star Records. According to her biographer Ellis Nassour, "It was probably the single biggest mistake Patsy had ever made in her professional life". Had she not signed to the small label she would probably have become a major star much sooner. Patsy was apparently prevented from recording anything other than Four-Star published songs, and this caused headaches for her producer, Owen Bradley, because much of the material was below standard. Patsy finally got free from the contract in 1960, giving her just a couple of years to achieve success.

O C T O B E R

1st OCTOBER

1932 Bonnie Owens born in Blanchard, Oklahoma. She married singer Buck Owens and they worked together in Arizona clubs. In the sixties she was divorced from Buck and became a part of the busy Bakersfield, California country scene having some solo success in the early sixties, then teamed up as duo with Merle Haggard, whom she married in 1965. Bonnie and Merle were divorced in the seventies, but she has continued to work for him — behind the scenes with his business affairs and as back-up singer — a situation only outsiders consider strange. As she explained in Haggard's book, *Sing Me Back Home:* "I was once part of his personal life and now I'm part of his family — his musical family, and that's the way I want it to be. We're all members, the band and I, and we care about each other, even though our personal lives are separate. We've all gone through periods of change, and when I think of me and Merle back in those early days I see two other people because, really, that's what we were."

1978 October, according to the Nashville-based County Music Association, is Country Music Month; the time when the annual CMA Awards are presented for the best musical achievements of the year and new members are elected to the prestigious County Music Hall of Fame. The CMA's attempts to gain national attention for country music in October received a substantial boost with the public support offered by Jimmy Carter, a life-long country fan, during his term as US President.

THE WHITE HOUSE
WASHINGTON

Country Music Month
October 1978

As modern American society becomes more and more hectic and complex, there is a desire in all of us to return to the simple things of life.

This perhaps in part explains the growing popularity -- even in our busiest metropolitan areas -- of country music. And designated as "Country Music Month," October invites us all to return, at least vicariously, to the hills and the farms of America and to retrace the everyday emotions and experiences of country life.

Country music is part of the soul and conscience of our democracy. It unfolds the inherent goodness of our people and of our way of life. It captures our indomitable spirit and pulsates with the sorrows, joys and unfailing perseverance of ordinary men and women who sustain our national vitality and strength.

I welcome the opportunity to applaud the Country Music Association on its sponsorship of this annual observance, and I encourage more Americans to share in the enjoyment and cultural enrichment that country music can bring.

Jimmy Carter

2nd OCTOBER

1896 Frank Leslie's *Illustrated Newspaper* reported the story of the Taylor Brothers' "War Of The Roses". Bob and Alf Taylor were old-time fiddlers who were competing against each other in the race for the Governorship of Tennessee. The story does seem to have been romanticised by the press — there is little evidence that either brother did much fiddling while on the campaign trail; but Bob (who won) was a very successful Tennessee politician for several years and much of his popularity was due to a down-home image that was fostered by his reputation as an enthusiastic fiddle-player.

1927 Leon Rausch, vocalist with Bob Wills and the Texas Playboys from 1958 until 1965 (he replaced Tommy Duncan), born in Springfield, Missouri. He is generally regarded as one of the finest western swing vocalists. When the

Original Texas Playboys were reformed for concerts and new recordings in the seventies, Leon was the featured vocalist.

194? Jo-El Sonnier, Cajun accordionist and singer, born in Louisiana. A performer since the age of seven, Jo-El played for many years in Cajun bands in the southwest Louisiana circuit, moved to California in 1972 and was with a country band, then travelled to Nashville where he established a reputation as a songwriter and first-class session man, working for Johnny Cash and others. Sonnier has also been acclaimed as a performer in his own right and has made several records, including the Rounder/Sonet *Cajun Life* album.

3rd OCTOBER

1938 Eddie Cochran born in Oklahoma City, Oklahoma. His family moved to California after World War II and Eddie was an enthusiastic guitarist in his early teens. He began playing professionally in the early fifties with singer Hank Cochran and though the pair weren't related, they toured as the Cochran Brothers. They made a couple of country records, but after seeing Elvis Presley switched to rock 'n' roll, they split-up in 1956, Hank going to Nashville where he eventually became one of country music's foremost songwriters, while Eddie established himself as one of the great rock 'n' roll singers with songs like 'Summertime Blues' and 'Twenty Flight Rock'. Eddie's career was cut tragically short when he was killed in a road accident while on tour in England on April 17, 1960. He was just 21.

1945 Elvis Presley's first public appearance, at the age of ten, in a talent contest at the Mississippi-Alabama Fair and Dairy Show. He had to stand on a chair to reach the microphone, then sang 'Old Shep', which he'd learnt from hearing Red Foley's version on the radio. Elvis won second prize, $5 and free admission to all the fair rides.

4th OCTOBER

1937 Lloyd Green, steel guitar virtuoso, born in Mobile, Alabama. He began having lessons on the Hawaiian guitar at seven, was playing professionally at ten, and as a teenager was working with country bands in rough and tumble honky-tonks. Lloyd moved to Nashville in 1957 and has been one of the city's busiest musicians ever since, though the situation when he arrived has changed a great deal over the years. As he explained, "This was right after Elvis had gotten so hot. Country music was at its lowest ebb. It had about bottomed out because most of the country singers were trying to go pop . . . Country music had almost no prestige - even the Chamber of Commerce refused to put anything about the Grand Ole Opry in their literature. There were only three recording studios in town and most of the music publishers had little hole-in-the-wall offices . . . Things were pretty slow when I arrived, but at least you didn't have the competition that you have today. I started working with Faron Young the day after I got here."

1944 Larry Collins, male half of the teenage Collins Kids duo, born in Tulsa, Oklahoma. Larry and Lorrie began singing country songs together at an early age and were featured on the California TV show "Town Hall Party" from 1953. They were very popular with country audiences in the fifties and, though their records didn't chart, several, including 'Hoy Hoy' and 'Beetle Bug Bop', are now held in high esteem by rockabilly enthusiasts. The ten-year career of the Collins Kids ended in the early sixties, when Lorrie married.

1956 Johnny Cash arrested in El Paso, Texas by a narcotics agent. He was returning from the Mexican border town of Juarez and was found to have several hundred Dexedrine and Equanil tablets. He was jailed for a night, then released on bail and subsequently fined $1000. According to his biographer, Christopher Wren, the experience had a sobering effect on Cash and he laid off pills for a time, but then slipped back into his old ways. It was several years before he finally kicked his pill-taking habit.

1975 Willie Nelson top of the country charts with 'Blue Eyes Crying In The Rain'. It was his first Top Ten hit since 1962 and the song that finally established him as a major performer. It was ironic that Nelson, long acknowledged as one of the all-time great country writers, should finally have broken through with a song written by someone else — the late Fred Rose.

5th OCTOBER

1925 The first programme broadcast over WSM, a powerful new radio station in Nashville and run by the National Life and Accident Insurance Company. The station was intended as a means of selling insurance to working people in the surrounding area, and the advertising even extended to the call letters, which stood for "We Shield Millions". WSM became internationally famous for the Grand Ole Opry, which originated from a musical show broadcast on November 28 1925.

1938 Johnny Duncan born on a farm near Dublin, Texas. He inherited a love of country music from his parents and was an accomplished musician as a youngster. Johnny was a DJ in Texas in the mid-sixties, then moved to Nashville where he took various jobs while he tried to break into the music business. Success finally came his way in 1967; signed to CBS he scored with 'Hard Luck Joe'. After a decade of small hits, he eventually cracked the Top Five in 1976 with 'Stranger', which he followed with his first number one, 'Thinkin' Of A Rendezvous'. The female voice on many of Johnny's successful records in the seventies belongs to Janie Fricke, who later became a star in her own right.

6th OCTOBER

1917 Bob Neal, country music promotor and manager, born in the Belgian Congo, Africa. He was a DJ on WMPS in Memphis and organising country shows when he met Elvis in the mid-fifties. Neal became Presley's second manager, from January 1955, until March 1956, then looked after the careers of other Sun performers Johnny Cash, Carl Perkins, Jerry Lee Lewis and Roy Orbison. He moved to Nashville in 1963 and helped several up-and-coming stars including Stonewall Jackson, Sonny James, Conway Twitty and Johnny Paycheck.

Jed Strunk

1981 Jed Strunk, singer/songwriter, killed in the crash of an antique plane near Carrabasset

Valley in Maine. He was 44. Jed had a number of small country hits, including the notorious 'Biggest Parakeets In Town' and one big-seller, the 1973 country-pop success 'A Daisy A Day'.

7th OCTOBER

1870 Uncle Dave Macon (David Harrison Macon), one of the great country entertainers, born on a farm near Smart Station, Tennessee. He was brought up in Nashville, where his family had acquired the Broadway Hotel, and as a child began playing the banjo, perfecting his own technique and entertaining friends and relatives with folk songs. He married in 1889 and bought a farm near Murfreesboro. He sang for his own enjoyment for many years and didn't make a public performance until 1921, at a charity show to raise money for a new church door. He impressed a talent scout for the Loew's chain of theatres and was signed up to perform in shows in Alabama and Tennessee. He was very well received, and at an age when most people would have been planning their retirement, Uncle Dave began a very successful new career. He teamed up with a young fiddler named Sid Harkreader and they made some of the earliest country recordings, for Vocalion, in New York on July 8, 1924. Dave was invited to appear on the Grand Ole Opry in 1926 and, though he was only able to make occasional appearances between tours for four years, he became the most popular performer. By the thirties he was a regular, playing both solo and with his band, the Fruit Jar Drinkers, featuring a wide ranging repertoire, from folk songs that pre-dated the Civil War to contemporary hillbilly material. Macon remained with the Opry until 1952, when he was 82. His influence was considerable, both as a musician and for his style of country entertainment, which can be traced through the careers of Grandpa Jones and Stringbean to the TV series "Hee Haw".

19?? Jim Halsey born in Independence, Kansas. A long established and very successful country music executive, Jim has been closely involved with the career development of Don Williams, The Oak Ridge Boys, Roy Clark, Hank Thompson and others. He played a key role in winning acceptance for contemporary country music from network TV and Las Vegas showrooms.

1967 Dolly Parton Day celebrated in Sevier County, Tennessee. 7000 locals turned up at the courthouse to hear Dolly sing. It had been intended as a small-scale event to celebrate her success in Nashville just three years after leaving home, but it coincided with her joining Porter Wagoner's show and signing with RCA. Dolly brought Porter and Mel Tillis along for the concert which was, by all accounts, an emotional and quite unforgettable experience.

1978 Merle Haggard and Leona Belle Williams married. It was a big wedding, which Merle described as "like a scene out of *Dr Zhivago* in his autobiography, *Sing Me Back Home*. "The wedding had been planned by Stu and Lorrie Carnell at their home in Gardensville, just outside of Reno. The setting was also right out of the movies. It was the old Crosby ranch and Lorrie had the wedding party stand in the back yard by a trout stream, surrounded by flowers and greenery, while we waited for the horse-drawn carriage to bring the bride."

8th OCTOBER

1932 Pete Drake born in Atlanta, Georgia. A leading Nashville-based session musician, Pete has played on hundreds of hits, including records by Elvis, Bob Dylan, Jim Reeves and Joan Baez. He was a country music enthusiast as a child, and by the fifties was recognised as one of the top instrumentalists in the Atlanta area, playing guitar and pedal–steel with his band, the Sons Of The South. Drake moved to Nashville in 1959 and was soon in demand as a session man, then had success in his own right with 'Talking

Steel Guitar', a pop hit in 1963. Angry at the way major record companies were neglecting traditional country performers, Pete formed First Generation Records in 1977, with Ernest Tubb as the first artist. "It really bothered me that a man like Tubb, who had done so much for the business, didn't have a record deal," said Drake. "If it weren't for Ernest, I certainly wouldn't be in the business, and so wouldn't a lot of other people. The man still performs over 200 days a year. That tells me he can still sell records." Drake's confidence was justified when the LP *Ernest Tubb: the Legend and the Legacy* sold over a quarter of a million copies. Pete has subsequently produced a critically acclaimed series of albums for First Generation, titled *The Stars of the Grand Ole Opry.*

1979 Canadian country star Hank Snow, and Hubert Long, the man who formed the first Nashville-based country talent agency, elected to the Country Music Hall of Fame.

9th OCTOBER

1899 Goebel Reeves, "The Texas Drifter", born in Sherman, Texas. He was one of the early recording stars and claimed to have taught Jimmie Rodgers his yodelling style. He came from the middle classes but chose to live as a hobo, and his songs like 'Railroad Boomer' and 'The Hobo And The Cop', which told of riding the rails, drinking sprees and jail, were based on his own experiences.

1965 'May The Bird of Paradise Fly Up Your Nose' by Little Jimmy Dickens, a favourite with collectors of bizarre songs, entered the country charts, eventually rising to number one and becoming a huge pop hit.

Paul Craft

1976 Another unusual song, 'Drop Kick Me Jesus (Through The Goal Posts of Life)' entered the charts; performed by Bobby Bare, it helped establish the reputation of a promising young songwriter named Paul Craft.

1978 Grand Ole Opry favourite Grandpa Jones elected to the Country Music Hall of Fame. The Kentucky born entertainer, real name Louis Marshall Jones, has been a Grandpa since he was just 22 years of age!

10th OCTOBER

1915 Owen Bradley, producer and record company executive, born in Westmoreland, Tennessee. He can take much of the credit for pioneering the slick Nashville Sound in the fifties, and for the development of the city as an important studio centre. He was a bandleader and musical director at WSM in 1947 when he was asked by Decca to produce records for them. He began with Ernest Tubb and Red Foley and continued with Decca/MCA for many years, producing the likes of Kitty Wells, Webb Pierce, Patsy Cline, Loretta Lynn, Bill Anderson and Conway Twitty. Owen began removing traditional country instrumentation at sessions, replacing them with lush strings and back-up vocals for a more pop-orientated style, which became known as the Nashville Sound. He was severely criticised for changing country music, but the technique proved to be very successful . He works today as a freelance producer, and also owns substantial real estate holdings, including much of Nashville's Music Row.

1946 John Prine, country/folk singer and writer, born in Maywood, Illinois. He began playing guitar in his mid-teens, around the same time that he was writing the poetry he later turned into distinctive songs. John came to prominence as a performer on the active Chicago folk scene, where Kris Kristofferson saw him, was very impressed, and helped arrange a record contract. John made a series of critically acclaimed albums in the seventies, though has to date met with little in the way of hit records.

1958 Tanya Tucker, teenage country sensation of the early seventies, born in Seminole, Texas. She loved country music as a child and had strong ambitions to be a performer. Tanya was singing seriously at the age of nine, and made a demo tape at 13, which so impressed Billy Sherrill that he signed her to CBS and produced her first record, 'Delta Dawn', which became a Top Ten hit. It was the first of many including 'Blood Red and Goin' Down' and 'Would You Lay With Me In A Field Of Stone'. The best-sellers continued after a switch to MCA in 1975, but then came a change in musical policy towards rock and pop, and after some initial success with the *TNT* album, her new material met with less success than her pure-country songs.

1971 English-born Arthur Satherley, who discovered Bob Wills, Roy Acuff and others, elected to the Country Music Hall of Fame.

11th OCTOBER

1932 Dottie West (Dorothy Marie) born on a farm near McMinnville, Tennessee, the oldest of ten children. Her career began while she was majoring in music at the Tennessee Tech. After working in nightclubs in the north, she cut her first record for Starday in 1959, was with Atlantic briefly, then Jim Reeves recommended her to Chet Atkins and she was signed to RCA, scoring her first hit with 'Let Me Off At The Corner'. A member of the Opry since 1964, Dottie's long run of country successes have included the songs 'Would You Hold It Against Me' and 'Paper Mansions'.

1943 Gene Watson, a firm favourite with fans of pure-country, born in Palestine, Texas. He was a professional singer at 13 and made his first record at 18, but for many years he spent his days doing body work on cars and his nights singing and recording. After notching up several local hits in the Houston area he was signed to Capitol and began having national best-sellers, with 'Love In The Hot Afternoon' the first of many Top Ten hits.

1976 Kitty Wells, "The Queen of Country Music", and Paul Cohen, the Decca executive who first recognised the potential of Nashville as a recording centre, elected to the Country Music Hall of Fame.

12th OCTOBER

1969 Merle Haggard entered the country chart with 'Okie From Muskogee', a controversial song that proved to be a goldmine for him. It started as a joke, composed by Merle and bandmember Eddie Burris in the back of their tour bus while driving through Oklahoma. Everyone heard what they wanted to in the song; conservatives took it as a rejection of the long-haired hippie youth movement, while left-wingers took it as a satirical joke, all singing along to the chorus—"We don't smoke marijuana in Muskogee/We don't take our trips on LSD". Merle planned a radical follow-up with his song about an interracial love affair, 'Irma Jackson', but his record company wouldn't allow it, releasing instead 'The Fightin' Side of Me', another controversial record that further boosted his popularity with the right. An unfortunate aspect of these successes was that for a long time it obscured, for many, the true depth of Merle's musical talents. "I didn't intend for 'Okie' to be taken as strongly from my lips as it was," said Haggard later. "Now, I'm not saying that I'm not proud of the song, or that I'm in disagreement with the song. But I think those two actually hurt me, because at the time I released them, there was such a strong movement in this country in the opposite direction that it alienated me from a lot of people who might otherwise have been fans of mine."

Merle Haggard

1971 Rock 'n' roll singer Gene Vincent died in Saugus, California from internal haemorrhaging. His successful career in the US was brief, but his popularity in Europe continued for many years. He was just 36.

13th OCTOBER

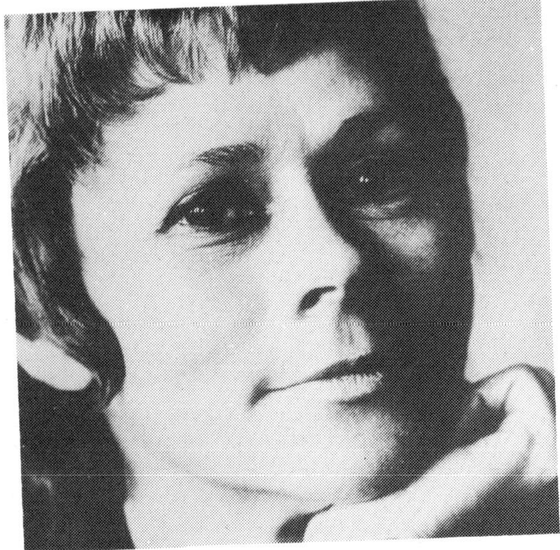

1927 Anita Kerr born in Memphis, Tennessee. She led the Anita Kerr Singers, who were featured as back-up vocalists on hundreds of country records in the fifties and sixties. Anita began playing the piano at four, encouraged by her mother who had a Memphis radio show, later leading a high school trio who sang on the programme. She moved to Nashville in the late forties and was a nightclub pianist, then formed her first group of Anita Kerr Singers in 1949. They had a solo contract with Decca in 1951 and began doing session work, making a significant contribution to the development of the so-called Nashville Sound that was being pioneered by Chet Atkins at RCA and Owen Bradley at Decca. Anita subsequently did A&R work for RCA, became one of the first women to produce country records, and formed several more singing groups, including the California-based Mexicali Singers.

1942 Grand Ole Opry star Roy Acuff gave Fred Rose $25,000 to start the Acuff-Rose publishing company, the first in Nashville. They began operations from a small, one-room office in the downtown area, developing into one of the most successful music business operations in the world.

1948 Lacy J. Dalton (Jill Byrem) born in Bloomsburg, Pennsylvania. Music played only a small part in her early life; she originally intended to be a painter but dropped-out of art classes at university and headed for California in the late sixties, where she became involved in a number of musical aggregations, including an acid-rock group called Office. In the late seventies she made a simple demo record of her songs and a copy reached Nashville producer Billy Sherrill, who'd made his name producing Tammy Wynette and Tanya Tucker. He was very impressed with her voice and songs, signed her to CBS and produced her country debut *Lacy J. Dalton* in 1979, which was a best-seller and spawned hits 'Crazy Blue Eyes' and 'Tennessee Waltz'.

1980 Johnny Cash received a standing ovation at the CMA Awards ceremony at the Grand Ole

Opry House when his election to the Country Music Hall of Fame was announced. Kenny Rogers made the presentation and said, "There are a lot of us who sing country music, there are only a few who are country music." In reply, Cash observed "June Carter is the only person with a mother, uncle, aunt and husband in the Hall of Fame."

14th OCTOBER

1897 Dorsey Dixon born in Darlington, South Carolina. He was one of the most talented performers and writers in the early days of country music, though he earned little money for his skills and had to spend most of his life working as a mill hand, playing music only during his off-duty hours. Dorsey performed with his brother Howard, as the Dorsey Brothers, who were popular in the thirties, and wrote several songs, including the classic, 'Wreck On The Highway', which was a big success for Roy Acuff.

1938 Melba Montgomery born in Iron City, Tennessee. She began singing as a child, at church, also playing guitar and fiddle. Her family moved to Nashville when she was a teenager and success in a talent contest in 1958 brought her to the attention of Roy Acuff, who asked her to join his group. After four years touring with the Smokey Mountain Boys, Melba branched out as a solo performer, scoring her first hit in 1963 with 'Hall of Shame' on United Artists. The same year she teamed up with George Jones and they had several successes as a duo, starting with 'We Must Have Been Out Of Our Minds'. She later teamed up on record with Gene Pitney and Charlie Louvin, while continuing to have hits as a solo artist.

15th OCTOBER

1899 Allen Britt shot Frankie Baker dead in St Louis, Missouri. The incident inspired the song 'Frankie and Johnny' which has subsequently appeared in various forms and with different titles in the repertoire of many blues and country singers. Jimmie Rodgers, Darby and Tarlton, Charlie Poole, Gene Autry, Johnny Cash and Elvis Presley have all recorded songs about the killing; Presley even appeared in a *Frankie and Johnnie* film in 1966.

1960 Loretta Lynn made her first appearance on the Grand Ole Opry. She sang 'Honky Tonk Girl' (her first hit) and received a very warm welcome. After the broadcast she was paid the obligatory $15 guest fee and was invited to appear again.

16th OCTOBER

1918 Stoney Cooper born on a farm in Harman, West Virginia. With his wife Wilma Lee, he was a leading performer of authentic mountain songs for many years. Traditional music was an important part of his family background; he began playing the fiddle and guitar as a youngster and joined the Leary Family singing group while in his teens. Soon afterwards he married the young Wilma Lee Leary and in the forties they left the group to perform as a duo. Music provided insufficient income in the early years and Stoney had to take other work, but by 1947 they had become established and were regulars on WWVA Wheeling Jamboree. They joined the Opry ten years later and began recording for Hickory, scoring hits with 'This Old House' and a version of Dorsey Dixon's 'Wreck On The Highway'. Stoney died in 1977, but Wilma Lee continued to perform their material on the Opry each week.

1960 George Hamilton IV made his debut on the country charts with 'Before This Day Ends'.

He was already known as a pop star, having scored a Top Ten hit in 1956 with 'Rose And A Baby Ruth', but this record marked a return to country, which had always been his favourite music, and the beginning of a long and successful career.

17th OCTOBER

1919 RCA — Radio Corporation of America formed. Ten years later it merged with the Victor Talking Machine Company and in over 50 years has been the most successful organisation manufacturing country records, with a catalogue ranging from Jimmie Rodgers and the Carter Family, through Elvis, Dolly Parton and Charlie Pride, to eighties superstars Alabama.

1960 Bob Luman's country debut with 'Let's Think About Living' which responded to a spate of songs with a lyrical obsession with death — like Marty Robbins' 'El Paso' — and urged performers to think of cheerful subjects. Luman had several more hits, including 'Everyday I Have To Cry Some' and 'Poor Boy Blues', but this was his biggest.

18th OCTOBER

1935 Bill Monroe married Caroline Brown in Spartanburg, South Carolina. They had two children, Melissa and James, both of whom later performed in their father's bluegrass band, James going on to lead his own group, the Midnight Ramblers.

1956 Elvis Presley arrested. A crowd had gathered when Elvis pulled into a Memphis gas station and the attendant, Ed Hopper became angry. There was a fist fight and both men were taken away by the police, then released on bail. At a court hearing later, Elvis was cleared but Hopper was fined.

1968 Bob Wills elected to the Country Music Hall of Fame. He accepted his award in person at a ceremony at the Ryman Auditorium. Taking off his trademark white hat he explained, "I never take this off to anybody, but I'm taking it off for all of you tonight."

1968 Tammy Wynette entered the country charts with 'Stand By Your Man'. It would complete a trio of chart topping hits for her in 1968 — the other two were 'D-I-V-O-R-C-E' and 'Take Me To Your World'. Seven years later, in the summer of 1975, the record topped the British pop charts.

19th OCTOBER

1889 Arthur Edward Satherley born in Bristol, England. He came to America in 1913 and was involved in the record business from 1919, watching the country music industry grow from "an acorn to a grand oak tree". He played a significant role in its development, as a talent scout from 1925, first for ARC (American Record Corporation) and then Columbia. His most important "discoveries" were Gene Autry, Bob Wills and Roy Acuff. His achievements were recognised by his election to the Country Music Hall of Fame in 1971.

1945 Jeannie C. Riley (Jeannie Stephenson) born in Anson, Texas. She was determined "to be somebody" as a child, learned songs from the radio and sang in local talent shows. Jeannie married Mickey Riley, her childhood sweetheart, and they moved to Nashville where she did the rounds of record companies, trying to get a deal. While Jeannie worked as a secretary for Plantation Records, a demo tape impressed her boss Shelby Singleton, who decided she'd be perfect for the Tom T. Hall song 'Harper Valley PTA'. The 1968 release sold millions of copies and made the 22-year-old singer an instant star. Jeannie was packaged with a sexy image and had a burst of fame, fortune and several other hits. But her private life and then her career fell apart. Divorced in 1970, she became increasingly unhappy. A turning point came in 1972 when she decided Christianity was more important then her career; she began singing gospel songs, and was eventually reunited with her ex-husband. She's subsequently told her remarkable story in the book, *From Harper Valley To The Mountain Top.*

1952 Hank Williams and Billie Jean Jones married, three times. First, in the middle of the night before a Justice of the Peace in Minden, Louisiana — because they were afraid that Hank's first wife Audrey might try and stop the scheduled ceremony — then at two wedding concerts at the New Orleans Municipal Auditorium before several thousand paying guests. Hank was too drunk to go on the planned honeymoon to Cuba and was ill for much of the time during their brief marriage. The New Orleans celebration seems to have been one of the few highlights.

20th OCTOBER

1908 Stuart Hamblen born in Kellyville, Texas. Singing turned from a hobby into a full time job for him in the late twenties — he moved to Southern California, formed a group and began singing western songs on the radio. He had a long recording career, with hits on Columbia and RCA including 'But I'll Go Chasing Women' and also several religious LP's and appeared in cowboy films (most often as a bad guy). A prolific songwriter, his best known song is 'This Old House', a country hit for Stuart in 1954, a pop success the same year for Rosemary Clooney, and then a British number one for Shakin' Stevens in 1981.

Grandpa Jones

1913. Grandpa Jones (Louis Marshall Jones), a popular country entertainer on the Grand Ole Opry and "Hee Haw" TV show, born in Niagra, Henderson County, Kentucky. His parents were musical and he followed their interests, learning the guitar by 11, later teaming up with a harmonica-playing neighbour to perform at social events. The family moved to Akron, Ohio and Louis soon had his own regular show on a local radio station. In 1935 he came to the attention of Bradley Kincaid who featured him on his radio broadcasts, and when listeners asked about the new singer with the "old voice", he had the idea for the Grandpa character. He disguised himself as an old man, switched from guitar to banjo and incorporated jokes and story telling into his act, with great success. He was a regular on the Boone County Jamboree in Cincinnati from 1938 then, after a period of war service, joined the Opry in 1947. Jones was in Washington for much of the fifties, but returned to Nashville in 1959 and has been an Opry fixture ever since.

1937 Wanda Jackson born in Maud, Oklahoma. She played guitar and piano as a child and had her own radio show at 13. She made country records for Decca in the mid-fifties, scoring her first success as part of a duo with Billy Gray in 1954, toured with Hank Thompson, then switched to rock 'n' roll and had a major hit with 'Let's Have A Party' on Capitol. In the sixties she was back in the country charts with songs like 'Right Or Wrong' and 'In The Middle Of A Heartache'.

1980 Bradley's Barn burnt to the ground. The famous Nashville landmark, a 50-year-old building owned by producer Owen Bradley, had been in operation as a studio since 1964 and used for recording numerous country stars including Conway Twitty, Loretta Lynn and Brenda Lee.

21st OCTOBER

1933 Singer Mel Street born. He sang in Virginia clubs for several years, then scored his first hit in 1972 with 'Borrowed Angel'. Mel recorded for Metromedia Country, GRT, Polydor and Mercury and has several more successes, including 'Lovin' On Back Streets' and 'I Met A Friend Of Yours Today'.

1958 Buddy Holly's last studio session, in New York City. He was no longer with The Crickets; instead producer Dick Jacobs and his orchestra provided musical support. The tracks recorded included 'True Love Ways' and 'Raining In My Heart'.

1978 Mel Street died at the Nashville Memorial Hospital after shooting himself at his Hendersonville home. According to music industry sources, Street had been very depressed due to a heavy workload and personal problems. It was his 45th birthday.

22nd OCTOBER

1961 Willie Nelson's classic song 'Funny How Time Slips Away' made its very first appearance in the country charts, on a record by Billy Walker. "I wrote this song one afternoon while driving to the office of Pamper Music," recalls Willie. "Somewhere during the trip the line that I had heard someone say probably a thousand times in my life, 'It's funny how time slips away', came to me. I thought 'It's funny there's never been a song by that title,' and it started coming to me. It has been my most financially successful song to date. It has been recorded maybe eighty or ninety times so far — on average, someone records it once a month."

1965 Ernest Tubb, "The Texas Troubadour" and Eddy Arnold, "The Tennessee Plowboy", elected to the Country Music Hall of Fame.

1966 Three men closely linked to the success of the Grand Ole Opry — George D. Hay, "The Solemn Old Judge" who introduced the show for many years; Uncle Dave Macon, the most popular star for 15 years; and talent booker Jim Denny — elected to the Hall of Fame.

George D. Hay

23rd OCTOBER

1960 Roy Orbison top of the British charts with 'Only The Lonely'. He was one of the most popular American singers in the UK during the sixties (along with Elvis Presley and Jim Reeves) and scored a total of 28 hits, of which 'Only The Lonely' was the first. One night in 1963, sharing top billing on a tour with The Beatles, Roy received ten encores. He is still a big star in Britain; in 1977 a compilation of his greatest hits topped the LP charts, and in 1982 he won several standing ovations from a full house at the Wembley Country Festival.

1978 Mother Maybelle Carter, of the Original Carter Family, died. She had been the most musically active of the three when the group split in 1941, touring with her daughters June, Helen and Anita, then when June married Johnny Cash, she'd worked with his roadshow and performed on Cash TV shows and specials. One of the most beloved figures in Nashville, Mother Maybelle's death brought numerous heartfelt tributes; Roy Acuff called her the "First Lady of Country Music", and Chet Atkins (who'd worked with her during the early years of his career) pointed out that the Carter Family and Jimmie Rodgers started country music as we know it today—"They deserve one of the highest niches in the history of country music."

24th OCTOBER

1930 The Big Bopper (J.P. Richardson) born near Sabine Pass, Texas. A larger-than-life Texas rock 'n' roll personality, he was a popular DJ in Beaumont, Texas in the early fifties playing country and swing jazz, then began recording as Jape Richardson, but found success as The Big Bopper with the huge rock 'n' roll hit 'Chantilly Lace' in 1958. A promising career ended tragically when he was killed in the same plane crash as Buddy Holly.

1980 The *Honeysuckle Rose* soundtrack album top of the country charts. Willie Nelson dominated the double LP and the movie; he played Buck Bonham a grizzled, grinning country troubadour from Cut-and-Shoot, Texas, "on the road" with his band playing Southern honky-tonks — a role clearly modelled on Nelson himself and his own rough and rocky life. Slim Pickens, Dyan Cannon and Amy Irving co-starred, Willie's own band were the featured musicians, and there were several fascinating cameo performances from fiddler Johnny Gimble, yodelling Kenneth Threadgill (the Dean of Austin's music scene), Augie Meyers and Hank Cochran. The album topped the charts for a month and a half, and the theme song 'On The Road Again' was a number one single.

25th OCTOBER

1881 Gunfight at the OK Corral. A feud between the Earp Brothers and ranching families in Tombstone came to a head when Wyatt, Virgil and Morgan Earp, plus their friend Doc Holliday, fought a brief, bloody gun battle with the Clantons and McLaurys. The Clantons were killed, the McLaurys fled, Virgil and Morgan were injured. The Earps were later cleared of any unlawful killing, but controversy surrounded the incident for years.

Minnie Pearl with Roy Acuff

1912 "The Queen of Country Comedy", Minnie Pearl (Sarah Orphelia Colley) born in Centerville, Tennessee. Dancing and acting were her first loves, and for much of the thirties she worked for the Wayne B. Sewell Production Company of Atlanta, directing amateur plays in schools. She began developing comedy routines and by 1940 had joined the Opry and, with her instantly recognizable costume of flower bedecked straw hat and long country dress, has been a favourite on the show for over 40 years.

26th OCTOBER

1936 Roy Acuff's first recording session, for the American Record Corporation, included a performance of 'The Great Speckled Bird', a popular number from his radio broadcasts. Acuff and his Crazy Tennesseans did another session for ARC in March 1937, but Roy was unhappy about the treatment they received—"They wanted 'The Bird', not me", he said later, and subsequently did no more recording for over a year, until Arthur Satherley convinced him he'd get a fair deal from Columbia Records.

1949 Wes McGhee, one of the most original British country singers and writers, born in Warwickshire. Much of his music is strongly influenced by Texas, a state where his records and live performances have been particularly well received.

1958 Charlie Walker made the first of many chart appearances, with his Columbia single, 'Pick Me Up On Your Way Down'. In the same chart, Roger Miller made his debut as a writer, Ray Price having entered with a recording of his 'Invitation To The Blues'.

27th OCTOBER

1933 Pianist Floyd Cramer born in Shreveport, Louisiana. He became interested in music at the age of five and learnt to play piano by ear. At 19 he was a regular on the Louisiana Hayride radio show, then took Chet Atkins' advice and moved to Nashville, where he joined the Opry, and became in demand as a session musician — playing on hundreds of RCA country recordings, also having considerable success in his own right, with hits including 'Last Date' and 'On The Rebound'.

1936 Ernest Tubb's first recording session, for RCA at the Texas Hotel in San Antonio. Jimmie Rodgers' widow Carrie had persuaded RCA to record Tubb singing a tribute to her late husband. He used Jimmie's guitar and sang six songs, including 'The Passing Of Jimmie Rodgers' and 'The Last Thoughts of Jimmie Rodgers', which were released on RCA's Bluebird label in December. The company did nothing to promote the record and sales were very low — Tubb's first royalty payment was just over two dollars. It was to be over five more years before his recording career took off, with Decca and 'Walking The Floor Over You'.

1939 Dallas Frazier, singer and writer, born in Spiro, Oklahoma. As a teenager he toured with Ferlin Husky, became a regular performer on Cliffie Stone's Hometown Jamboree and had a recording contract with Capitol. His first big success came as a writer: his 'Alley Oop' was a smash hit for the Hollywood Argyles in 1960. Dallas moved to Nashville in the sixties and wrote several more hits including 'Elvira', which was a million-seller for the Oak Ridge Boys in 1981. He also had some modest country hits as a performer, for Capitol and then for RCA, including 'Everybody Ought To Sing A Song'.

1951 Four Lefty Frizzell songs in the country Top Ten. 1. 'Always Late', 2. 'Mom And Dad's Waltz', 6. 'I Love You A Thousand Ways', 8. 'Travelling Blues'.

28th OCTOBER

1917 Bill Bolick, elder of the two brothers who comprised The Blue Sky Boys, a popular mandolin/guitar and harmony vocals duo of the late thirties and forties, born in Hickory, North Carolina. Bill and Earl Bolick were traditional music enthusiasts in their teens and began playing local dates around Hickory and were invited to perform on a radio station in Ashville, North Carolina. This exposure led to records on the Bluebird label, which spread their popularity throughout the South. Country favourites in the forties, their traditional, acoustic sound had gone out of fashion in 1951 when their record company wanted them to add an electric guitar to the line-up. Unwilling to change, they split up and took non-musical jobs, though re-formed on a part-time basis in the sixties for some folk festival appearances.

1936 Charlie Daniels, who has successfully combined hard-driving rock and country music, winning fans in both markets, born in Wilmington, North Carolina. The son of a lumberman, Charlie grew up listening almost exclusively to bluegrass. At 15 he began playing guitar and by his late teens was determined to be a rock 'n' roll musician. He spent over a decade playing honky-tonks in the South and Midwest with a group called The Jaguars. In Texas his guitar and fiddle playing impressed producer Bob Johnston, who suggested he try his luck in Nashville. Daniels started doing sessions in Music City and his work on Bob Dylan's *Nashville Skyline* LP earned him a reputation as one of the best musicians in the city. He was very successful, but missed life on the road and wanted to make his own records, so, in 1971, the Charlie Daniels Band was formed. The group became very popular on the concert circuit and notched up best selling albums. Now established as one of the leading Southern rock/country bands, they've had big pop hits with 'Uneasy Rider' and 'The Devil Went Down To Georgia'. They host the prestigious annual Volunteer Jam in Nashville each January, which attracts some of the biggest names in contemporary country and rock.

29th OCTOBER

1936 Hank Snow's first recording session for Canadian RCA. Though he became a very popular country singer in his home country, it was 13 years before Hank's records were issued in the US. Snow's association with RCA lasted for 45 years.

Hank Snow

1937 Sonny Osborne, baritone singer and 5-string banjo player with bluegrass trio, the Osborne Brothers, born in Hyden, Kentucky. With elder brother Bob, he grew up in a traditional music environment and they began playing on a Knoxville radio station when Sonny was just 16. They were featured on other stations, then joined the WWVA Wheeling Jamboree in 1956. Three years later they added another member to the group, Bennie Birchfield (later replaced by Ronnie Reno, then Dale Sledd). They became very popular in the sixties, with their three-part harmonies and "progressive" blue-grass style, which involved electric instruments and the steel guitar and were featured on TV, at folk festivals and on successful LP's and singles.

1971 Dolly Parton entered the country charts with the autobiographical 'Coat Of Many Colours'. "This is a true story, and means more to me than any other song I've ever recorded," Dolly told Dorothy Horstman, "There were twelve children in our family, and we were real poor. We had food to eat, because we raised it, but as far as money to buy clothes, all we had was what Mama made . . . Somebody had sent her a box of scraps and she took them and made me a little coat. This was the first time I was going to have my picture taken. That's why it hurt me so bad when the kids laughed, because I was so proud of it."

30th OCTOBER

1914 Patsy Montana (Rubye Blevins), "The Yodelling Cowgirl", born in Hot Springs, Arkansas. She was the first female country singer to have a million-selling record — 'I Want To Be A Cowboy's Sweetheart', in 1935, and was a very popular performer on the Chicago WLS Barn Dance radio show for 25 years. She was singing in public from her mid-teens and began a lengthy recording career in 1933. The following year she began a long association with the Prairie Ramblers, who supported her at numerous shows around the US and on record. Patsy retired in 1959, but was back performing and recording a few years later and was still going strong in the eighties.

1976 Razzy Bailey made his first appearance on the country chart with 'Keepin' Rosie Proud Of Me', on his own Erastus label. It wasn't a great success, managing two weeks on the listings and a highspot of 99, and Razzy had to wait two more years for his first bona-fide hit.

Razzy Bailey

31st OCTOBER

1912 Dale Evans (Francis Smith) born in Uvalde, Texas, She was a promising amateur singer and began a professional career as performer in 1930 after a brief and unsuccessful marriage. Dale was featured on several radio shows during the thirties and early forties, then landed the role of a cowgirl in the 1943 movie, *Swing Your Partner.* It was the first of dozens of westerns that she'd make with co-star Roy Rogers, a young singer from the popular Sons of the Pioneers, who was being groomed as a rival to Gene Autry. Roy and Dale were a favourite couple with audiences for many years (they married on New Year's Eve 1947), had their own network TV show and made several successful records.

1944 Kinky Friedman (Richard Friedman), one of the most bizarre singers in any field, born in Rio Duckworth, Texas. He made his first record, as King Arthur and the Carrots in 1967, then fled the country as part of the Peace Corps, returning to form a band called the Texas Jewboys. Performed by almost anyone else, Kinky's songs about toilets, mass murders and Jesus, would be extremely offensive, but he somehow gets away with them and has even played that pillar of country music sobriety, the Grand Ole Opry. He's made three albums *Sold American, Kinky Friedman* and *Laso From El Paso,* which have won him cult status. In the early eighties he was based in New York and was a mainstay of Manhattan's leading country venue, the Lone Star Cafe.

N O V E M B E R

1st NOVEMBER

1926 Uncle Jimmy Thompson, early star of the Grand Ole Opry, made his first recording, for Columbia in Atlanta, Georgia. He performed some traditional fiddle tunes, including 'Karo' and 'Billy Wilson'.

1929 Bob Wills' first recording session, in Dallas, Texas for the Brunswick Recording Corporation. It was unsuccessful and nothing was released, but is nevertheless of significance, demonstrating that Wills had a very open-minded attitude to music from his early years. With guitarist Herman Arnspiger, Bob cut a blues song—'Gulf Coast Blues', which had been popularised by black singer Bessie Smith, and an old-time fiddle tune—'Wills Breakdown', which he'd learnt from his father.

1937 Bill Anderson, a successful country singer, songwriter and TV personality, born in Columbia, South Carolina. He began writing songs and performing with a local country band while at high school, but didn't give serious thought to a musical career. Anderson attended the University of Georgia, graduating with a degree in journalism, and was a sports writer for a time, but then became a disc jockey on a Commercial Georgia station and found himself increasingly involved with music. His song 'City Lights' was a hit for Ray Price in 1958, and Bill signed to Decca, recording the first of over 50 hits and 40 albums. His big hits, many of which were self-penned, include 'Still', 'Po' Folks' and 'Tip Of My Finger'. Bill's touring band are called the Po' Folks, after his hit, and he's corporate spokesman for a Po' Folks chain of restaurants in America. A pioneering country artist through his work on TV, his numerous apperances have included hosting a network game show, several spots on the daytime soap opera 'One Life To Live', and the syndicated 'Backstage At The Grand Ole Opry', which Bill introduces each week.

1980 Waylon Jennings recording of the theme song from "The Dukes Of Hazzard" TV show, topped the country charts.

2nd NOVEMBER

1920 Radio station KDKA in East Pittsburgh, Pennsylvania, became the very first regular broadcasting service in the United States.

1925 George D. Hay lured away from WLS in Chicago, where he was the leading announcer and originator of the popular WLS Barn Dance show, to WSM, the new radio station in Nashville, Tennessee.

Charlie Walker

1926 Charlie Walker, popular disc jockey and country singer, born in Collin County, Texas. A country fan as a youngster, Charlie joined Bill Boyd's Country Ramblers as a teenager in 1943, starting his radio career a few years later. By the fifties he was regarded as one of the leading DJ's in America. Continuing with his broadcasting duties, Walker began recording for Columbia and had hits from 1958, starting with 'Pick Me Up On Your Way Down', until the early seventies.

1971 Sonny James in the charts with 'Here Comes Honey Again', which would be his 20th number one record, and his 16th in succession.

3rd NOVEMBER

1957 Jerry Lee Lewis' 'Great Ball's Of Fire' released by Sun. It rose to the top of the country and pop charts. The record's success was helped by Jerry Lee's sensational stage act, his appearance singing the song in the Warner Brothers film *Jamboree,* and a remarkable TV performance on Dick Clark's 'Saturday Night Show' which was accompanied by explosions going off in the background.

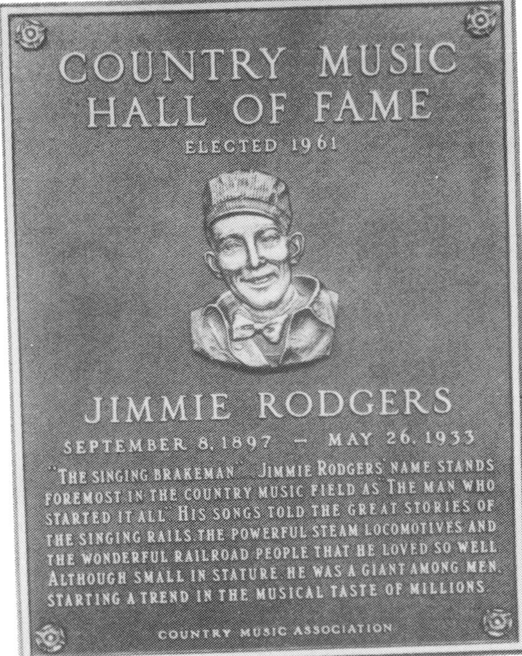

1961 The first members elected to the Country Music Hall of Fame in Nashville, Tennessee. Established by the Country Music Association, the Hall of Fame honours people who have made valuable contributions to country music. Each year several names are nominated and CMA-selected voters participate in a secret ballot. The first three people to be elected were Jimmie Rodgers (a unanimous choice), Hank Williams and publisher Fred Rose. The plaques describing the achievements of the members of the Hall of Fame were originally hung in the Tennessee State Museum, but since 1967 have been displayed at the Country Music Hall of Fame at 4 Music Square East, in Nashville.

1967 Jerry Reed's tribute to Elvis Presley, 'Tupelo, Mississippi Flash', entered the country charts. It was a rare example of a subtle Presley tribute, which made no effort to cash-in on his popularity and didn't even mention him by name.

1973 The first appearance of Dolly Parton's 'Jolene' in the country charts.

4th NOVEMBER

1899 Kirk McGee, banjo-playing half of the McGee Brothers, born in Franklin, Tennessee. He grew up on a farm with his elder brother Sam where they inherited a love of traditional music from their fiddle-playing father. They worked with Uncle Dave Macon's Fruit Jar Drinkers in the twenties, teamed up with Fiddlin' Arthur Smith and recorded with him as The Dixieliners, played with Bill Monroe's band and then began appearing as a separate act. They were popular performers on the Grand Ole Opry for several decades.

1940 Delbert McClinton born in Lubbock, Texas. He moved to Fort Worth as a child and grew up with a musical background of blues and country. He spent over 20 years playing Southern honky-tonks before finding chart success as a performer—in 1980 with the funky, R&B flavoured 'Giving It Up For Your Love'—and headlining big concerts. Despite a lack of commercial success, Delbert was highly rated by fellow musicians and critics for many years; his 1975 ABC album, *Victim Of Life's Circumstances* is regarded as a progressive country classic. It includes his original version of 'Two More Bottles Of Wine', which was a chart-topping success for Emmylou Harris (a keen McClinton fan) in 1979.

1957 The first country music show on Broadway in New York City. Roy Acuff, Kitty Wells and Johnny and Jack topped the bill at the Palace Theatre.

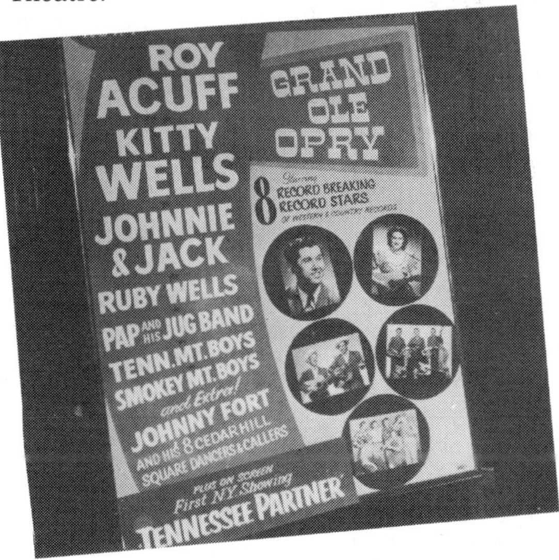

5th NOVEMBER

1912 Roy Rogers (Leonard Slye), 'The King of the Cowboys', born in Cincinnati, Ohio. He migrated to California when he was 18 and took a variety of menial jobs while trying to put together a successful western group. After several short-lived outfits, he met up with Bob Nolan and Tim Spencer in 1933 and they formed the Pioneer Trio, which became the Sons of the Pioneers when Karl and Hugh Farr joined. They popularised western harmony singing and had many imitators, though were rarely bettered. Roy had keen ambitions to be a film star and debuted in *Under Western Skies* in 1938. He was a great success and subsequently made over 100 cowboy movies, many featuring his wife, Dale Evans, horse Trigger and dog Bullet. Rogers' film commitments forced him to drop out of the Pioneers, but he retained strong links with them and they appeared in many of his films. Roy and Dale made several records together for RCA and had their own network TV show in the fifties.

1946 Gram Parsons, the most influential figure of the country-rock movement, born in Winter Haven, Florida. As a teenager, Gram led The Legends, whose members included Jim Stafford, then joined The Shilos who played Greenwich Village folk clubs in the early seventies. His enthusiasm for country music became apparent with the band he formed while at Harvard, the International Submarine Band. Now rated as an important and pioneering outfit, their unfashionable combination of country and rock interested only a few people at the time, and their only album, *Safe At Home,* was released in 1968 after they'd broken-up and Gram had joined The Byrds. He had a profound effect on their country album, *Sweetheart of the Rodeo,* and achieved his ambition of playing the Grand Ole Opry when The Byrds performed at the Ryman Auditorium later that year. Parsons quit the band after a few months, hung-out with the Rolling Stones in London, then formed a new country-rock outfit called The Flying Burrito Brothers, who made the landmark LP *The Gilded Palace Of Sin*. In 1972 Gram launched a solo career with Warner Brothers, releasing the critically acclaimed *G.P.* and *Grievous Angel,* which featured Emmylou Harris (then little known outside Washington DC) on back-up and harmony vocals. Parsons had lived fast—he died young, aged 26 in 1973, soon after completing his last album. Death was from a heart attack, brought on by his lifestyle that had involved consumption of excessive quantities of alcohol and dangerous narcotics.

Gram Parsons

1960 Johnny Horton, singer best known for 'The Battle Of New Orleans' and 'North To Alaska', killed in a car accident while driving to Nashville for a DJ convention. His widow was Billie Jean Jones, who had suffered a previous tragedy in 1953, when her first husband Hank Williams had died.

6th NOVEMBER

1932 Stonewall Jackson born in Tabor City, California. As a child he taught himself to play the guitar and began composing rudimentary songs; while in the Navy he found himself in demand as an entertainer and on his discharge

he was determined to become a professional entertainer. Stonewall travelled to Nashville in 1956 and attracted the attention of publishers Acuff-Rose and Columbia Records. Success came quickly; he had his first hit with 'Life To Go' in 1958, followed by the pop smash, 'Waterloo', which remains his best known song, though he had many more hits including 'BJ The DJ' and 'A Wound that Time Can't Erase'.

1941 Guy Clark born in Monihans, Texas. A singer and songwriter who emerged from the fruitful Houston folk scene, his best songs are autobiographical tales drawn from memories of his early days and include 'Texas 1947', 'Desperados Waiting For A Train'—successfully covered by Jerry Jeff Walker and David Allan Coe—'The Last Gunfighter Ballad', a hit for Johnny Cash. Guy's solo albums have been critically acclaimed, particularly his RCA debut in 1975 *Old No. 1,* but commercial success has eluded him to date.

1942 Doug Sahm, one of the most versatile and accomplished musicians from Texas, born in San Antonio. He had a huge pop hit in 1965, as leader of the Sir Douglas Quintet, with 'She's About A Mover', and was one of the leading personalities of the so-called "progressive" scene in Austin during the seventies, making several interesting LP's, including the country-orientated *Mendocino* and *Texas Rock For Country Rollers*.

1948 Glenn Frey, guitarist and vocalist with the Eagles, born in Detriot, Michigan.

1964 Tex Ritter, America's most beloved cowboy, elected to the Country Music Hall of Fame.

7th NOVEMBER

1914 Archie Campbell, country comedian, born in Bulls Gap, Tennessee. His successful career began with the "Mid-Day-Merry-Go-Round" on WNOX in Knoxville, Tennessee in the forties. He became a regular on the Grand Ole Opry in 1958, which led to an RCA recording contract and success with comedy singles like 'Trouble In The Amen Corner', 'The Men In My Little Girl's Life' and duets with Lorene Mann, like 'Dark End Of The Street', which revealed his serious side. Archie was voted Comedian Of The Year by the CMA, and in the seventies he became a key figure on the "Hee Haw" TV show, both as writer and performer.

1960 A. P. Carter died at Maces Spring, Virginia. His career as a performer had more or less ended with the demise of the Carter Family in 1941, though there was a reunion with Sara in 1952, to record for an obscure Bristol label called Acme, but little came of these sessions.

1970 '(I Never Promised You A) Rose Garden' by Lynn Anderson released. It sold over two million copies, and won a Grammy Award for the "Best Female Country Performance" of 1970. The song was written by Joe South, who took the title from a novel written by Hannah Green, though the lyrics have no connection with the book.

8th NOVEMBER

1909 Scotty Wiseman, of the popular Lulu Belle and Scotty duo, born in Spruce Pine, North Carolina. While training to be a teacher in the late twenties, he had sung on West Virginia radio stations as Skyland Scotty. Putting aside his teaching ambitions, he joined the Chicago-based WLS National Barn Dance in 1933, and soon teamed up with singer/guitarist Lulu Belle. They were popular stars of the show for 25 years, recorded for several labels, appeared in films, and from 1949 had their own daily TV show on Chicago's WNBQ. They retired from performing in 1958 and Scotty finally became a teacher, 30 years after his training.

1927 Patti Page (Clara Ann Fowler) born in Tulsa, Oklahoma. She began as a country singer on a local radio station, joined Jimmy Joy's band and headed north, then began a very successful solo career in the Chicago/Milwaukee area. Signed to Mercury, Patti had several hits, including the phenomenal 'Tennessee Waltz' in 1950 which sold over six million copies. The song, written by Redd Stewart and Pee Wee King, had previously been a big country hit for Cowboy Copas in 1948.

1950 Bonnie Raitt, contemporary rock singer and guitarist, born in Los Angeles, California. Her music has strong roots in blues, plus some country influences, and she was featured in the *Urban Cowboy* film.

9th NOVEMBER

1895 George D. (Dewey) Hay, "The Solemn Old Judge" of the Grand Ole Opry, from its humble beginnings in 1925 until 1951, born in Attica, Indiana. He was a journalist on the *Commercial Appeal* in Memphis and when the paper set up a radio station, he became an announcer, making his debut in June 1923. The following year he was chief announcer at WLS in Chicago, where he originated the long-running WLS Barn Dance (later the National Barn Dance). George was then lured away to head Nashville's new WSM station, where he started the WSM Barn Dance in 1925, changing the name two years later. The show was preceeded by classical music and one night, in a moment of inspiration, Hay announced, "For the past hour we have been listening to music largely from the Grand Opera, but from now on we will present the Grand Ole Opry." George can take much of the credit for the early success of the show, from hiring performers like the very popular Uncle Dave Macon, to increasing the potential audience, with the 1929 decision to make WSM a clear-channel station; boosted to 50,000 watts the Opry could be heard across much of the South and Midwest. Hay continued with WSM until his retirement in 1951, announcing the acts and bringing each show to a close with a blast on his steamboat whistle.

George D. Hay

1944 James Talley, gifted writer and performer who is strongly influenced by Woody Guthrie's "dust bowl" songs and John Steinbeck's novels, born in rural Oklahoma. His socially conscious songs made him a favourite with President and Mrs Jimmy Carter, and many music critics. Talley's record company, Capitol, said they hadn't had such good press on an act since The Beatles, though sadly his critical acclaim wasn't matched with popular success. In 1974 he helped construct a Nashville studio, then traded his services for recording time, and cut the classic debut LP, *Got No Bread, No Milk, No Money, But We Sure Got A Lot Of Love*.

1955 George Jones made his first appearance on the country charts with 'Why Baby Why', on Starday.

1962 Roy Acuff elected to the Country Music Hall of Fame.

10th NOVEMBER

1910 Paul Cohen, Decca Records talent scout and country music director, born. He was the first to recognise the potential of Nashville as a recording centre, starting with Red Foley at WSM's Studio B in the spring of 1945. By the fifties several other companies had followed his lead. Paul hired producer Owen Bradley, and together they helped boost the successful careers of Decca artists Kitty Wells, Ernest Tubb, Red Foley, Webb Pierce and Patsy Cline.

1927 Darby and Tarlton recorded 'Columbus Stockade Blues' and 'Birmingham Jail' in Atlanta, Georgia. The songs have become classics and featured in the repertoire of dozens of country performers, yet the duo never received more than the initial $75 fee for their recording.

1949 Donna Fargo (Yvonne Vaughn) born in Mount Airey, North Carolina. She sang at church as a child, but her big ambition was to be a teacher. While studying in California, Donna met producer Stan Silver, who was very impressed with her singing and convinced her she could be a very successful country performer. Stan and Donna, who were later married, wrote 'The Happiest Girl In The Whole USA', which launched Donna to international stardom in 1972. Several more big hits followed, including 'Funny Face' and 'Superman'.

1973 David "Stringbean" Akeman, a star of the Opry and the "Hee Haw" TV show, and his wife Estelle, murdered after they had disturbed burglars at their Tennessee farm following a performance at the Grand Ole Opry.

11th NOVEMBER

1938 Narvel Felts, "Narvel the Marvel" to his fans, born in Missouri. He started performing on a Saturday morning radio show in Bernie, Missouri as a teenager, then worked in various bands, backing Conway Twitty (when he was still Harold Jenkins) and Charlie Rich among others, before making his own records and having rock 'n' roll success with 'Honey Love' in 1959. Narvel moved to Nashville in the seventies and had several country hits including 'Drift Away' and the best-selling 'Reconsider Me' which was chosen as "Record of the Year" by both *Cashbox* and *Billboard* magazines in 1975.

1944 Jessie Colin Young (Perry Miller) born; he was one of several American rock musicians of the seventies who had strong country influences. He started out as a folk singer on the East Coast, then led the Youngbloods who made several albums, including *Ride The Wind,* which was produced by Charlie Daniels; Jessie later performed as a solo artist.

12th NOVEMBER

1945 Neil Young, outstanding singer-songwriter, born in Toronto, Canada. He worked as a folk singer in Canada in the early sixties, then travelled to California and was a key member of the seminal country-rock band Buffalo Springfield, subsequently working as part of Crosby, Stills, Nash and Young, and with Crazy Horse, then making a highly acclaimed series of solo albums.

1950 Barbara Fairchild, singer best known for the 'Teddy Bear Song' hit in 1973, born in Knobel, Arkansas. Her professional singing career began at 12 on a local Missouri TV station. Barbara moved to Nashville and was orginally signed up as a songwriter, but demos of her songs brought her to the attention of CBS producer Billy Sherrill and a recording contract followed in short order. Her other hits include 'Baby Doll' and 'Kid Stuff'.

1981 Bud Strevel, MC and singer with the Blue Ridge Quartet, died after suffering a heart attack after a concert in Pennsylvania. Bud had been a member of the popular gospel quartet since its inception in 1948.

13th NOVEMBER

1954 Jeannie Kendall born in St Louis, Missouri. She began singing with her father Royce (a successful St Louis barbershop owner) in the living room of their house when she was 15. In 1969 they decided to take a stab at the professional music business and came to Nashville to record a custom session. That record caught the attention of steel guitar ace, Pete Drake, and he promptly signed them to his Stop Records. Royce was a dyed in the wool country fan and, though Jeannie enjoyed country, she liked other music as well. Their first commercial recording represented a compromise — a country version of Jeannie's favourite folk song, 'Leaving On A Jet Plane'. It was their first hit, in 1970. The Kendalls made records for several labels over the next few years, then arrived at Ovation where they scored a huge hit with 'Heaven's Just A Sin Away', which won a Grammy award in 1977 and was voted CMA 'Song of the Year' in 1978. More country successes have followed, including 'It Don't Feel Like Sinnin' To Me' and 'Pittsburg Stealers'.

1973 Another tragedy for Jerry Lee Lewis. His eldest son, the child of his second marriage to Jane Mitchum, Jerry Lee Jnr, killed in a car accident in Mississippi.

14th NOVEMBER

1950 Popular Canadian country singer Colleen Peterson, born in Peterboro, Canada.

1975 Waylon Jennings top of the country charts with the value for money, double-sided hit, 'Are You Sure Hank Done It This Way'/'Bob Wills Is Still The King', from the successful RCA LP *Dreamin' My Dreams*. In his book *Waylon and Willie,* writer Bob Allen described 'Are You Sure Hank Done It This Way' as the closest Jennings had come to having an anthem; "the song sums up the frustration and desperation of Waylon's first decade in the music business." 'Bob Wills Is Still The King' was a live recording, a tribute to the western swing bandleader who'd died earlier in the year.

1981 Rosanne Cash top of the country chart with 'My Baby Thinks He's A Train', a country-rockabilly song which had originally been recorded (from a male standpoint) by the Texas-based band Asleep At The Wheel.

15th NOVEMBER

1929 C. W. McCall (William Fries) born in Audubon, Iowa. He studied art at university and had a successful career in advertising, culminating in a 1973 campaign for the Metz

Bread Company which involved a truck driving character named C. W. McCall. Fries did the voice-overs for the TV commercials and they were so well received that he was encouraged to develop the character on record. 'The Old Home Filler-Up And Keep On A-Truckin' Cafe' was released by MGM and became a country Top 20 hit in 1974. C. W. McCall made several more records, mainly recitations about truck drivers, then struck gold with the story of a convoy of vehicles communicating by CB radio. 'Convoy' sold millions of copies, topped the country charts for six weeks in 1976, and inspired a movie, directed by Sam Peckinpah and starring Kris Kristofferson and Ali MacGraw.

1940 Unique and very funny British country star Hank Wangford (also Sam Hutt, a London-based gynaecologist) born in Wangford, Suffolk, England. Hank, whose motto is, "It's better to have bad taste than to taste bad," has had cult success in the UK with songs like 'Cowboys Stay On Longer' and 'Joggin' For Jesus', on the Cowpie label.

16th NOVEMBER

1938 Troy Seals born in Big Hill, Kentucky. He began playing guitar as a child and had his own country/rock band while in his teens. Troy married singer Jo Ann Campbell and they toured as a duo, then quit the music business, disillusioned at their lack of success. After a spell as a manual worker, Troy went to Nashville to pitch some of the songs he had written. Encouraged by other aspiring young writers like Donnie Fritts and Will Jennings, he had success, with Conway Twitty taking 'There's A Honky Tonk Angel' to number one, and several artists recording his 'We Had It All'. In the seventies Seals was signed to Atlantic, then Columbia, as a performer, and had some small hits of his own.

1955 The name Johnny Cash appeared on the American country charts for the very first time. His debut single for Sun, with the Tennessee Two, 'Cry Cry Cry' stayed on the charts for one week, at number 14. Cash's name can be counted over 1000 times since—he's appeared in every subsequent year and scored well over 100 hits, many of which have gone to number one, including 'Ballad Of A Teenage Queen', 'Ring Of Fire', 'Folsom Prison Blues', 'A Boy Named Sue' and 'One Piece At A Time'.

17th NOVEMBER

1938 Gordon Lightfoot, singer-songwriter with strong country influences, born in Orilla, Ontario. He studied orchestration in Los Angeles, then returned to Canada and was involved in the booming folk movement, encouraged by Ian Tyson, who had formed the successful Ian and Sylvia duo. 1966 was an important year for him—his song 'Early Morning Rain' was a major pop hit for Peter, Paul and Mary, and a country success for George Hamilton IV, while his debut solo LP *Lightfoot* won him several 'Singer Of The Year' accolades. He's made several well received solo albums, but remains best known as a writer, having composed several hundred songs including 'If I Could Read Your Mind' and 'For Lovin' Me'.

1941 Country-rock musician Gene Clark born in Tipton, Missouri. His recording career began with the folk-rock band the New Christy Minstrels, but his best work can be found on the early LPs by The Byrds, some records made with banjo-picking Doug Dillard, and a series of solo releases.

1973 Honky-tonk singer Gary Stewart made his chart debut with the RCA release, 'Ramblin' Man'. Florida-based Gary credits Charley Pride with helping him to get started as a solo performer. In the early seventies he was playing piano and opening Pride's road show—"Charley Pride is a great person and he was the first to

give me an opportunity to do it. I played a little too loud for his audiences, so eventually I went out on my own, and that's where I've been ever since."

18th NOVEMBER

1946 Jacky Ward, the country singer whose lively stage show inevitably includes some wickedly accurate impersonations of other performers, born in Grovetown, Texas. At one time, Jacky was doing three jobs — salesman in the morning, disc jockey in the afternoon, and country singer in the evening. He had some success in the Houston area, most notably with the single, 'Big Blue Diamonds', which brought him to the attention of Mercury Records in Nashville, with whom he's had chart success including 'Fools Fall In Love' and 'A Lover's Question', plus the duet hit with Reba McEntire, 'Three Sheets In The Wind'.

1978 Barbara Mandrell top of the country charts for the third straight week with 'Sleeping Single In A Double Bed'. It was her first number one record and provided the vital boost necessary to push her into the superstar class of country performers.

19th NOVEMBER

193? Jerry Foster born in Tallapoosa, Missouri. A first generation rockabilly artist, Jerry's great success has been as part of the Foster-Rice song-writing team, though he's had sporadic periods as performer and recording act ever since. He teamed up with Bill Rice, in 1959, for a partnership that lasted just over 20 years. They won 61 ASCAP awards and wrote hits for many acts, including Johnny Paycheck ('Song And Dance Man'), Mickey Gilley ('Here Comes The Hurt Again') and Jerry Lee Lewis ('39 And Holding').

1960 Johnny Horton entered the charts with 'North To Alaska', one of his biggest hits, a success in the country field, and on pop charts around the world.

1977 Television actress Mary Kay Place, in the role of Loretta Haggers from the series "Mary Hartman, Mary Hartman", entered the country chart with 'Something To Brag About', which featured harmony vocals from Willie Nelson and musical support from Emmylou Harris' Hot Band. The record eventually reached the Top Ten.

20th NOVEMBER

1887 Eck Robertson (Alexander Campbell Robertson) born in Delaney, Arkansas. He began making music at the age of five with a fiddle made from a long-necked gourd and a cat's hide.

Eck began his professional career working with a travelling medicine show, later playing at dances. He gained a reputation as an excellent fiddle player and, though far too young to have fought in the Civil War, travelled each year to an Old Confederate's Reunion, where he took part in fiddling contests. With another fiddle star, Henry Gilliland, he travelled to New York City and on June 30, 1922, the pair presented themselves at the offices of Victor and asked to make a record. They cut several tunes, and Eck's solo version of 'Sallie Goodin' was the first to be released, Robertson thereby becoming the first Southern country musician to make a commercial recording. He subsequently recorded a few more tunes for Victor; though none were particularly big sellers, his influence on other fiddlers was considerable.

1978 An extremely bizarre country concert at the Keystone Club in Palo Alto, California, featuring the one and only appearance of Cowboy Fee and the Heffers (who were really the satirical rock band The Tubes). Their set included 'The Theme From Rawhide', 'Tumbling Tumbleweeds' and 'Jackson Browne's Version Of White Punks On Dope'.

21st NOVEMBER

1933 Jean Shepard, one of the first ladies of country music and a firm favourite of the "Keep It Country" movement, born in Paul's Valley, Oklahoma. Jean began her career in California as the leader of her own group, The Melody Ranch Girls. Soon she was spotted by Red Foley, who signed her to appear on his network TV show "The Ozark Jubilee", then she travelled to Nashville and joined the Opry. Her professional and personal life took a tragic turn when her husband and singing partner, Hawkshaw Hawkins, died in a plane crash along with Patsy Cline and Cowboy Copas. Jean bravely continued her own career and organized a new band, the Second Fiddles. Her hit-making career has spanned three decades and includes 'Satisfied Mind', 'Beautiful Lies' and 'Slippin' Away'.

1950 Flatt and Scruggs' first recording session, for CBS. Lester and Earl had become established as a leading bluegrass act and had developed a powerful, driving sound, which was very different from that of their former boss, Bill Monroe, and brought them considerable success.

1970 George Jones entered the country charts with 'Good Year For The Roses'. Eleven years later the song was a big British hit for Elvis Costello, a single from his Nashville-produced album of country standards, *Almost Blue*.

22nd NOVEMBER

1955 Steve Sholes of RCA Records paid Sam Phillips $35,000 for Elvis Presley's contract and master tapes. Elvis received an additional $5,000 in lieu of royalties he'd have received from Sun Records—he spent most of the money on a pink Cadillac. In retrospect it is the best deal ever made in the music business, though it was an unheard of sum at the time. For Sam Phillips' part, the money was very welcome for developing the careers of other Sun artists, and he's never publicly regretted his decision, "We had two up and coming stars in Johnny Cash and

Carl Perkins under contract at the time we sold Presley," said Sam, "I haven't regretted selling his contract because I figured then, and still think, that you can't figure an artist's life for more than six months in advance".

1980 A new Jim Reeves single, 'There's Always Me', entered the country charts, marking the 25th anniversary of his signing with RCA Records. Reeves died in an air crash in 1964 and 'There's Always Me' was his 30th posthumous hit for the label.

23rd NOVEMBER

1951 The first broadcast of the "Town Hall Party" show over Channel 11 from Compton in Southern California. The Saturday night TV show ran for over 10 years and featured many of the big names in country music. Johnny Bond (who wrote most of the scripts), Merle Travis and Joe and Rose Maphis were regulars. Frequent visitors to the show included Johnny Cash, The Collins Kids, Rex Allen, Tex Ritter, Lefty Frizzell, Martha Carson, Ted Daffan, Freddy Hart, Tommy Duncan and Mac Wiseman.

1969 Spade Cooley, western swing bandleader, died in California. He was in prison for the murder of his wife and had been given an evening leave to appear at a concert in Oakland. He died during the intermission after suffering a heart attack.

1976 Jerry Lee Lewis arrested in the early hours of the morning in his Lincoln Convertable, demanding to see Elvis, and waving a Derringer pistol. The police came and charged the singer with public drunkenness and carrying a gun but, the following May, a Memphis judge declared Jerry Lee "not guilty".

24th NOVEMBER

1940 Johnny Carver born in Jackson, Mississippi. His breakthrough came as featured singer with the house band at North Hollywood's famed Palomino night club, in the mid-sixties. This job brought him to the attention of Imperial Records and he had his first country hit on the label in 1967, 'Your Lily White Hands'. Johnny moved to Epic, then ABC with whom he made his Top Ten debut with a country version of 'Tie A Yellow Ribbon Round The Old Oak Tree'. He also had success as a songwriter, composing hits for the likes of Ferlin Husky and Connie Smith.

1973 Charlie Rich crowns a phenomenal year with 'The Most Beautiful Girl' at the top of the country charts for the first of three weeks. The song was an even bigger hit than 'Behind Closed Doors', earning platinum status for two million sales. Both songs came from the same Billy Sherrill-produced album, *Behind Closed Doors,* on Epic and, not unsurprisingly, won the CMA 'Album Of The Year.' Rich received many other awards in 1973, including a Grammy and CMA 'Best Male Vocalist.'

1979 *Willie Nelson Sings Kris Kristofferson* entered the country LP charts, a tribute from one great songwriter–performer to another. Nelson gave his own distinctive treatment to most of Kris's best known songs, including 'Me And Bobby McGee', 'Help Me Make It Through The Night', 'For The Good Times' and 'Sunday Mornin' Comin' Down'.

25th NOVEMBER

1926 Biff Collie (Hiram Abiff Collie), one of the best known personalities in the history of country music radio, born in Little Rock, Arkansas. He started work as an announcer at the age of 17 on KMAC in San Antonio, progressing to be leading DJ on the powerful Houston stations, KNUZ and KPRC. In the fifties Biff was involved in promoting country tours and by the sixties he was firmly established as one of the top jocks in the US, working for KFOX in Southern California and broadcasting on syndicated shows.

1978 New entries in the country chart included

the Bee Gees with 'Rest Your Love On Me' and Dolly Parton with 'Baby I'm Burning'. America was at the height of the disco craze, fuelled by the runaway success of the film *Saturday Night Fever* and its soundtrack album which was dominated by the songs of the Bee Gees. 'Rest Your Love On Me' was picked up by country DJs and stayed on the chart for 12 weeks. Meanwhile 'Baby I'm Burning' was given a special "disco mix" and Dolly became the only country artist to score a major disco hit. The version that eventually topped the country charts, however, (in January 1979) was the untainted original.

26th NOVEMBER

1955 Rock 'n' roll finally hit Britain. Bill Haley and the Comets took up residency at the top of the pop charts with 'Rock Around The Clock', spurred by the success of the controversial film, *Blackboard Jungle,* which featured the song as its theme tune. The record stayed at number one until January. Haley was the only rock 'n' roll singer to have made in-roads on the British charts in 1955; the rest of the hit parade continued to be dominated by middle-of-the-road ballad singers, plus Slim Whitman's 'Rose Marie' (which had been in the Top Ten for six months) and a bizarre record by the Singing Dogs. But a change was coming. There were a growing number of "teddy boys", sporting a new fashion that included drainpipe trousers and drape jackets, eager for more exciting music.

1963 Dottie West made her debut on the country charts as a performer, with 'Let Me Off On The Corner'. She'd won an RCA contract after proving herself as a successful songwriter, composing 'Is This Me', a hit for Jim Reeves that won Dottie the first of her many awards.

27th NOVEMBER

193? R. J. Blackwood, leader of the popular gospel group the Blackwood Singers, born in Memphis, Tennessee. A contemporary of Elvis Presley, he attended the same First Assembly of God Church in the city and sang at the funeral of Gladys Presley. One of the best known gospel groups in the US, R. W. Blackwood and the Blackwood Singers have had best-selling records, including 'Turn Your Radio On' and 'Put Your Hand In The Hand'.

1944 Eddie Rabbitt born in Brooklyn, New York, of Irish ancestry. His enthusiasm for music was encouraged by a fiddle and accordion-playing father. Eddie began performing in New Jersey clubs in the mid-sixties, then travelled to Nashville in 1968. Within days he'd found a taker for his song 'Working My Way Up From The Bottom', which became a hit for Roy Drusky. "Boy, this is going to be easy," Eddie remembers thinking at the time; "but it wasn't easy, I soon found that Nashville is where all the best musicians in the world gather, and I was in competition with every one of them." It took years before he achieved his ambition of being a successful recording artist, but he had more hits as a writer, most notably with 'Kentucky Rain' for Elvis, and 'Pure Love' for Ronnie Milsap. Signed to Elektra, Eddie first made the charts as a singer with 'You Get To Me', in 1974. Voted 'Best New Artist of 1977' by the CMA, Rabbitt subsequently reached superstar status with hits like 'Every Which Way But Loose' and 'I Love A Rainy Night'.

28th NOVEMBER

1925 The very first broadcast of WSM Barn Dance, from the WSM studio on the fifth floor of the National Life and Insurance Company building in Nashville, Tennessee. George D. Hay introduced Uncle Jimmy Thompson, an 80-year-old fiddler who claimed that he could fiddle "the taters off a vine." "Uncle Jimmy told us he had a thousand tunes," Hay recalled several years later; "he was given a comfortable chair in front of an old carbon microphone. While his niece, Mrs Eva Thompson Jones, played the piano accompaniment, our reporter presented Uncle Jimmy and announced that he would be glad to answer requests for old time tunes. Immediately telegrams started to pour into WSM. One hour later at nine o'clock we asked Uncle Jimmy if he hadn't done enough fiddling, to which he replied, 'Why shucks, a man don't get warmed up for an hour. I just won an eight-day fiddling contest down in Dallas, Texas, and here's my blue ribbon to prove it." The WSM Barn Dance began regular Saturday night broadcasting soon after this historic session, and was renamed the Grand Ole Opry in December 1927.

1938 Bob Wills and the Texas Playboys recorded 'San Antonio Rose' for the first time. Originally performed as an instrumental, Tommy Duncan recorded a version with vocals in April 1940. The tune is the best known in the Bob Wills catalogue, and was a major pop hit for Bing Crosby in 1941.

1964 Willie Nelson made his debut on the Grand Ole Opry.

29th NOVEMBER

1917 Multi-talented Merle Travis, influential guitarist, actor, gifted songwriter and successful performer, born in Rosewood, Kentucky. His father taught him to play the banjo at the age of six, then his brother built him a guitar that he taught himself to play, unconsciously developing a new style by playing the instrument in the same way as a banjo. He became a musical vagabond, travelling around the US, then joined the Tennessee Tomcats in 1935 before working with Clayton McMichen's Georgia Wildcats who were regulars on a Cincinnati radio show for several years. After war service, Merle migrated to California where he worked with Cliffie Stone and others, then signed to Capitol and had successful records, including 'Divorce Me COD' and 'So Round, So Firm, So Fully Packed'. Travis somehow found time to act in some movies and write hit records, including 'Sixteen Tons' for Tennessee Ernie Ford. In the fifties he was a regular on the two big California country TV shows, "Town Hall Party" and "Hometown Jamboree", and in the sixties spent a lot of time in Nashville and joined the Opry, but then returned to the West Coast. He was elected to the Hall of Fame in 1977.

1941 Singer Jody Miller born in Phoenix, Arizona. She grew up in a musical family, her father was a fiddler, and she led a folk group at school. Jody worked as a secretary for several years, but after a move to California began a musical career. Her debut record, for Capitol, was a huge hit—'Queen Of The House' in 1965—the first of several country successes, including 'He's So Fine' and 'Baby I'm Yours'.

30th NOVEMBER

1736 The first fiddling contest in America, in Hanover County, Virginia. Researcher Dick Hulan has discovered a story in the *Virginia Gazette* announcing a St Andrew's Day celebration that offered a "fine Ceremona Fiddle to be plaid for, by any number of Country fiddlers."

1931 Teddy Wilburn (Thurman Theodore Wilburn) of the Wilburn Brothers, born in Thayer, Missouri. Teddy and his elder brother Doyle were performing together from an early age and debuted at the Opry in 1941 as the Singing Wilburn Children. They have had a long and busy career, run a booking agency and are successful publishers; their company Surefire Music published seven of the songs in the movie *Coal Miner's Daughter*, including the title song.

The Wilburn Brothers

1974 David Allan Coe made his chart debut as a performer with '(If I Could Climb) The Walls Of A Bottle'.

D E C E M B E R

1st DECEMBER

1954 Fred Rose, founder of the mighty Acuff-Rose publishing house, died in Nashville. He had considerable success as a songwriter, his best known compositions being 'Blue Eyes Crying In The Rain', which was Willie Nelson's first big hit, 'Take These Chains From My Heart', a success for Ray Charles in the sixties and several of Hank Williams' best known songs, including 'Kaw Liga', 'Settin' The Woods On Fire' and 'I'll Never Get Out Of This World Alive'. Rose also had a big hand in several songs that didn't bear his name because he frequently helped young writers, including Williams and Gene Autry, to complete their compositions. He was the first music industry figure to be elected to Country Music Hall of Fame.

1966 Bluegrass musician Carter Stanley, guitarist and vocalist with the influential Stanley Brothers, died in hospital in Bristol, Virginia. A few months before he'd made a triumphant UK debut, with his brother, at London's Royal Albert Hall.

1968 Texas songstress Billie Jo Spears made her first appearance in the country charts, with 'He's Got More Love In His Little Finger' on Capitol.

2nd DECEMBER

1898 Herman Crook, harmonica playing leader of the Crook Brothers, a favourite hoedown band from the early days of the Grand Ole Opry, born.

1950 John Wesley Ryles born in Bastrop, Louisiana. As a small boy he sang with his family in the Ryles Family Singers, was playing the Dallas club circuit at the age of 13, and three years later arrived in Nashville. He worked as a studio engineer and demo singer, then signed to Columbia and cut 'Kay', his first Top Ten hit, at the age of 19. More hits followed, but when they slowed down a disillusioned John moved to Missouri. He carried on singing, however, and six years later he was back in the charts, realising perhaps that he'd been a little too young to handle fame the first time around. His seventies hits for ABC/Dot included 'Once In A Lifetime Thing' and 'Liberated Woman'.

1967 Porter Wagoner and his new partner Dolly Parton appeared in the country chart with their first duet hit, 'The Last Thing On My Mind'. With help from their regular TV appearances, Dolly and Porter scored a further 18 chart entries together, including 'Please Don't Stop Loving Me' (a number one in 1974), 'Daddy Was An Old Time Preacher Man' and 'Better Move It On Home'.

3rd DECEMBER

1910 Rabon Delmore of the Delmore Brothers duo, born in Elkmont, Alabama. He grew up on a farm with his elder brother Alton and they sang together as children. In their teens they were local fiddle champions, then in 1931 were "discovered" by Columbia and began a long recording career, switching to King Records in the forties. They were radio favourites in the thirties and forties, beginning at the Grand Ole Opry in 1932. Most of their material was written by Alton, though Rabon was also a writer, and their best known songs included 'Blues Stay Away From Me' and 'Beautiful Brown Eyes'. The Delmore Brothers moved to Houston in the late forties and their successful partnership ended when Rabon became very ill; he died the day after his 42nd birthday in 1952.

1923 Hubert Long, far-sighted and very successful Nashville manager, publisher and talent booker, born in Proteet, Texas. He worked for Colonel Tom Parker, doing advance publicity for Eddy Arnold, then set up Nashville's first talent agency in 1953, subsequently helping and developing the careers of many country stars, including Bill Anderson, Ferlin Husky, George Jones, Skeeter Davis and David Houston. A founder of the Country Music Association and the Country Music Foundation, Hubert Long died in 1972.

Ferlin Husky

1927 Ferlin Husky born on a farm near Flat River, Missouri. Investigation of his early years in the music business reveals a confusion of different names and spellings. He moved to Bakersfield, California and worked as a DJ, calling himself Terry Preston, later performing under the same name. He recorded briefly for Four Star, then signed to Capitol in the early fifties and made country-pop records as Ferlin Huskey and also as hayseed satirist Simon Crum. His first chart success came as part of a duo with Jean Shepard, singing 'Dear John Letter'. Ferlin had reverted to the correct spelling of his real name in 1955 when he began a long string of solo country successes, including the chart-toppers 'Gone' and 'Wings Of A Dove', though he continued to make occasional records as Simon Crum and had a huge hit in 1958 with 'Country Music Is Here To Stay'.

1973 Bob Wills last recording session, in Dallas, Texas. He assembled several members of the Texas Playboys, including Leon McAuliffe, Al Stricklin, Eldon Shamblin, Leon Rausch and Johnny Gimble, plus guest Merle Haggard, a long-time fan of Wills and his music.

4th DECEMBER

1915 Hondo Crouch (John Russell Crouch), who found fame as owner of the tiny Texas hamlet of Luckenbach, born in Hondo, Texas. A multi-talented man, he was a journalist (using the pen name of Peter Cedartaker), actor, whittler, philosopher and prankster.

1944 Chris Hillman born in Los Angeles, California. A musical enthusiast since childhood, he played mandolin in his first group, the bluegrass-orientated Scottsville Squirrel Barkers, later finding fame as guitarist and singer with The Byrds. When Gram Parsons joined the band, Chris had the necessary support for his project to make a country LP with the band—*Sweetheart Of The Rodeo,* the pioneering country-rock album of 1968, was the result. Chris and Gram left the band soon afterwards, developing their country-rock ideas as the Flying Burrito Brothers, with pedal steel guitarist Sneeky Pete Kleinow, bassist Chris Etheridge and making the acclaimed *Gilded Palace Of Sin* album.

1952 Raban Delmore, of the Delmore Brothers, died in Athens, Alabama.

1956 The Million Dollar Quartet recorded at the Sun studio in Memphis. According to a report in the *Memphis Press Scimitar* the next day, Carl Perkins was recording at Sun when Johnny Cash, Jerry Lee Lewis and Elvis Presley (who was now signed to RCA) dropped into the studio, and the four sang several songs together. The *Press Scimitar* reporter wrote, "If Sam Phillips had been on his toes, he'd have turned the recorder on . . . ". But Sam was on his toes—he'd already had the foresight to alert the journalist and photographer for what he obviously realised was an historic occasion, though it was 25 years before the tapes of the session were available in record form as *The Million Dollar Quartet* (Sun 1006). The delay was caused because Sam was no longer the owner of Presley's contract.

1973 Bob Wills suffered a stroke after a two-day recording session for United Artists at Dallas. He never regained consciousness, though he didn't die until May 1975.

5th DECEMBER

1947 Jim Messina, West Coast country-rock musician, born in Maywood, California. After working as a recording engineer in Hollywood, Jim joined Buffalo Springfield in the late sixties, was one of the founder members of Poco, then had a string of successful LPs with Kenny Loggins, as part of the Loggins and Messina duo.

1964 Lorne Greene, star of the TV western series "Bonanza", entered the charts with 'Ringo', a recitation about a notorious gunfighter and the sheriff who had saved his life. The record was a phenomenal international success, but Lorne's only big hit.

1981 Nine years after breaking up, the John Fogerty-led rock band, Creedence Clearwater Revival, scored their first country hit, with a version of the Leadbelly classic, 'Cotton Fields'.

6th DECEMBER

1877 The first sound recording made, on a machine invented by Thomas Edison. The first recorded words were the nursery rhyme 'Mary Had A Little Lamb'. Edison was granted a patent for his invention, which he called the phonograph, a year later.

194? Helen Cornelius born in Hannibal, Missouri. After winning the Ted Mack Amateur Contest three times in a row, Helen decided to make a career of music. Her first success came as a songwriter, composing hits for Jeannie C. Riley, Lynn Anderson and Dottsy, then she signed to RCA, who teamed her with Jim Ed Brown. They became very popular, were voted 'Vocal Duo of the Year' by the CMA in 1977, and had hits including 'I Don't Want To Have To Marry You', 'If The World Ran Out Of Love Tonight' and 'Lying In Love With You'. Since 1980 Helen has been concentrating on a solo career.

1949 Black folk singer Leadbelly died in a New York hospital. Many of his songs are still being performed by folk and country artists, including 'Good Night Irene', 'Cotton Fields' and 'Black Betty'.

7th DECEMBER

1931 Bob Osborne, eldest of the Osborne Brothers, born in Hyden, Kentucky. Bob played mandolin and sang tenor with the popular bluegrass group. They were regulars on the WWVA Wheeling Jamboree show and had several best-selling records for Decca, from the mid-sixties.

1941 A reporter from the prestigious *Life* magazine came to Virginia to interview the Carter Family. Country music was rarely considered worthy of treatment by national magazines in those days, so this was a special event. June Carter recalls what happened. "He was from New York and we couldn't understand one word that he said. He made motions, we all smiled. Anita did her sitting-on-the-head routine and, not to be outdone, I showed him that I was still a pretty good stomach mover. We fed him good, he photographed the Carter family, and we were all set to have ourselves in *Life* magazine. But it was December 7, 1941. That day the Japanese bombed Pearl Harbor. All that we ever saw to remind us that we had an interview was a bushel basket of burned out flash bulbs. I cherished them for months."

1961 June Carter and Johnny Cash appeared together for the first time, at a concert in Dallas, Texas.

Johnny Cash and June Carter

1977 Bill Boyd, western singer and film actor, died. He had been brought up on a ranch in Texas and sang western songs as a child. He had a daily radio show on WRR in Dallas, "Bill Boyd and his Cowboy Ramblers", which ran from 1932 until the sixties, had a lengthy association with RCA Records and appeared in many cowboy films.

8th DECEMBER

1914 Multi-talented Floyd Tillman, successful songwriter, singer and instrumentalist, born in Ryan, Oklahoma. He began playing honky-tonks in the Houston, Texas, area in the thirties, working with a variety of bands, including the Blue Ridge Playboys, with whom he began songwriting in earnest. In the forties he had several country hits, many of which were also pop successes for other artists. The best known of his 200 or more songs are 'It Makes No Difference Now' (which was his first record) 'Slippin' Around', 'I Love You So Much It Hurts' and 'I'll Never Slip Around Again'.

1922 Jean Ritchie, the traditional folk performer who has done much to keep alive the traditional music of the Appalachian Mountains, born in Viper, Kentucky. She's the best known member of the Ritchie Family, who have a folk song tradition that goes back several generations. During the folk revival of the fifties and sixties, Jean was greatly in demand for festivals where she sang and played the Appalachian dulcimer —a stringed, zither-like instrument.

1941 On the day after the bombing of Pearl Harbour by the Japanese, Tommy Duncan, vocalist with Bob Wills and the Texas Playboys, rrived for the band's regular noon radio show in Tulsa and announced, "I don't know about you guys, but I'm going to join 'this man's Army' and fight these sons-of-bitches" Before the end of the year Wills had lost most of his best musicians to the armed forces. It was one of many examples of how World War II had a profound effect on country music—altering, shortening or ending the careers of several important acts. Another significant effect of the War was the drastic reduction of the amount of vinyl available for discs; few new acts were recorded, the limited resources being kept for the releases of established stars.

9th DECEMBER

1932 Billy Edd Wheeler born in Whitesville, West Virginia. Best known as a writer, he composed 'Jackson'—which was a country hit for June Carter and Johnny Cash, also a pop success for Nancy Sinatra and Lee Hazelwood—and 'The Reverend Mr Black' for the Kingston Trio. Billy also had some success as a performer, most notably with 'Ode To The Little Brown Shack Out Back' in 1964.

1938 David Houston, a major country star of the sixties and early seventies, born in Shreveport, Louisiana. David is a descendant of General Sam Houston, after whom the famous Texan city is named, and Robert E. Lee. He learnt to play the guitar early in life and made his first appearance on the locally-based "Louisiana Hayride" a the age of 12, later becoming a regular performer. He was signed to Epic Records and had the first of many hits with 'Mountain Of Love' in 1963. Houston's six number one's include 'Almost Persuaded', 'You Mean The World To Me' and 'Already It's Heaven'. In 1970 David began a successful partnership with Barbara Mandrell and they had duet hits like 'After Closing Time' and 'I Love You, I Love You'.

10th DECEMBER

1952 Chicano country star Johnny Rodriguez (Juan Raul Rodriguez) born in Sabinal, Texas, some 90 miles from the Mexican border. He began playing guitar and singing as a child and led a rock band while at high school. His "discovery" had a bizarre beginning—when he was 17, Johnny was arrested for stealing and barbecuing a goat. In jail he sang songs to pass the time and was overheard by a patron who passed the word along. As a result, he was offered a singing job at the nearby Alamo Village Amusement Park where he was heard by visiting Nashville stars Bobby Bare and Tom T. Hall. Both were sufficiently impressed to invite him to Music City. Eventually he did just that, was soon fronting Tom T.'s road band and writing songs for his publishing company. In a short time, Hall helped Rodriguez land a recording contract and in 1972, aged just 20, he had his first hit with 'Pass Me By'. A long string of hits followed, including chart-topping successes, 'Ridin' My Thumb To Texas' and 'That's The Way Love Goes'.

1966 The very first appearance in the country charts of Tammy Wynette, with 'Apartment Number 9'. The Billy Sherrill-produced record only reached 44 on the listings, but her next 21 singles made the Top Ten. Tammy (plain Virginia Wynette Pugh then) had come to Nashville in the hope of becoming a country singer and spent six months "living in a one-room efficiency in Nashville on my own with three kids, an old beat-up car, no work and nobody to call for help." Just as she was about to give up she met Billy Sherrill, boss of Epic Records. He heard her sing only three songs and knew that he'd discovered a star.

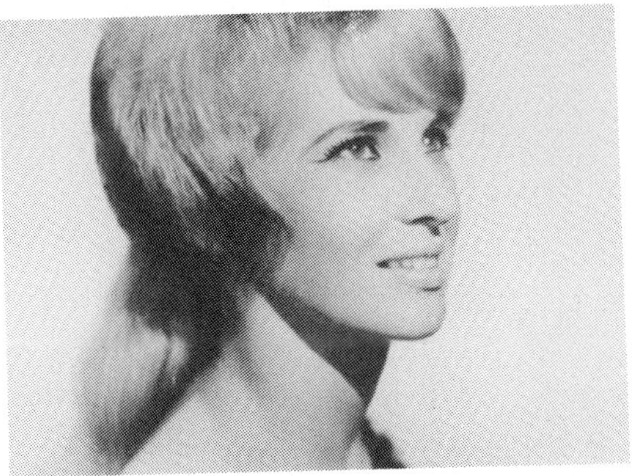

11th DECEMBER

1915 Dorothy Laverne Good, better known as Dolly from The Girls of the Golden West, born in Muleshoe, Texas. The Girls were two of the first female country stars, popular in the thirties and forties through appearances on WLS National Barn Dance, then the Boone County Jamboree and the Midwestern Hayride radio shows.

1944 Brenda Lee (Brenda Mae Tarpley) born near Augusta, Georgia. She started singing at the age of four, worked on local TV shows, graduating to Red Foley's Ozark Jubilee and a recording contract with Decca, all before she'd reached her teens. She had her first country success in 1957, with 'One Step At A Time', then scored a string of Nashville-produced rock and pop hits like 'Dynamite' (which earned her the Little Miss Dynamite label—she's just 4' 9" tall) and 'Sweet Nuthins'. Brenda was back with country music in the seventies, her big sellers including a version of Kris Kristofferson's 'Nobody Wins' in 1972. Still making country records in the eighties, Brenda somehow finds time for extensive TV and film work, plus a syndicated radio series, "Brenda Lee's Country Profile".

1946 Hank Williams' very first recording session, for the small Sterling label in New York City.

1949 Fiddlin' John Carson, one of the recording pioneers of country music, died in Georgia.

12th DECEMBER

194? LaCosta, elder sister of Tanya Tucker, born in Snyder, Texas. She worked for a while in a band with Tanya, called the Country Westerners, then pursued a career in a hospital as medical records technician. But Tanya's remarkable success encouraged her to return to music; signed to Capitol, LaCosta had numerous country hits in the seventies, including 'Get On My Love Train' and 'He Took Me For A Ride'.

1955 John Anderson, up-and-coming young star with a sound deeply rooted in fifties honky-tonk country music, born in Apopka, Florida. He came to Nashville after graduating from high school and went through the time-honoured process of taking part-time jobs while trying to break into the music business. Hard work, persistence and talent eventually landed him a publishing contract and then a deal with Warner Brothers in 1977. After three years of minor hits, John broke into the Top Ten with '1959', and then 'I'm Just An Old Chunk Of Coal'.

13th DECEMBER

1934 Lulu Belle and Scotty Wiseman married. They had teamed up as a musical duo the previous year, on the Chicago-based radio show WLS National Barn Dance. Known as "the Sweethearts of Country Music", they were popular regulars on the programme for 25 years. Lulu Belle had been singing with Red Foley prior to Scotty's arrival on the show, and some listeners wrote angry letters to WLS accusing Wiseman of stealing Foley's girlfriend!

1974 Bill Swan top of the country charts with 'I Can Help'. He had been trying to break through as a performer since the early sixties, when he recorded with Mirt Mirley & The Rhythm Steppers for Bill Black in Memphis. Swan had subsequently worked for Elvis as gateman at Graceland, and was in the bands of his musical friends Kris Kristofferson, Kinky Friedman and Billy Jo Shaver. 'I Can Help' was phenomenally successful, selling five million copies worldwide and reaching the best-selling charts in over a dozen countries, including England, France, Finland and Australia.

1980 *Any Which Way You Can,* the soundtrack album from the Clint Eastwood film, entered the country charts. It had been a remarkable year for country music soundtrack LPs: *Bronco Billy, Coal Miner's Daughter, Electric Horseman, Smokey And The Bandit 2, Honeysuckle Rose* and *Urban Cowboy* all made the Top Ten.

14th DECEMBER

1932 Charlie Rich born in Colt, Arkansas. While in the Air Force he formed a jazz/blues band called the Velvetones, which featured his wife Margaret on vocals. Returning to Arkansas, they were farmers for a while, then moved to Memphis where Charlie worked on the local club scene. He was "discovered" by Bill Justis of Sun Records, who persuaded him to change to a rock 'n' roll style and then produced his hit single 'Lonely Weekends'. After Sun, Rich was on various labels, including Smash, with whom he had another hit, 'Mohair Sam'. In 1967 he was signed to Epic by Billy Sherrill (they'd previously worked together at Sun) and their partnership led to several small country hits before 'Take It On Home' cracked the Top Ten in 1972. The next two releases, 'Behind Closed Doors' and 'The Most Beautiful Girl', made Rich a superstar and began the phenomenal crossover boom in country music sales to pop audiences—a trend that increased dramatically during the late seventies, with artists like Kenny Rogers capitalising on the sophisticated "countrypolitan" formula that Rich and Sherrill had developed. Charlie has had successful records since, though nothing to top his two biggest hits.

1962 Ned Miller entered the country charts with 'From A Jack To A King', later a big hit on the pop charts and a crossover hit ten years before the term was in regular usage in Nashville music industry circles.

15th DECEMBER

1918 Alvin Pleasant Delaney Carter, better known as "A P" or "Doc", leader of the Carter Family, born in Maces Springs, Virginia. He had a strict religious background and grew up in an area rich in traditional music. A P sold fruit trees for a living, and while on a trip to Copper Creek, Virginia, with his wares, met Sara Dougherty, who later became his wife. They shared a love for music, and when Sara's cousin Maybelle Addington married A P's brother, the three began singing and playing together. When A P saw a newspaper report in the summer of 1927 about a record company audition for local musicians in Bristol, on the Virginia/Tennessee border, they travelled to the town and made their first recordings as the Carter Family. When they'd recorded all the folk material they knew, A P began collecting more, thereby preserving many traditional American songs that might otherwise have been lost. He was the organizer of the group and held them together through some difficult times, especially after he and Sara separated in 1932. A P, along with Sara and Maybelle, was elected to the Country Music Hall of Fame in 1970.

1926 Rose Maddox born in Boaz, Alabama. She was vocalist with the Maddox Brothers and Rose, one of the most popular country acts in the post war years, and performed regularly on the "Louisiana Hayride" show. When the family group split up in 1960, Rose went solo and scored several big hits, including 'Sing A Little Song Of Heartache'.

1928 Ernie Ashworth, popular country star of the sixties, born in Huntsville, Alabama. His biggest hits include the chart-topping 'Talk Back Trembling Lips' and 'I Love To Dance With Annie'.

1933 Country music's "Mr Smooth" Jerry Wallace born in Kansas City, Missouri. Jerry's first taste of chart success came as a rock 'n' roller in the fifties, but he switched to country music in the sixties and had many hits, including 'Primrose Lane', 'Do You Know What It's Like To Be Lonesome' and 'If You Leave Me Tonight I'll Cry'.

1955 Randy Parton, eighth of the 12 Parton siblings, born in Sevierville, Tennessee. At 19 he was playing bass with Jean Shepard, then spent five years playing with Dolly, who introduced him every night by saying, "Here's my brother, he's Randy!" Now a solo artist, Randy is signed to RCA.

16th DECEMBER

1919 Earl Bolick, who formed the Blue Sky Boys with his younger brother Bill, born in Hickory, North Carolina. The duo performed old-timey and religious material and were very popular from 1935 until the late forties, through regular radio broadcasts over North Carolina stations and several record releases.

1937 Jim Glaser, youngest of the three Glaser Brothers, born on the family farm in Spaulding, Nebraska. He had already begun a successful solo career when the trio split in the early seventies, scoring several modest hits, including 'Woman, Woman', which he co-wrote and which was a big pop hit for Gary Puckett and the Union Gap. The Glaser Brothers split came after much feuding. "We tried to be too involved," Jim explained, "we had too much going on, running publishing companies and staying on the road all the time. Things got to be very hectic and the tension just mounted until it peaked in 1973." However, after seven years the brothers were happily reunited.

Jim Glaser

1972 Don Williams made his very first appearance on the charts as a solo performer, with 'The Shelter Of Your Eyes'.

17th DECEMBER

1905 Karl Victor Davis, half of the Karl and Harty team, born in Mount Vernon, Kentucky. Karl and Harty were a popular guitar and mandolin duo who were featured on the WLS National Barn Dance show from 1930 until 1951. Karl was the songwriter of the pair, composing most of their material, including 'I'm Just Here To Get My Baby Out Of Jail', 'The Prisoner's Dream' and 'Kentucky', all of which have subsequently been hits for other country performers.

1938 Nat Stuckey born in Cass County, Texas. Nat's involvement in the music business began as a disc jockey, and he was featured on KWKW in Shreveport, Louisiana for several years. Then he became a writer, composing hits like 'Waitin' In Your Welfare Line' for Buck Owens and 'Pop A Top' for Jim Ed Brown. His efforts to win a Nashville recording contract were unsuccessful, so he signed with the Shreveport-based Paula label, and his faith in his own ability was rewarded when he reached the country Top Five with his song 'Sweet Thang'. After several more hits with Paula, Nat joined RCA and had success with 'Plastic Saddle', 'Joe and Mabel's 12th Street Bar And Grill' and others.

18th DECEMBER

1904 Wilf Carter, the cowboy singing star who was sometimes known as Montana Slim, born in Guysboro, Nova Scotia, Canada. An authentic cowboy, Wilf initially sang for his own amusement, but then found himself in demand as an entertainer at rodeos. He made his radio debut in 1933 on CFCN in Calgary, moved to Radio Vancouver, and was then signed up by CBS for a New York radio show, where he first adopted the persona of Montana Slim. Carter is said to have written several hundred cowboy songs, including 'Swiss Moonlight Lullaby' and 'I'm Hittin' The Trail', and recorded for RCA Victor, Bluebird, Decca and Starday.

1970 Kris Kristofferson's classic song 'Help Me Make It Through The Night' made its very first chart appearance; performed by Sammi Smith, it was a version that would be a major country and pop hit in 1971. The song has subsequently been an international soul hit for Gladys Knight and the Pips in 1972, a reggae smash, in Jamaica and England, for John Holt in 1974, and most recently a country success again, for Willie Nelson.

19th DECEMBER

1908 Bill Carlisle, country singer, instrumentalist and comic, born in Wakefield, Kentucky. He formed a duo with his younger brother Cliff, and they played shows and made frequent radio broadcasts in the Louisville, Kentucky area from the late twenties until the late forties. After separating from his brother, Bill formed The Carlisles, signed to Mercury Records and had several hits, including 'No Help Wanted' and 'Is Zat You Myrtle?'. Their popularity increased with appearances on the "Louisiana Hayride", and then membership of the Grand Ole Opry from 1954. When The Carlisles disbanded, Bill

The Carlisles

continued as a solo performer and had another hit, with 'What Kind Of Deal Is This' in 1965.

1925 Little Jimmy Dickens, diminutive (4' 11") country star of the fifties and sixties, born in Bolt, West Virginia. He began singing professionally in 1942, as Jimmy The Kid, with Johnny Bailes and his Happy Valley Boys, then started performing as a solo artist, joining the Opry in 1948 and beginning a long association with Columbia records soon afterwards. His numerous hits include 'Country Boy' (his first, in 1949) and the international pop success 'May The Bird Of Paradise Fly Up Your Nose', in 1965.

1945 John McEuen, multi-instrumentalist and a central figure of the Nitty Gritty Dirt Band, born in Long Beach, California.

195? Janie Fricke born near South Whitney, Indiana. She came from a musical family; her father was a guitarist and her mother taught piano and played the organ at the local church. After college, Janie worked in Memphis and Dallas, had an unsuccessful time trying to break into the Los Angeles session scene, but fared much better in Nashville where she was soon the most popular back-up singer in the city. She sang on over 1000 records and made numerous jingles—everything from 7-UP to United Airline advertisements. Billy Sherrill signed her to CBS in 1977 after realizing her potential as solo performer during sessions with Johnny Duncan. Her run of hits began the following year and included 'Please Help Me, I'm Falling' and 'Down To My Last Broken Heart'.

20th DECEMBER

1907 Skeeter Willis, fiddler and vocalist with the Willis Brothers, born in Coalton, Oklahoma. Guy, Skeeter and Vic Willis grew up in a strong country music background and had a reputation as talented musicians and harmony singers while in their teens. They made their radio debut in 1932 and were soon one of the most popular musical outfits in the state of Oklahoma. After a four year break because of World War II, they re-formed in the mid-forties, joined the Opry, worked briefly with Hank Williams—featured on his early sides for the Sterling label—then began an eight year association with Eddy Arnold. The Willis Brothers recorded prolifically, both in their own right—scoring hits like 'Give Me 40 Acres (To Turn This Rig Around)'—and as back-up musicians for others. Skeeter died in the mid-seventies, Guy retired, but Vic was still performing at the start of the eighties.

1957 Elvis Presley, at the height of his popularity as rock 'n' roll performer, received a draft notice. He had been expecting to be called up for Army service, but the notice came sooner than expected. Presley wrote a polite letter to the Memphis Draft Board asking for a delay so that he could complete the filming of *King Creole,* pointing out that he wasn't asking for himself, but for the movie company, who stood to lose a lot of money if the picture was cancelled. His request was granted.

21st DECEMBER

1933 Freddie Hart born in Lochapoka, Alabama. From the age of five, Freddie's great ambition was to be a country star. He ran away from home several times and invariably headed towards Nashville, Tennessee, where he tried to join the Grand Ole Opry, though always without success. On his return he'd tell his family that he'd been on the legendary radio show, "when you weren't listening". He joined the Marines at the age of 14 and found that his singing was popular with the other soldiers. After his tour of duty was complete he took to travelling again, as a footloose musical itinerant. In 1951 he met the great Lefty Frizzell, who was impressed with the youngster's singing and determination "to be a star". Lefty helped him get a recording contract with Capitol, and Freddie was soon a regular on the California TV show "Home Town Jamboree". He made his chart debut in 1959 with 'The Wall', and after 12 years of small hits he recorded 'Easy Loving', which shot to number one in 1971 and made Freddie Hart a major country star. Several more best-sellers followed, including 'My Hang Up Is You' and 'Bless Your Heart'.

Albert Lee

1943 Albert Lee, gifted guitarist who made his name with Eric Clapton and Emmylou Harris' Hot Band, born in Hertfordshire, England. He started with a skiffle group, then played with the semi-legendary British bands, Country Fever, and Heads, Hands and Feet, before moving to America and working with The Crickets, Jackson Browne, Joe Cocker, Don Everly and others. He then hitched up with the Hot Band, making an indelible stamp on Emmylou's LPs with his unique guitar and mandolin style. In 1979 Albert made a critically acclaimed solo LP for A&M called *Hiding*.

22nd DECEMBER

1921 Hawkshaw Hawkins (Harold Hawkins) born in Huntingdon, West Virginia. He had his first success as a musician at the age of 15, winning a local talent show where the prize was a regular radio show. Hawkshaw became a popular local performer and, after a period of war service, his career took off with appearances on the famed WWVA Wheeling Jamboree show. He signed to King Records and had several hits, including 'I Wasted A Nickel' and 'Slow Poke'. In 1954 he began appearing on Red Foley's "Jubilee USA" TV show and a year later joined the Opry. Hawkshaw's life ended tragically in 1963, in the same plane crash that killed Patsy Cline and Cowboy Copas.

19?? Red Steagall (Russell Steagall) born in Gainsville, Texas. His left arm was paralysed after he had polio as a teenager, but he overcame his disabilities and taught himself to play guitar and mandolin, and found success as a country performer. His hits include 'Lone Star Beer And Bob Wills Music', in 1976.

1973 Merle Haggard began a four week stay at the top of the country charts with 'If We Make It Through December', his sixth chart-topping record in two years.

23rd DECEMBER

1949 Hank Snow made his debut in the American country charts (he'd been a big star in his native Canada for over a decade, but RCA hadn't released his records in the US) with 'Marriage Vows'. Hank subsequently scored at least one hit every year until 1970.

1978 Kenny Rogers' version of 'The Gambler', one of the most popular country songs of the seventies, top of the country charts. The song was written by Don Schlitz, a young writer from North Carolina. "I wrote the song after the death of my father, and in many ways it's about him. He was a policeman in Durham, and the most incredible man I've ever known. When someone who's really close to you dies, you go through a whole process of channelling it out one way or another. For me it came out in this song, 'The Gambler'. I had a dry period after his death when I just couldn't write anything, then one day I went for a walk and when I came back I wrote it very quickly. It was almost like automatic typing."

24th DECEMBER

1913 Lulu Belle (Myrtle Eleanor Cooper), of the popular husband and wife team, Lulu Belle and Scotty, who were favourites with the WLS National Barn Dance audiences for 25 years, born in Boone, North Carolina. She had begun performing in public while a teenager, and was only 19 when she joined the Chicago-based radio show. Her future husband joined in 1933 and the following year they began recording together; their best known songs including 'Whippoorwill Time', 'Mountain Dew', 'Empty Christmas Stocking' and 'In The Doghouse Now'. Lulu Belle and Scotty also appeared regularly on the WLS Breakfast In The Blue Ridge show and on Chicago's WNBQ TV station, from 1949. They retired from performing in 1958.

19?? Black country singer Stoney Edwards born in Oklahoma of Afro-Indian parents. Stoney grew up listening to country music on the radio and says that Bob Wills and Hank Williams had a profound influence on his becoming a singer. Based in California, he's best known for hits like 'Blackbird' and 'She's My Rock'.

25th DECEMBER

1908 Alton Delmore, eldest of the Delmore Brothers, born in Elkmont, Alabama. He wrote most of the duo's material and is said to have composed over 1000 songs. Alton and Rabon Delmore began singing together as children and built a large following through countless radio appearances, on stations in Alabama, Arkansas, North and South Carolina and Tennessee. They recorded for Columbia and then King, and their best known songs include the Top Ten hit, 'Blues Stay Away From Me', 'Prisoner's Farewell', 'Midnight Special' and 'Pan American Boogie'.

1946 Jimmy Buffett born in Mobile, Alabama. He's a rock musician who flavours his easy-going music with liberal doses of country. After earning a degree in journalism at the University of Southern Mississippi, he began a musical career, recording for Barnaby, then ABC, scoring big hits with 'Magaritaville' and 'Changes In Latitude, Changes In Attitude'. Since his success Buffett has been spending an idyllic-sounding life, dividing his time between music making and frequent boat trips from his home base in Florida.

1948 Barbara Mandrell, one of the most successful contemporary country performers, born in Houston, Texas. She came from a musical family and was learning to play a variety of instruments before she could read. By her teens she had mastered the steel guitar, saxophone, banjo and bass. Barbara made her TV debut on "Town Hall Party" when she was 11, and then joined her father's group The Mandrells. In 1967 she married the band's drummer, Ken Dudney, and temporarily stopped performing, but was back two years later, signed to CBS. She had several hits with country versions of rhythm and blues songs, and duet success with David Houston. In 1975, after a move to ABC (which was later merged into MCA), her career took off dramatically. She had number one hits with 'Sleeping Single In A Double Bed' and '(If Loving You Is Wrong) I Don't Want To Be Right', had a very successful network TV series with her sisters and won numerous awards, including CMA 'Entertainer of the Year' in 1980 and 1981.

26th DECEMBER

1926 The WSM Barn Dance (later The Grand Ole Opry) began regular Saturday night broadcasting, with Uncle Dave Macon, "the oldest banjo player in Dixie" and Uncle Jimmy Thompson playing requests for "old time melodies". The first shows were broadcast from the WSM studios in downtown Nashville. Fans began coming to the studios to see their favourite performers and a special Studio B was built that could accommodate an audience of 500. The Opry subsequently made several moves, to increasingly larger premises. From the Hillsboro Theatre, an old movie house, the show moved to a tabernacle in East Nashville, then, in 1939, to the War Memorial Auditorium, and in 1943 to the Ryman Auditorium, which was the home of the Opry for over 20 years.

1943 Ronnie Prophet, singer and comic, born in Calumet, Quebec, Canada. He arrived in Nashville in 1969 and began playing the Carousel Club. He was a firm favourite with the country fans who visited Music City in droves each week, and the club was re-named Ronnie Prophet's Carousel Club; he now has a lifetime contract to appear whenever he can. Ronnie is particularly popular in his native Canada and in Britain, where he's introduced the important Wembley Festival on a number of occasions, linking each act with segments from his acclaimed one-man show. This remarkable act includes the use of electronic gadgetry which allows him to sing duets with himself. Classics from the Ronnie Prophet repertoire include 'Harold The Horny Toad' and an impersonation of Donald Duck singing 'Help Me Make It Through The Night'.

27th DECEMBER

1931 Scotty Moore (Winfield Moore), gifted guitarist who played on Elvis' first records, born in Gadsden, Tennessee. He came from a country music background and was featured on Washington DC's WBRO in the early fifties, then came to Memphis and was working with the country band, Doug Poindexter's Starlight Wranglers, in 1954, when he met Elvis. Scotty was extremely important in helping Presley develop his rockabilly style and his guitar sound on those early Sun recordings have influenced thousands of rock and country guitarists since. Scotty is now a Nashville-based record producer who rarely plays music in public.

1947 Tracy Nelson born in Madison, Wisconsin. She has sung in a variety of styles—folk, blues, rock and country; she was lead singer with Mother Earth in California in the late sixties, then moved to Nashville where she made the classic *Mother Earth Presents Tracy Nelson Country,* which featured rare guitar performances from Scotty Moore. Tracy has a cult reputation, is a "musician's musician" who's never achieved the commercial success that many expected. She has sung back-up vocals on numerous records, including those of Willie Nelson (no relation), Michael Murphey and Steve Young.

1963 Merle Haggard made his very first appearance on the country charts with 'Sing Me A Sad Song', on the small, California-based Tally label.

28th DECEMBER

1932 Dorsey Burnette, rockabilly pioneer, songwriter and country star, born in Memphis, Tennessee. He was a boxer in his teens, then was employed at the Crown Electric Company in Memphis, where Elvis worked soon after leaving school. The success of Elvis, Scotty and Bill inspired Dorsey's younger brother Johnny to form a similar group. Johnny Burnette's Rock 'n' Roll Trio featured Dorsey on bass and a friend, Paul Burlison, on guitar. They never achieved chart success but their records are now held in the highest regard by rockabilly enthusiasts. Dorsey quit the Trio in 1959 and had success as a pop balladeer with 'Tall Oak Tree' and 'Hey Little One', then did well as a writer, composing hits for Jerry Lee Lewis, Rick Nelson and others. In the seventies Dorsey was a country star and had several hits on Capitol.

1962 Glen Campbell's first appearance on the country charts, with 'Kentucky Means Paradise' on Capitol. It was another four years before Glen was back on the best-sellers, though he had experienced chart success before: in 1958 he was one of the West Coast session men who recorded as The Champs and had a million-selling instrumental hit with 'Tequila' in 1958.

29th DECEMBER

1922 Rose Lee Maphis of the vocal and instrumental duo, Joe and Rose Lee Maphis, born in Baltimore, Maryland. She was singing and playing guitar before she reached her teens, and at 15 was performing on the radio as "Rose Of The Mountains". She met Joe on the WRVA Old Dominion Barn Dance show in Richmond, Virginia, in 1948. They married and then moved to California where they were regulars on the "Town Hall Party" TV show for over ten years. Joe and Rose Lee made numerous records, also doing several back-up vocal sessions, for Rick Nelson, Tex Ritter and others.

19?? Ed Bruce born in Keiser, Arkansas. He started his musical career as Edwin Bruce, rock 'n' roller, then turned to country in the sixties, starting a decade of small hits with 'Walker's Wood', on RCA in 1967. Ed's early successes came as a writer, often with his wife Patsy (who is also his manager). He was frequently employed for advertisements, including a famous series where he was cast as "The Tennessean", dressed in buckskins and carrying a musket, for a campaign to attract tourists to Tennessee. His big song has been 'Mamma's Don't Let Your Babies Grow Up To Be Cowboys', a hit for Ed in 1976, later a best-seller for Waylon and Willie. With increased media attention focussed on him, Bruce moved to MCA Records and scored Top Ten hits, including 'You're The Best Break This

Old Heart Ever Had', and was then a star in the TV series "Bret Maverick".

1945 The first important Nashville recording session since RCA Victor's unsuccessful sessions in 1928; Opry announcer Jim Bulleit launched his Bullet label by recording singer Sheb Wooley.

30th DECEMBER

1931 Skeeter Davis (Mary Frances Penick) born in Dry Ridge, Kentucky. She teamed up with Betty Jack Davis while at high school, they performed as the Davis Sisters and had a country hit with 'I Forgot More Than You'll Ever Know'. Their promising career together was cut tragically short by a car accident in which Betty was killed. After a period away from the music business, Skeeter returned for a long and fruitful solo career; she's been a member of the Opry for over 20 years, had a major pop hit with 'The End Of The World' and a long string of country successes including 'Gonna Get Along Without You Now' and 'I'm A Lover (Not A Fighter)'.

1937 Multi-instrumentalist and entertainer John Hartford, born in New York. An accomplished musician by his early teens, John's early jobs included DJ, sign painter and deckhand on a Mississippi river boat. He's had a lengthy recording career, for RCA and then Flying Fish, and his best known song, 'Gentle On My Mind', is among the most frequently recorded compositions of the sixties. Hartford is a regular performer on TV shows, usually appearing solo and accompanying his singing with banjo, fiddle, guitar and percussion effects from an electrified board, on which he dances!

John Hartford

1942 Mike Nesmith born in Dallas, Texas. In the sixties he was a teeny-bop star as one of the Monkees, then became a country-rock cult figure, writing Linda Ronstadt's first hit (when she was vocalist with the Stone Poneys), 'Distant Drum', and making albums with the First, and then Second National Band. Nesmith is now an innovative director/performer in the video field.

1950 Arkey Shibley's 'Hot Rod Race' entered the country charts, the first hit song about hot-rod cars.

31st DECEMBER

1924 Rex Allen, "The Arizona Cowboy", born in Willcox, Arizona. He came from a genuine western background, learning to rope cattle as a youngster. A popular entertainer at rodeos, Rex made his radio debut in the mid-forties and was soon a regular on the WLS National Barn Dance, then had his own show in California. In the fifties he was the star of several cowboy films and had hit records, including 'Crying In The Chapel' and 'Don't Go Near The Indians'.

Rex Allen Snr. and Rex Allen Jnr.

1933 Fred Carter born in Winnsboro, Louisiana. A top session guitarist, Fred is supposed to have played on 90 per cent of the country records made in Nashville during the sixties. With Chet Atkins, Owen Bradley, Anita Kerr and a few other session men, Carter was one of the creators of the so-called Nashville sound.

1943 John Denver (John Henry Deutschendorf), soft-rock musician whose records are frequently flavoured with country, born in Rosewall, New Mexico. He was a folk singer in the sixties, a member of the Chad Mitchell Singers, then began a solo career which blossomed with smash hits like 'Rocky Mountain High' and 'Annie's Song'. He's made several best-selling LPs all characterized by his use of the best available musicians—James Burton, Glen D. Hardin, Hal Blaine and Emory Gordy are regulars on his albums.

1947 The King and Queen of the Cowboys, Roy Rogers and Dale Evans, married.

INDEX

Bibliography

The following publications were used as general reference for some of the facts and figures in this book.

Encyclopedia Of Folk, Country & Western Music *Irwin Stambler & Grelun Landon* (St Martin's Press)

The Illustrated Encyclopedia of Country Music *Fred Dellar, Roy Thompson & Douglas B. Green* (Salamander)

Country Music USA *Bill C. Malone* (University of Texas Press)

The Stars Of Country Music *Edited by Bill C. Malone & Judith McCulloh* (University of Illinois Press)

Who's Who In Country & Western Music *Edited by Kenn Kingsbury* (Black Stallion Country Press)

Top Country & Western Records *Joel Whitburn* (Record Research)

The Guinness Book Of British Hit Singles *Jo & Tim Rice, Paul Gambaccini & Mike Read* (Guinness)

Country: The Biggest Music In America *Nick Tosches* (Stein & Day)

The Illustrated History of Country Music *Edited by Patrick Carr* (Doubleday/Dolphin)

The Grand Ole Opry — The Early Years *Charles K. Wolfe* (Old Time Music)

The Nashville Sound *Paul Hemphill* (Ballantine Books)

Watermelon Wine *Frye Gaillard* (St Martin's Press)

Sing Your Heart Out Country Boy *Dorothy Horstman* (E P Dutton & Co Inc)

The American West *Edited by Howard R. Lamar* (Crowell)

The Illustrated NME Encyclopedia Of Rock *Compiled by Nick Logan & Bob Woffinden*

Pete Frame's Rock Family Trees (Omnibus)

The History Of Rock (Orbis)

The Encyclopedia Of Rock *Edited by Phil Hardy & Dave Laing* (Panther)

All About Elvis *Fred L. Worth & Steve D. Tamerius* (Bantam)

The Storyteller's Nashville *Tom T Hall* (Doubleday)

Your Cheatin' Heart *Chet Flippo* (Simon & Schuster)

Sing A Sad Song *Roger M: Williams* (Ballantine Books)

Waylon And Willie *Bob Allen* (Quick Fox)

Coal Miner's Daughter *Loretta Lynn* (Warner Books)

The Intimate Biography of Dolly Parton *Alanna Nash* (Granada)

Patsy Cline *Ellis Nassour* (Tower Books)

Buddy Holly *John Goldrosen* (Granada)

Stand By Your Man *Tammy Wynette with Joan Dew* (Arrow)

Sun Records *Martin Hawkins & Colin Escott* (Omnibus)

Sing Me Back Home *Merle Haggard with Peggy Russell* (NY Times Books)

Johnny Cash *Christopher S. Wren* (Abacus)

Timeless Flight *John Rogan* (Scorpion/Dark Star)

Magazines consulted include The Journal of Country Music, Country Music, Country Rhythms, Omaha Rainbow, Sing Out, ZigZag, Country Music People, Old Time Music, Melody Maker, and Country Music World.

Acknowledgements

This book would not have appeared without the help of a large number of people. I am especially grateful to Peter O'Brien, editor of Omaha Rainbow, who provided information, photographs and much needed encouragement in the early stages; the multi-talented Robert K Oermann of Nashville, Tennessee, whose Country Music History Calendar (Country Music Foundation Press) was one of the initial inspirations for the project; Tony Russell, who loaned many of the atmospheric old photographs; "Big" John Shotton, editor of *Country Music World*; and Catherine Cardwell, my unflappable and hard-working editor.

Thanks to the following for their swift response to my requests for photographs and information: Paul Fenn, Stoney Byworth, Sharon Poling, Kathy Gangwisch, Sanford Brokaw, Kathy McClintock, photographer Bob Hooper, illustrator Pete Coffey, Mervyn Conn, Ed Benson, Johnnie Allan, Meme Coe, Susan Jarrett, Tom Adkinson, Lee Williams, Kay Shaw, Lee Simmonds, Sue Foster, Barbara Charone, Sue Humphris, Louise Collins, Debbie Bennett, Martha Haggard, Jerry Bailey, Cynthia Leu, Jody Denburg, Jan Simmons, Bonnie Rasmussen, John Lomax III, Luis Castresana, Bruce Adelman, Judy Vulcano, Bryan Chalker, Sam Cox, Bernie Slater, Ken Hunt, Richard Hoare, Brian Gibson, Andy Childs, Jonathan Morrish, John Tobler, John Atkins, Arthur Anderson, Bob Claypool, Fred Dellar, Spencer Leigh and Judith Newton. Apologies to anyone I've left out.

Additional thanks are due to the following record companies and organisations: PolyGram. MCA, CBS, Epic, Austin City Limits, Tree International, F Beat, Capitol, United Artists, RCA, Warner Brothers, Elektra/Asylum, MGM, DJM, Tomato, Kaleidoscope, Arhoolie, First Generation, Jet, Sonet, Rounder, Flying Fish, Swansong, BBC, Gilley's, A&M, Fate, Charly, Monument, Ovation. EMI, Starday, RSO, Fantasy and Big R.